Doris Day

Reluctant Superstar

Doris Day
RELUCTANT SUPERSTAR

DAVID BRET

BOOKS

This book is dedicated to
Marlene, Barbara, Amalia, Axel and *Les Enfants de Novembre*
Novembre
N'oublie pas . . .

La vie s ⸻ *rs*

First published in Great Britain in 2008 by
JR Books, 10 Greenland Street, London NW1 0ND

www.jrbooks.com

ISBN 978-1-906217-50-1

1 3 5 7 9 10 8 6 4 2

Mixed Sources
Product group from well-managed forests and other controlled sources
www.fsc.org Cert no. TT-COC-2082
© 1996 Forest Stewardship Council
FSC

Printed by Cromwell Press, Trowbridge, Wiltshire

Contents

Acknowledgements

Writing this book would not have been possible had it not been for the inspiration, criticisms and love of that select group of individuals who, whether they be in this world or the next, I will always regard as my true family and *autre* coeur: Barbara, Irene Bevan, Marlene Dietrich, René Chevalier, Axel Dotti and Roger Normand, *que vous dormez en paix*; Montserrat Caballé, Lucette Chevalier, Jacqueline Danno, Héléne Delavault; Tony Griffin, Betty and Gérard Garmain, Annick Roux, John and Anne Taylor, Terry Sanderson, Charley Marouani, David and Sally Bolt, Dorothy Squires and Maria da Fe. Also a very special mention for Amalia Rodrigues, Joey Stefano, those *hiboux* and *amis de foutre* who happened along the way, and *mes enfants perdus*.

A deep debt of gratitude to Jane Donovan. And *where* would I be without Jeremy Robson and the munificent team at JR Books. And also, where would I be without my agent Guy Rose? Also to my wife, Jeanne, for putting up with the bad moods and for still being the keeper of my soul!

And the final *chapeau* for Mrs Kappelhoff's daughter, for having lived.

David Bret, February 2008

Introduction

She was known as 'the girl next door' – the archetypal, perennial virgin one could always be confident of taking home to Mum for Sunday tea. Her heyday years were lived wholly without scandal because the gossip columnists truly believed in the wholesome image promoted by Warner Brothers, who were, of course, only interested in using her to line their coffers – and to be fair, they never saw her as anything but the dippy, happy-go-lucky blonde with the bubbly personality. In her memoirs, published in 1975, Doris Day revealed the tears of the clown, declaring her life had been nothing like the sunny excursion portrayed in most of her films. Yet in trying not to offend her readers and risk many of them losing the respect for her that had built up over the years, and on account of her strong, if not frequently misguided religious principles, she was not always entirely honest about herself and those around her. Rock Hudson, who appeared with her in a trio of phenomenally successful (so-called) sex comedies, claimed that beneath the giggles, she was just another lonely little child looking for help; also, that when riled she could out-curse any woman he had ever known with the exception of Elizabeth Taylor.

After watching the rushes for *Love Me Or Leave Me*, Ruth Etting refused to meet her, declaring Doris's portrayal of her was so inaccurate that it would be as if she was looking through a shattered mirror. Like Etting, Doris had the knack of always ending up with the wrong man – thugs, crooks, thieves and rapists all flocked to her banner to ensure that she never went too long without being made to suffer. And in a similar way to Judy Garland, perhaps her nearest contemporary, looking back on her life she gives every impression that she actually enjoyed being dragged through the mire, along with the acts of contrition which followed from whosoever she was involved with at the time. Only now, with most of the characters in her Pirandello-style drama dead, can one dip into the archives (somewhat repressed at times) and reassemble the pieces to say what really happened.

Of course what we must never forget is that Doris Day is unique, inimitable and if not an authority on the human condition then certainly one where animals are concerned – a comedic and dramatic genius, a sincere, consummate artiste the like of which we shall never see again.

Chapter 1

With A Song in My Heart

'I found Doris Day sexy in a very acceptable, very chaste way. She wasn't down and dirty . . . she was above that and that's what made her a star.'

Norman Jewison, director, 1989

Like many of her contemporaries, much of what we know of her early life comes post-fame from Doris Day herself. With almost all the major players in the scenario now dead, it often becomes difficult to separate truth from hearsay. She was born Doris Mary Anne Von Kappelhoff on 3 April 1924 in Evanstown, Cincinnati, the third child of Frederick William and Alma Sophia Welz, Catholics of German descent, who were thought to have dispensed with the 'Von' at the time of Hitler's rise to power. Kappelhoff on its own, Frederick declared, sounded Jewish, and as such would see the family discriminated against. Doris was the couple's third child: a son, Richard, had died aged 2 in 1920 and Paul was born the following year. Her maternal grandparents, known only as Frau and Herr Welz, emigrated from Berlin to the United States some years before because her grandfather, a conscientious objector, wished to avoid military service. They used their savings to open a pretzel factory in the city's German quarter and various members of the family, including Alma and Frederick, lived in the apartments above.

Alma and Frederick are known to have fought a lot – largely on account of their differing musical tastes, which each of them wanted to pass on to their offspring. As a couple, they were totally incompatible. In her ghosted memoirs (*Doris Day, Her Own Story* by A. E. Hotchner, 1975) Doris describes her father as, 'A handsome man, tall, slender, thick auburn hair, large brown eyes topped by heavy auburn eyebrows,' adding that he had had very little time for family life. A music teacher by profession, Frederick also directed the choir at St Mark's Catholic Church. He appears to have been a strict disciplinarian, barring the front of the house from everyone, especially his family, when he was working in the music room – a tell-tale sign was that if his car was parked in front of the building, everyone had to use the back entrance. Doris describes Alma as 'very barrelhouse', into country music, parties and the local social calendar while her father preferred to stay at home, listening to opera on the radio – the heavier, the better.

From early on, Alma nurtured hopes for both of her children to have a stage career. Doris was named after one of her idols, silent star Doris Kenyon (1897–1979), forgotten today but a sizeable name in 1924 as Rudolph Valentino's leading lady in *Monsieur Beaucaire*. The two children were enrolled at Golden's School For Tap and then at Martin's Ballet School, Cincinnati, where, in addition to dance they were taught comportment. For his part Frederick aspired to a more classical future and attempted to teach them the piano and violin, failing miserably where Doris was concerned.

In 1934 Frau Welz died, bequeathing the pretzel factory to her sons, Frank and Charley. Alma and Frederick were devastated and the tragedy appears to have decimated Alma's sex-drive, resulting in Frederick embarking on a series of affairs, the first of them with his wife's best friend. Doris said she listened to them having sex in the room next to hers and then cried herself to sleep. Alma threw him out of their apartment and such was the scandal when she announced why she was divorcing him that most of Frederick's music students deserted him and he was fired from his directing post at St Mark's Church.

The bottom dropped out of Doris' world and her idyll was shattered. 'It was the only ambition I ever had,' she said. 'Not to be a dancer or Hollywood movie star but to be a housewife in a good marriage.' She would go on to achieve one ambition with flying colours but sadly the other one would pass her by, largely on account of her own bad choices in men.

For some time after her parents' divorce Doris and Paul took turns at sleeping in their mother's room – not a healthy proposition for Paul, who was by then going on 15. They saw their father once a week, an exercise Doris dismissed as a chore because Frederick insisted on dragging them round to visit various members of their extended family rather than spending quality time with his children. Nor does he appear to have made an effort to support his family, though this might have been because his income was by now so depleted that he could barely support himself. He had also ditched Alma's best friend and taken a new (unnamed) mistress, a classical singer whom he would later marry but soon afterwards lose to cancer.

In the days before National Assistance Alma was compelled to take a job on the production line at the pretzel factory; though struggling to keep afloat, she still found the extra few dollars to pay for her children's dancing lessons. By this time they were enrolled at the slightly more prestigious Hessler's Studio in the city's Mount Adams district, where the curriculum also included elocution. To avoid spending 24 hours a day at the factory Alma moved her family to a small apartment in Cincinnati's College Hill suburb, where the children were enrolled at Our Lady Of Angels School. Why Alma never found another man, given her love of socialising and the fact that she was still quite an attractive woman well into old age, has never been explained. Once bitten, twice shy perhaps – maybe she was terrified of ending up with another man like Frederick. Doris certainly inherited her trait of choosing the wrong partner. Later she would confess how pleased she was that Alma had elected to lead a single existence. 'My mother's lack of interest in developing a new life for herself had an enormous advantage for me,' she rather egotistically declared, adding that it had left Alma free to devote all her time to her in the wake of her own disastrous marriages.

At the age of 12 Doris formed a dance partnership with a fellow student of the same age called Jerry Doherty, courtesy of their respective mothers. Like most student dancers of the time they aspired to be the next Fred Astaire and Ginger Rogers. Together, they performed in church, at charity and Masonic lodge functions and frequently in minstrel sketches which today would be regarded as racially offensive but were very much in vogue in those days. Although they earned next to nothing, expenses mostly, they soon developed a local following. They also made the newspapers when, costumed by their mothers, they entered a talent contest sponsored by Almes & Doepke's department store and walked off with the first prize of $500, a tidy sum indeed for a song-and-dance patter executed to the vaudeville ditty, May Ward's 'The Bird On Nellie's Hat', popularised some years before Doris' birth by Maidie Scott. Doris later recalled in her memoirs that whenever she heard the song afterwards she cringed because the title had been so silly, though later in her career she was to sing much sillier songs.

Unlike many show-business mothers – for example, those of Elizabeth Taylor, Judy Garland and Joan Crawford – Alma Kappelhoff was no megalomaniac. She was purely interested in her daughter's wellbeing and placed no emphasis on forcing her to be something that she herself had failed to become through lack of talent. Doris was given her share of the winnings and Alma suggested that maybe it would be a good idea for the youngsters to further develop their abilities by taking a shot at the Hollywood dance circuit. Mrs Doherty agreed and they were booked in for a four-week course with Fanchon and Marco, then one of Tinseltown's leading tap-dance academies, to begin in July 1937 during the school holidays.

Fanchon and Marco (Fanny and Mike Wolff) were a brother-and-sister ballroom dance act that started out as cabaret dancers in the early 1920s and then branched out into theatre management. During a lengthy partnership they kickstarted the careers of Cyd Charisse, Bing Crosby, Dorothy Lamour and Judy Garland. Besides numerous West Coast theatres they also managed The Mickey Mouse Circus (a feature of the 1935–6 California Pacific Exposition) and at the time of their involvement with Doris Kappelhoff five separate troupes of Fanchon and Marco Girls, who worked the circuits around San Francisco, Seattle, Portland, Vancouver and Los Angeles.

Alma rented a room in a cheap downtown apartment block and while she and Mrs Doherty slept comfortably, Doris and Jerry took turns in sleeping on the floor or in a truckle bed. Fanchon and Marco's dance teacher at their Los Angeles academy was the soon-to-be legendary Louis Da Pron (1913–87) whose big break occurred the previous year when he was taken on by Paramount Studios. From 1941 he choreographed 13 films for Donald O'Connor. During the 1950s he choreographed *The Perry Como Show* and towards the end of his career in 1975 he worked with Barbra Streisand in *Funny Lady*. Doris and Doherty made such an impression on him that he put in a good word with his employers which resulted in them being assigned to a month-long Fanchon and Marco tour running concurrently with the course and performing at small venues in and around Hollywood. The mothers were also approached by a Paramount talent scout who wanted to assign Doris to a trial contract: Alma insisted

Doris herself should decide but when she learned that the studio was only interested in her and not Jerry Doherty she turned them down.

The Kappelhoffs and the Dohertys returned to Cincinnati early in September 1937 and with both mothers unattached with nothing to keep them there, they made plans to relocate to Hollywood. Recently Doris had been going steady with Doherty's elder brother Larry and on 13 October – a Black Friday, if ever there was one – the trio set off for a leaving party with two friends – Albert Schroeder and Marion Bonekamp, who lived in Hamilton, 25 miles out of Cincinnati. At some stage during the evening the youngsters drove to a hamburger joint on the out-skirts of town. Caught in a rainstorm, they tried to make it across an unmanned railway crossing, even though the signal heralded an approaching train. The train clipped the car, swung it round but luckily none of the occupants were killed. Albert (who was driving) and Marion were catapulted through the windscreen and sustained severe facial cuts. But the Doherty brothers remained unhurt and Doris managed to escape from the back of the car. 'I probed my leg and discovered I was bleeding,' she observed in her memoirs, 'Then my fingers came to the sharp ends of the shattered bones protruding from my leg . . . I fainted in the gutter.'

Surgeons at the nearby Mercy Hospital discovered a double compound fracture of her right leg and with little hope of Doris ever dancing again the move to Hollywood was abandoned. Her primary concern was not for herself but for Jerry Doherty who told her he would never dance with anyone else. In fact he ended up becoming a milkman! Compelled to undergo several operations, Doris' splintered bones were reassembled and a steel pin inserted. Her leg was encased in a thick plaster cast and she spent four months confined to a wheelchair. Further examination revealed the leg was not healing, resulting in more surgery. Around the same time the Welz brothers put the pretzel factory on the market.

Charley Welz then purchased a tavern in Sailor Park. Alma was hired as cook and she and her children moved into the small apartment above the kitchen.

It was here that the seeds were inadvertently sewn for Doris' singing career. The tavern had a jukebox full of big band and jazz records that were played non-stop every evening. Doris developed a fascination for Duke Ellington and Benny Goodman but Ella Fitzgerald was her own particular favourite and she proved to be a natural mimic. Much to the delight of the customers she would 'duet' with Ella. However, in a moment's madness while listening to 'Tea For Two' – a song that would one day be associated with her worldwide – Doris forgot all about the cast on her leg. She tried to dance and took a tumble, undoing in one fell swoop all the good work of the surgeons and physiotherapists during the last four months. Back at the Mercy Hospital, where she was rushed for yet more surgery, she was told she would have to wear the cast for at least another year and that another similar accident might result in her losing her leg altogether. Instead of dancing she concentrated on her singing. To encourage her daughter Alma decided to give her lessons herself, mindless of the fact that she appears to have been tone deaf and that for her repertoire she selected a clutch of songs made famous by Jeanette MacDonald, who Doris could not stand.

Realising her faux pas, Alma enrolled Doris with Grace Raine, then the voice-coach for WLW Radio. The curious thing about her was that she herself could not sing – indeed she is believed to have been tone deaf! Despite this, her reputation was legendary. WLW was more than a local radio station: in those days it was relayed to around two-thirds of the country and was one of the most widely listened to networks in the United States. Raine had a singular theory for success: the singer should focus on the shape of a member of the audience in the darkened auditorium, preferably someone in the gallery, rather than on the audience collectively. As there was no gallery within the radio station theatre and since Doris would never sing in a legitimate theatre or concert other than as a band singer, she found it hard to put this into practice. Usually she concentrated on an inanimate object such as the exit sign – which she said was always in her sights!

Raine's services were not cheap ($5 for a single lesson) but unlike Louis Da Pron, she was so impressed by Doris' innate talent that she agreed to two more lessons a week at her own expense. Later Doris accredited Raine as being the one person who had had the greatest effect on her career. It was she who introduced her to WLW Radio's Andrew Carlin whose top-rating show – *Carlin's Carnival* – was broadcast live every Saturday morning from a Cincinnati department store. An early version of *Opportunity Knocks*, this was a sponsored showcase for local talent whose unpaid contestants were judged by audience applause; no easy task as more often than not the auditorium was packed with their families and school friends. Doris' greatest problem was not to do with any lack of confidence – 'I have never had any doubts about my ability in anything I have ever undertaken,' she cockily boasts in her memoirs – but to do with singing before an audience. In these early performances – one also hears it in her first recordings – she was reported as standing too close to the microphone, which resulted in her 'popping' the letters 'b' and 'p', most particularly with words such as 'baby' and 'people'.

Grace Raine subsequently taught her how to avoid this by moving just an inch or so away from the microphone. One of Doris' greatest qualities (then, as later in her career) was when she aimed for a high note, giving every impression that she would sail spectacularly off-key only to slant the note beautifully half an octave and send shivers down the spine. For her *Carlin's Carnival* audition piece, she chose Howard Dietz and Arthur Schwartz's 'Day After Day' and caused a minor sensation. Carlin's producer liked what he heard, told her to forget about the competition and signed her up as a regular guest artist. Almost always she was requested to sing this song.

Among those listening in to WLW was Charlie Yee, proprietor of the Shanghai Inn Chinese restaurant and also mayor of Chinatown, who was on the lookout for a resident singer to entertain his Saturday evening clientèle. For some reason, probably on account of a surfeit of *Fu Manchu* films, Doris had a fear of anything Chinese and she makes no secret of it in her memoirs, when she remembers describing them as 'the yellow peril'. In those days the population of Evanstown included few foreigners other than Germans. Doris recalls with horror how her father would refer to the Jews as 'kikes' or 'sheenies' and of her own aversion to the Chinese family who ran the local laundry; in particular the pigtailed gentleman who terrified her each time she saw him through the window. This was of course so-called 'mother's milk' racism and anti-Semitism, the way things were in Middle America at the time. 'It wasn't until I began singing with the bands that I learned about the real people who lived inside the skins of those prejudices,' she recalled later, admitting how wrong she had been.

Doris was hired for $5 a session, which was enough to pay for her lesson with Grace Raine. Every evening she opened her set with 'Ain't Misbehavin' – technically she was doing just that for Raine had lied to the establishment about the age of her protégée when she told Yee and the press who visited the restaurant that Doris was actually 18, adding three years to her age.

Physically and vocally, Doris was almost a younger version of Jane Froman (1907–80), who was without doubt the greatest American realist singer of her day. During World War II, Froman was critically injured in an air crash and following this, she was to fight her way back to health and spend much of her remaining career singing on crutches or attached by a steel wire to a post while on stage. Asked to name his Top Ten favourite girl singers, showman Billy Rose famously quipped, 'Jane Froman – and nine others!' Ironically Doris was a Froman fan and incorporated several of her numbers into her act including 'Tea For Two', which Froman would re-record for Susan Hayward to lip-synch to in the 1952 biopic of her tragic story *With A Song In My Heart*. Naturally Doris' crutches evoked pity from Charlie Yee's customers and the tips she received after her performances enabled her to double her nightly fee.

One great source of comfort to her during her recuperation was her little mongrel Tiny. They were a familiar sight in Evanstown – Doris hobbling along on her crutches with Tiny trotting behind her – until one day when he dashed out into the road and was hit by a car. For the rest of her life Doris blamed herself for his death and she would always go out of her way to return a dog to its owner whenever she found one in the street, tagged and straying, to give that person a piece of her mind.

Another local entrepreneur alerted to Doris' budding talents, meanwhile, was bandleader Barney Rapp (Barnaby Rappaport, c.1900–70), the first in a succession of men who would take advantage of her extreme naivety and childlike trust, while she herself was blinded – either by love or ersatz admiration – from seeing them as they really were. Rapp was about to open his own club Sign Of The Drum in Bond Hill's Reading Road, and was auditioning for girl singers, not just for his new enterprise but also for a proposed hotel lobby and ballroom tour with his band The New Englanders.

Doris was but one of over one hundred hopefuls who turned up, clutching her portfolio of sheet music, at the Hotel Sinton in downtown Cincinnati but because she was more attractive than most and therefore an easy catch, Rapp assumed, she soon found herself at the top of his audition list. Whether she actually ended up in his bed is not known but considering his unsavoury nature and fondness for under-age girls this was more than likely. Having formed his first orchestra in Connecticut during the 1920s, Rapp moved to Cleveland, Ohio where he married Ruby Wright, one of The Call Sisters, in 1936. When Doris entered the equation Ruby was pregnant with the first of four daughters and Rapp was involved with another discovery: Dorothy Schaub, part of a roller-skating act. Later he helped launch (and also seduced) 17-year-old Rosemary Clooney who, like Doris, also lied about her age to perform on the circuit. Effectively Rapp could have been arrested and jailed for statutory rape even if his 'victims' were submissive.

Doris planned on singing 'Day After Day' for her audition but Barney Rapp insisted that *he* would choose her programme if she was to work for him. This included 'A Foggy Day In London Town', 'That Old Black Magic' and the number he asked for at the audition: Harry Warren and Johnny Mercer's 'Jeepers Creepers', which she herself loathed. Though this was sung by Louis Armstrong in a horseracing film, supposedly about one of the horses, the term was a euphemism for 'Jesus Christ!' In any case, Rapp liked what he heard – and saw – and hired her on the spot for $25 a week. What Doris did not know was that he actually claimed $50 for her on his expense account and pocketed the balance.

She made her debut at Sign Of The Drum in March 1940. For all of Rapp's promises, this was not an entirely respectable establishment and many of the clients were as shady as the proprietor himself. Doris also had to suffer the indignity of having to get changed in the ladies' because there was no dressing room. What she would later have to thank Rapp for (though she claimed that she always hated her moniker) was that he persuaded her to change her name. Doris Kappelhoff, he argued, still sounded too Jewish and in any case it would never fit onto the playbills. His first choice was Doris Kapps, which she flatly refused but then, thinking of the song 'Day After Day', which had brought her to him, he re-baptised her Doris Day.

Chapter 2

You Won't Be Satisfied Until You Break My Heart

'She looked so clean-cut. You expected her voice to be clean-cut but it wasn't at all. It was very smoky . . . very sultry.

Barbara Bonney, opera singer

Not content with swindling Doris out of half her salary, Barney Rapp was clearly keen to get his money's worth out of his protégée. She was contracted for 18 sets – three four-song spots each evening for six nights a week. Additionally she was still appearing on Carlin's Saturday morning Carnival and fulfilled her contract at the Shangai Inn that evening. As her club work meant that she was working until two in the morning, she was initially chaperoned by her mother but the long hours soon became too much for Alma since she was still running the kitchen at Charley Welz's tavern. She began to entrust Doris to the care of various dates.

When she began working at Sign Of The Drum, Doris was going steady with Fred Foster, the 21-year old presenter of WLW Radio's Saturday night dance-band programme featuring live concerts by the Cincinnati Symphony Orchestra. Two years previously, on 30 October 1938, Foster had gone on air while working for CBS immediately after Orson Welles' infamous *The War Of The Worlds* broadcast and was commended for calming his listeners down and convincing them this had not been a real Martian invasion but a mere dramatisation of H. G. Wells' novel. Doris met Foster in the radio canteen, they started chatting and went on a date that same evening (with Alma chaperoning) to nothing more innocuous than the local drugstore.

The other man in her life, very reluctantly at first on his part, was Barney Rapp's trombonist, 23-year old Al (Albert) Jorden, who lived near the Kappelhoffs in Price Hill. Doris found him attractive enough but surly. It was she who broke the ice, asking him if he would not mind collecting her each evening and then dropping her back home after the show. She subsequently described him as one of the glummest personalities she had ever met but she stuck with him all the same. In retrospect she was the first to admit that she should never have bothered with him in the first place. Maybe she was searching for some sort of rugged excitement that the quiet, good-natured Fred Foster could not guarantee. All her life Doris, like Judy Garland, Edith Piaf, Joan Crawford and many other icons, was to attract mean and moody types and she was to expect (and enjoy) rough sex while frequently wearing her bruises with pride. Also, like these other women, she would never learn from her mistakes.

From the time of their first date Jorden was bad news. He lived with his equally unpleasant mother who, on meeting Doris for the first time, hammered home the point that no woman was good enough for her son and that he would never marry her or anyone else. In turn, Doris' own mother Alma detested Jorden on sight but being the archetypal Johnny Opposite, Doris went to great lengths to prove them both wrong. Though he was also dating another singer from Barney Rapp's band, there is every possibility that Jorden's psychosis stemmed from an ambiguous sexuality: a heterosexual relationship unless he was in complete control of the sex, with violence and fear providing the essential aphrodisiac.

13

'He's a creep and I wouldn't go out with him if they were giving away gold nuggets at the movie!' Doris told Alma the first time Jorden asked her out to the cinema. And yet to her eternal regret step out with him was exactly what she did. 'This Jekyll-Hyde switch from grump to charmer should have forewarned me about Al Jorden,' she later observed in her memoirs.

Jorden cheated on Doris, knocked her around and humiliated her in public. One might just about excuse him for criticising her table manners; something that can be said to leave much to be desired in her formative years, however. Doris had a fondness for wolfing down hamburgers with huge portions of ketchup and raw onions after the show (usually in Jorden's car on their way home) and dropping chunks of food everywhere because of his reckless driving. She also had a habit of talking with her mouth full and spitting, which cannot have helped his mood swings.

Soon into their relationship, she accompanied him and some of the musicians from Sign Of The Drum on a weekend trip along the Ohio River in his 15-foot speedboat. Jorden attempted to hit top speed while racing in the swell of a paddleboat. The resulting waves overturned the craft and the occupants very nearly drowned; in the end they were rescued by a passing boat manned by a local reporter and their near-tragedy made the front page of the *Cincinnati Star*. Declaring him an uncertified lunatic, Alma begged Doris not to have anything to do with Jorden again but the incident only drew her closer. Fred Foster was unceremoniously dumped and when Jorden asked her to marry him, she agreed. The ceremony, she said, would take place as soon as she turned 18. For the second time in less than a year (the third, had her relationship with Foster been consummated), Doris risked becoming a subpoenaed witness in a statutory rape case.

It was a case of absence making the heart grow fonder when Al Jorden left Barney Rapp to join forces with Benny Goodman's former drummer Gene Krupa, who had recently started up his own band and was about to embark on a nationwide tour. The move coincided with Rapp selling Sign Of The Drum and hitting the road himself, taking Doris with him – an arduous enterprise that would see them travel up to one hundred miles a day from Cincinnati but always return to base afterwards to save on hotel bills. With Jorden swearing to remain faithful, Doris in turn promised to wait for him and not to date anyone else until they were together again.

In May 1940, halfway through her tour, Doris was contacted by Grace Raine. The singer-bandleader Bob Crosby was searching for a female vocalist and Raine recommended her for the job. Bob Crosby (1913–93), the youngest of Bing's five siblings, was different from other bandleaders in that he was just a frontman who was unable to play a musical instrument or write arrangements. He began his career in 1931 singing with Anson Weeks then briefly worked with the Dorsey Brothers, before forming The Bob Crosby Orchestra. From there he poached several others to form his most famous band The Bobcats, a Dixieland jazz group and precursor of the trad-jazz revival of the next decade.

Raine accompanied Doris to Chicago for an audition, which did not take place in an empty auditorium (as had happened with Barney Rapp) but at the Blackhawk Restaurant when the place was full. Records do not state what she sang, but Crosby took her on and his musician-manager Gil Rodin (they played together in Ben Pollack's Orchestra) assigned her to a legitimate contract which would see her getting $75 a week, half of which Doris sent home to Alma. Her brother Paul, who recently joined the Cincinnati Reds baseball team and had fractured his skull during a game, was having hospital treatment for the injury-related epilepsy that was to plague him for the rest of his life.

Doris' tenure with The Bobcats lasted but three months and was a far from comfortable experience. Bob Crosby saw red over Alma's interference in her daughter's personal life and refused to have her anywhere near the theatres where the band was working.

His dictum was 'play hard, live hard' and after each show he and the boys – and Doris – would hit a club and let their hair down until the early hours. Unfairly or not, and possibly because of her association with a louse like Al Jorden, her reputation as a possible 'easy lay' preceded her and several members of the band are known to have pestered her for sex. The sudden severance from Crosby occurred not on account of this, but in the wake of a concert at the Strand Theater on Broadway. Fearing Doris might ask for a raise after experiencing her first standing ovation, Crosby asked Gil Rodin to fire and replace her with Bonnie King, the singer who appeared with the band in radio broadcasts instead of Doris. There was, however, some compensation: before giving Doris her marching orders Gil Rodin arranged for an even more acclaimed bandleader, Les Brown, to sit at the back of the auditorium of New York's Edison Hotel where Doris gave her final performance with Bob Crosby with a view to engaging her. Though girl vocalists were basically two-a-penny in those days and almost always secondary to the musicians and Doris' singing voice was not particularly distinctive compared with those of Frances Langford and Helen O'Connell (she would very soon surpass them), what attracted Brown was her innate warmth and charisma, qualities that would later transcend the limitations of the airwaves.

Pennsylvania-born Les Brown (1912–2001) was educated at Ithaca College and Duke University, where he led The Duke Blue Devils Dance Orchestra. The band left college in the summer of 1936 and after touring for a year took up summer residence at the Playland Casino in Rye, New York. Following this, he worked as a freelance arranger with Glenn Osser, writing material for Don Bestor, Larry Clinton and other jazz-swing outfits. In 1938 he formed his 12-piece Band Of Renown, achieving notoriety after a three-month season at New York's Edison Hotel. By this time he had acquired the considerable talents of tenor-saxophonist Wolffe Tannenbaum and alto player Steve Maddrick. 'Leap Frog', the band's signature tune, aptly described their bouncy, staccato style.

Brown was astonished by Doris' laid-back approach and honeyed tones. Later when he was approached (along with a number of others) by her to include an essay in her autobiography *Doris Day, Her Own Story*, he insisted his opinion be included:

> She was every bandleader's dream, a vocalist who had natural talent, a keen regard for the lyrics, and an attractive appearance . . . As a singer, Doris belongs in the company of Bing Crosby and Frank Sinatra . . . I'd say that next to Sinatra, Doris is the best in the business for selling a lyric.

And of his own unique set-up, he observed,

> I ran a tight ship – no booze, no dope, no hard language. One reporter wrote that the X band played on booze, and the Y band played on dope, but Les Brown and His Band Of Renown became known as the Milk Shake band. And if ever there was a milk-shake girl, it was Doris!

However, when Brown offered to hire her there and then Doris knocked him back, arguing that she was so fed up with the long hours on the road and being the only girl among a bunch of rowdy, swearing, hard-drinking men that she was seriously considering a return to Cincinnati. It took several days for him to persuade her otherwise, declaring anyone who broke his no drugs-booze-cursing rules would be out on their ear. Never reported to have dabbled with drugs, Doris was drinking, albeit in moderation, and smoking like a chimney – upwards of two packs a day.

In a tour that would see The Band Of Renown zigzagging across the country, her first engagement took place in August 1940 at the

Theater Cafe in Chicago, showman Mike Todd's establishment, where stripper Gypsy Rose Lee topped the bill. As with Barney Rapp, she joined the band on stage halfway through their set and sang four songs. Minutes before, she received a good luck telegram from Al Jorden, who had left Gene Krupa and was currently touring with the Jimmy Dorsey Orchestra. Henceforth, wherever she appeared, Doris would get a cable or telephone call and on 6 February 1941 in New York Jorden surprised her by turning up at the recording studio where she had just cut 'Anapola', her first shellac disc with Les Brown (one of 12 sides and the only one which appears to have survived) and asked her to marry him. With her usual impetuosity, Doris accepted his proposal though no date was set for the wedding, as both were about to hit the road again. In any case, as she was still legally a minor, Doris would have to seek her mother's approval and she knew that in the current climate this would not be forthcoming.

The tour concluded where it started: with a month-long stint at Mike Todd's Theater café. Following this, Doris informed Les Brown that she was leaving the band to get married. With Al Jorden there was absolutely no compromise: a wife's place was in the home or hanging around hotel rooms with other orchestra wives. Les and Alma, together with several other friends, advised Doris against the union (correctly, as it turned out). In fact Jorden was subsequently diagnosed schizophrenic and it was to emerge that he had a proven history of violence towards women. Doris was so enamoured of him at the time that she refused to listen, however. Her career, she declared, was of no importance – she wanted to stay home, to keep house and have children.

Making the best of a bad situation and promising to pick up the pieces when it all fell apart – in her mind, there was no question of *if* – Alma helped to arrange the ceremony which took place at New York's City Hall during the late spring of 1941. Doris does not give the exact date in her 1975 memoirs: clearly her first wedding day was something she never wanted to be reminded of. Writing about it when Jorden was dead must have been her way of exorcising the demons from her mind but all she tells us is that she was working her notice for Les Brown at the Strand Theater while Jorden was playing with the Jimmy Dorsey Band at the Martin Beck and the ceremony was slotted in between matinee and evening shows. The reception, a last-minute affair, was held at a nearby greasy spoon.

The day after the wedding Jorden witnessed Doris giving a fellow musician a peck on the cheek for a belated wedding present. Later she admitted that he dragged her out of the theatre and through the streets, then up the stairs to their two-room apartment at the Whitby Hotel off Times Square, where he beat her senseless. Another reported incident occurred when she and Jorden were walking past a newsstand in New York and she pointed to a photograph of herself wearing a swimsuit on the cover of a magazine. In front of dozens of shocked fans he slapped her repeatedly across the face and then dragged her back to their apartment for more of the same.

Not only did he cheat on her from the beginning of their marriage, but Jorden was the classic schizoid wife-beater, laying into Doris with his fists, feet or whatever was to hand and leaving her body bruised, her face a bloodied mess and her mind in a state of turmoil. He would then collapse in tears, twisting the scenario around so that *Doris* was the one always made to feel guilty because *she* had brought it all on herself by flinging herself at other men and forcing them to flirt with her. In fact her husband was the one doing the cheating with a stand-in vocalist from the Dorsey band, who he also knocked around, according to the letter found in his jacket pocket by Alma when she was preparing to send his suit to the dry-cleaners. Doris later admitted that she lost count of the number of times he called her 'dirty whore'. After every manic episode, he would fling her on the bed and make passionate love to her. Many years later her friend Rock Hudson repeated to a French reporter how Doris had told him, 'In bed Al was a good fuck all right, but what he liked most of all was to fuck my face with his fists.'

In 1977 the Day-Jorden love-hate relationship was to be resurrected with the usual Hollywood blend of fantasy, wishful thinking and invention as part of the plot for Martin Scorcese's groundbreaking parody of the Hollywood musical *New York, New York* with Robert De Niro and Liza Minnelli. De Niro played the ebullient saxophonist who knows no difference between sexual passion and violence while Minnelli is the girl-next-door (the kind of role she could never quite get to grips with after *Cabaret*), who only realises what she has got herself into when it's too late. She divorces her beast of a husband and heads to Hollywood with her young son, where she becomes a major star. Of course there were heavy references to the tempestuous marriages of her own mother, Judy Garland, but not even the De Niro character was as odious as Al Jorden.

Doris was several weeks' pregnant when she married. She was delighted and assumed Jorden would only share her joy, bearing in mind the fact that he had ordered her to give up working. Sadly this was not to be the case. Within hours of her giving him the news, her husband arranged an appointment with a back-street abortionist. This brought out the very worst in the usually placid Alma, who confronted him with what would happen should Jorden force Doris to kill her grandchild. 'My knees were shaking,' Alma later recalled, 'But I knew that if any real trouble developed I could depend on my brother who loved Doris with a passion and would have gladly killed Al Jorden on the spot if need be.'

Undeterred Jorden visited a quack and bought an emetic that he forced Doris to swallow several times a day, the quack's theory being that excessive vomiting would cause her to miscarry. She was so terrified that she went along with this. Next, he somehow got it into his head that the child was not his and consequently gave Doris such a beating – at his parents' house while the Dorsey band was playing Cincinnati – that she almost miscarried. Although her father-in-law was sympathetic, by now his wife had decided that Doris was bad for her son. Doris called Alma who, just as she had helped plan her daughter's wedding, now set about talking her into a divorce.

Once again Doris refused to listen. Al, she declared, had been put under undue pressure by having fatherhood thrust upon him so soon after his marriage – in other words, inasmuch as her husband always held her responsible for the beatings he administered, so he now convinced her that she had somehow managed to con him into getting her pregnant. Therefore there was a reconciliation of sorts with floods of tears from the 'wronged' husband, who, four weeks before the baby was due, elected for a joint murder-suicide pact. He bought a gun that he kept in the glove compartment of his car, waiting for the right moment. This came while the couple cooled off in a lay-by after an argument. He pushed the nozzle of the gun into Doris' stomach, intent on killing her and their baby before blowing his brains out. Somehow she managed to talk him out of this only to have him beat her black and blue when they got home. For the rest of her life, Doris had a horror of riding in the front of a car.

From that point on she recognised another aspect of her husband's schizophrenia: the fact that he had started out on a trail of self-destruction that, so long as they stayed together, would see him treat her not just as a punch-bag but always on the verge of self-harm. For a while she was terrified of what he might do to her next, but she was even more scared of what he might do to himself, should she leave him. Again, this was another case of Jorden convincing her that she alone was responsible for their marital strife.

In January 1942, leaving Doris alone in their Whitby apartment and vowing never to return, Jorden travelled to Buffalo with the Jimmy Dorsey Orchestra with his latest mistress. Doris had already contacted her mother and within hours Alma arrived and announced that she had found a house for just the two of them and the baby in Cincinnati. On 8 February Doris was rushed into hospital and after a gruelling 12-hour labour she gave birth to an eight-pound son whom she named Terry after *Terry And The Pirates*, a favourite book from her childhood.

But if she was hoping to have seen the last of Al Jorden, she was in for an even bigger shock. A few days after Terry's birth, he returned to New York with the news that once he had tied up a few loose ends there, he also intended to move into the Cincinnati house and take over the mortgage payments. He had turned over a new leaf, he said, and having left the Dorsey band, his intent was to find session work locally to support his new family provided Doris forgave him and accepted him back into her life. She was foolish enough to believe him.

While Alma Kappelhoff pleaded with her daughter for the umpteenth time to have nothing to do with him, Doris decided to give Jorden one more chance, convinced he would never dare knock her around with her family close at hand: Alma was sleeping in the next room, Charley Welz's tavern was but a stone's throw away and her Aunt Marie (possibly Frank's wife) lived next door. Jorden's housewarming gift was a dog – a deliberate play on Doris' emotions because he knew how fond she was of animals. He fussed over the dog, insisting it should sleep on their bed while Terry was farmed out to Alma. If the child cried during the night, Doris was prohibited from going in to comfort him and if she disobeyed he rewarded her with a swift backhander.

It was Jorden's treatment of his son and his fondness for wife-bashing that made Doris finally see sense. After a night on the town with his latest squeeze he would stomp up the stairs, roaring drunk, barge into Alma's room and rattle the bars of Terry's cot, half-frightening him to death with his bellowing. Doris put up with this a few times but then called in a locksmith while her husband attended an audition. In doing so, she was effectively breaking the law because by now the house was in his name. When Jorden finally arrived home not only was he unable to get in, but his bags were packed and left on the porch. Just in case things got rough, Doris, her mother and the baby moved in with Aunt Marie. For the time being, he accepted things at face value and jumped into his car and drove to his parents' place.

Alma took Doris to see a lawyer with a view to filing for divorce proceedings that she envisaged would see her sue Jorden for cruelty and be awarded the house as part of the settlement. In the meantime, to help out with the repayments Doris went to see WLW Radio's Andrew Carlin in the hope that she might be allowed back on his Saturday morning show. But Carlin did better than that: he introduced her to the station's new director, a Mr Weiner, and he hired her as a headliner in *The Lion's Roar*, a weekly variety show sponsored by MGM to advertise their latest movies. She was also given a regular spot in another showbusiness extravaganza, *Moon River*, which went out four evenings a week. Accompanied by Jimmy Wilber's Little Band, Doris sang with The Ink Spots, The Mills Brothers and on one occasion shared the bill with Jane Froman.

The divorce now going ahead, Al Jorden was visited by the police and served with a restraining order. This only had the opposite effect and he began to stalk Doris – often sitting outside the radio station entrance in his car and then driving off at top speed down the wrong side of the road when assured that she had seen him. Alternatively, he would park outside her house for hours on end or follow her into a restaurant and sit at the next table, just staring. On the eve of the divorce, which unsurprisingly was granted on the grounds of extreme mental and physical cruelty, the most extraordinary swansong took place. Jorden had left to complete his military service at the Great Lakes Naval Station and when Doris came off stage he was shown into her dressing room. Still wearing his uniform, he was home on leave and he swore he had changed his ways. Doris agreed to have dinner with him but this time she stood her ground. There was no violence, just the usual floods of tears from Jorden. Rather than simply sending him on his way, she spent the night with him before telling him that no matter how much he pleaded with her, they would never have a future together.

The judge granted Jorden partial access to Terry with Doris' wholehearted approval. She then set about removing every trace of him from her life: destroying his clothes and effects, asking friends and acquaintances for photographs so that they could be burned. Terry, she declared, should never know what his father looked like. Jorden subsequently remarried and had another child. Some years later when Doris learned that Al Jorden had put a bullet through his skull after one angry episode too many, she shed no tears.

Chapter 3

My Dreams Are Getting Better All The Time

'I have the unfortunate reputation of being Miss Goody Two-Shoes . . . so I'm afraid it's going to shock some people for me to say this, but I staunchly believe no two people should get married until they've lived together.'

Doris Day, 1975

Hoping Al Jorden was well and truly out of the picture and having had him sign the house and its crippling mortgage repayments over to her, Doris soon realised that her meagre salary from WLW Radio was insufficient to keep her afloat. When her lawyer (Alma's cousin) informed her that Jorden was legally obliged to send money to support their son, she refused to have anything to do with the idea. Her theory was that while she was healthy, there was no reason why she could not go on supporting herself. She even consulted her priest with the idea of having her marriage annulled because the ceremony had not been conducted in church. She might even have gone through with it, had the priest not responded that should the union be declared void, Terry would be regarded as illegitimate. In those overtly moral times this would almost certainly have put an end to her career.

For the last time, she fell into a deep depression. Her girlhood dream of marriage and a blissful family life was destroyed and now it seemed as though nothing would take its place. Despite her insistence that her only ambition was marital bliss, she was in fact using this as an excuse because at the time she sincerely believed that she would never get anywhere with her singing career unless she had someone to lean on. In her eyes even a low-life such as Al Jorden was better than no man at all. During the autumn of 1944 she appeared on the same WLW bill as The Williams Brothers, the original 'boy band' formed in the late 1930s. Years after, when describing 17-year-old Andy in her memoirs, it appears she developed a crush on him, though the fact that he was at the time of writing almost as a big a star as Doris herself might have caused her imagination to work overtime. Williams started out as a chorister at his local Presbyterian church before joining forces with his older brothers Don, Rick and Bob. Shortly before their first meeting, they sang together on Bing Crosby's hot recording of 'Swinging On A Star'. For a little while there was talk of Doris joining them and they rehearsed fervently at the Williams' house in Cincinnati.

The brothers then relocated to New York, where they worked briefly with singer Kay Thompson before splitting up. Andy Williams' solo career was to get truly underway in 1952. Doris recalls in her memoirs how Les Brown called her the day after the Williams' Brothers left for New York and asked her to work with him again. Actually, it was the other way round, though for two years he had begged her to return to the fold. Brown was by now at the height of his popularity. Ironically, his first hit record was released in July 1941, two months after Doris left the band: 'Joltin' Joe Di Maggio', a tribute to the legendary baseball player who would later marry Marilyn Monroe.

Touring with Les Brown meant leaving baby Terry with Alma although since the divorce there was always the danger Jorden might turn up and snatch the child. Doris decided to take the risk and over the next three years she enjoyed tremendous success with Brown, both on the road and in the recording studio. Between November 1944 and September 1946 she cut around 30 sides for Columbia's Okeh label, which were released commercially and sold well, and at least six others which have since disappeared. Her big hits at the time included 'My Dreams Are Getting Better All The Time' (a misnomer if ever there was one), 'Till The End Of Time', and 'Aren't You Glad You're You?'. None of them matched the phenomenal success of 'Sentimental Journey', which she recorded on 20 November 1944. 'I always feel a rise in my scalp or in the backs of my wrists when something is special,' she observed, 'whether it be a song or a man.' Fortunately, she was always a far better judge of the former! Written by Brown in collaboration with Bud Green and Ben Homer, the song was originally considered beyond her then-limited vocal range and his musicians did not like it at all – they considered it too syrupy for the younger members of their audience who liked to get up and jive. The introduction at the Hotel Pennsylvania's Cafe Rouge was there-fore suitably low-key but the kids loved it so much that it became the highlight of every subsequent Brown-Day concert, and for many years served as Doris' signature tune, occupying the Number One spot in the charts for nine weeks. Millions of copies were sold and it became as readily accepted as a 'Forces Sweetheart' song as Vera Lynn's 'We'll Meet Again' and Marlene Dietrich's 'Lili Marlene'. Like Marlene, Doris was the first to confess that she was sick of hearing it, not that this prevented her from singing the song hundreds of times.

Working with Brown the second time around was no bed of roses for some of the other players, however. Like Frank Sinatra, Doris was rarely modest when discussing her talents – a facet of her character that her peers forced themselves to accept because she was so genuinely talented. Ted Nash in particular often spoke of her temper tantrums when things were not going all her own way – she would slam doors, curse the air blue and threaten to leave. According to her, she always had something to go back to if push came to shove – Cincinnati – though she never lost her cool with Brown himself. It is doubtful whether she would have carried out her threat once she became popular but once again ill-chosen love got in the way of her career. Within days of returning to Brown, she announced she was in love again: with alto saxophonist George Weidler (1926–89), the brother of child actress Virginia, who appeared briefly in Shirley Temple's *Dimples* (1936). Weidler was not a regular with Les Brown but a replacement for Steve Madrick, who had recently received his call-up papers. As usual by now this was to be a case of Doris' heart ruling her head. Like Al Jorden, Weidler would only cause her pain.

Just as Brown imposed a no drugs-drinking-swearing embargo on his band members so too did he frown on them fraternising together. Gossip columnists such as Hedda Hopper and Louella Parsons did not restrict their activities to the film community and to have ended up as fodder for one of their scoops might have produced disaster but Doris and Weidler made no secret of the fact that they were sharing a hotel room. Neither cared much for public opinion, declaring what they did away from the concert platform was no one's business but their own. Both Doris' parents and the Catholic Church hammered it into her that sex outside of marriage was morally reprehensible and maybe this was why, with her Johnny Opposite tendencies, she had always gone out of her way in her attempts to ruffle feathers and prove them wrong.

Even in 1975, when the sexual climate had changed drastically from what it had been in 1945 when Doris had just turned 21, fans of this 'perennial virgin' were shocked, on reading her memoirs, to discover that she had been no saint. Les Brown, who always considered himself some sort of surrogate father figure, was mortified by her behaviour and asked Doris to stop seeing Weidler. According to him, Weidler was only marginally less obnoxious than Al Jorden and, in any case, fraternisation among band members was forbidden. When this did not work, he ordered the pair to separate, a move which coincided with Steve Madrick returning from the forces on open-ended injury leave, causing a rift between Weidler and Brown. Weidler promptly headed for California, where he believed he could earn far more money than on the road but not before he announced that he and Doris were getting married and she would once again be leaving the band to spend more time with her family.

The wedding took place at Mount Vernon on 30 March 1946, with Doris declaring how this time she really had found the right man and they were going to live happily ever after. To celebrate her 'newfound joy', three days earlier she recorded 'I Got The Sun In The Morning' with Les Brown. Secretly, she did not love Weidler at all. As with Al Jorden, in her memoirs she pretends to have forgotten the date of her marriage, the names of the witnesses, why the wedding took place at Mount Vernon or where the couple spent their honeymoon. 'No bride ever went to her wedding with more misgivings,' she concludes. 'I should have worn black.' Which of course begs the question: why marry him in the first place?

Like the marriage to Jorden, this ceremony was slotted in between a matinee performance when George Weidler was filling in for another musician and Doris' evening performance with Les Brown. It also coincided with The Band Of Renown being offered a regular guest slot on *The Pepsodent Show*, Bob Hope's radio extravaganza (sponsored by the toothpaste company), which had topped the ratings since 1938. Initially Hope wanted only the band because he already had a singer, Frances Langford, but when Brown offered the ultimatum – no Doris, no band – he capitulated and this led to a huge row with Langford, who accused 'that

Cincinnati bitch' of muscling in on her territory. In fact, Doris' arrival on the scene was heaven-sent for the producer of the programme who had been trying to get rid of Langford for some time on account of her escalating personal problems.

Trained as an opera singer, Frances Langford (1913–2005) underwent throat surgery while young and this left her with a mellow tone more suited to singing with big bands. Discovered in 1935 by crooner Rudy Vallee, who nicknamed her 'The Florida Thrush', her signature tune was 'I'm In The Mood For Love', which Doris performed regularly on the circuit. Years later, she was amused when the song was taken up by Popeye's rubber-limbed girlfriend, Olive Oyl. Langford starred in several successful movies, most notably *Broadway Melody Of 1936*, and had just completed *Yankee Doodle Dandy* with James Cagney. She began work with Bob Hope in 1941 as one of his 'three gypsies', the others being guitarist Tony Romano and bug-eyed comic Jerry Colonna. Langford also accompanied Hope on his USO tours to combat zones at home and overseas and continued to work with him after the War and as late as 1989 in commemorative shows. She was, however, currently fighting a battle with the bottle, which Hope, ever the undisputed megalomaniac, refused to notice, fearing the slightest acknowledgement might be regarded as him supporting her and would therefore be damaging to his own career. Langford was also involved in several humiliating episodes with the military including having sex with a fighter pilot while at the controls of his plane. This incident resulted in her being let go from *The Pepsodent Show* and replaced by Doris, already described in newspaper columns as 'The Girl Next Door', though had the journalists known more about her, they might have argued that this particular girl-next-door suffered more traumas in the last few years than might have been considered appropriate for her 'wholesome' image.

Her first appearance on *The Pepsodent Show* took place on Christmas Eve 1946. Over the new four years, she became Hope's regular guest on his shows, at home or touring between movies. Despite his initial dislike of her, the two became friends. She would say, 'He's one of the few genuinely compassionate people in our business,' though away from the spotlight Hope was far removed from the happy-go-lucky, wisecracking icon adored by millions, being described as bitchy and surly. He always addressed her as 'J. B.' even on the air. This was a private joke for the initials stood for 'Jut Butt' on account of her shapely derrière. Through Hope, Doris was introduced to her first agent, Al Levy, yet another shady character who ran Century Artists with Richard Dorso and Marty Melcher.

It was Levy who recognised her enormous potential, not as a band and radio singer where he believed her talents were being wasted, but as a solo performer and potential movie star. Doris, for all her pretence that fame did not interest her, was sufficiently interested to take him seriously when he mentioned Hollywood but only if she relocated there so that she and Terry could be reunited with George Weidler, who immediately after their wedding had (like Al Jorden) hit the road. He was playing with Stan Kenton's orchestra in Los Angeles.

Levy secured Doris a regular spot on *The Sweeny & March Radio Show*, hosted by comedians Bob Sweeny and Hal March. She therefore cabled ahead to ask Weidler to find them some suitable accommodation. The best he could come up with was a trailer parked on the Midway Camp, off Sepulveda Boulevard – hardly a good start to married life forced as they were to live among drug dealers and other low-life. Matters could not have been helped when Doris insisted Alma should move in with them. For Terry's sake, she coped with the appalling conditions but the writing was clearly on the wall so far as her marriage was concerned. Though Weidler is not thought to have been violent, he was already cheating on her.

Neither was he overtly fond of his stepson. Brought up more or less single-handedly by Alma, Terry had had far too much of his own way and insufficient discipline. One incident made the press when Alma took the boy for a walk using a safety harness. He broke free just as a mounted policeman was passing. The horse reared up and a terrified Terry wrapped his harness straps around Alma's ankles, bringing her down to the pavement and shattering her leg in 14 places. As far as Weidler was concerned, the best place for Terry was as far away from him and Doris as possible.

Even after a matter of weeks, aware that her second marriage was not working out, Doris came up and asked Al Levy to find her work as far away from her husband as he could. He managed to secure her a four-week contract with ex-Vaudevillian Billy Reed, who was about to open his Little Club on New York's East 55th Street. Reed, not to be confused with British bandleader Billy Reid (then making a star of Dorothy Squires on the other side of the Atlantic), started out at 14 with a travelling minstrel show then worked in burlesque before appearing in George White's *Scandals*. By the age of 21, as a member of Gordon, Reed & King, he topped the bill at the Palace. From the late 1930s he enjoyed a secondary career writing gags for Bob Hope, Ed Wynn and Al Jolson *and* directed the danceband at the Copacobana. He had recently returned to New York after serving four years with the US Navy, followed by a lengthy stay in Paris where he was influenced by the clubs that were springing up on the Left Bank. The Little Club, with its peppermint-striped decor, was criticised by many as being way over the top but despite this the concept was to work well and earn him a fortune.

On the opening night, 26 February 1947, while performing in front of a hypercritical audience and with a pressman at almost every table, Doris suffered terrible stage fright. In an interview she confessed that moments before stepping up to the microphone she was so nervous that whatever she had eaten that day, 'suddenly came out of one end or the other.' In this respect she was very much like Barbra Streisand who, for a while after making *Funny Girl*, would do anything to get out of making live appearances – though in her case the nervousness owed more to terrorist attacks in the wake of the Arab-Israeli War when Streisand, a practising Jew, enjoyed an open affair with her Egyptian co-star Omar Sharif. Setting a precedent for the future and following in the tradition of Barney Rapp, Doris was not permitted to choose her own songs: this job went to Al Levy and partner Marty Melcher. During her opening number, 'Come To Baby, Do', she was completely ignored by the diners. It was only when she began singing 'Sentimental Journey' that they stopped chattering, put down their cutlery and listened. By her third song, 'My Dreams Are Getting Better All The Time' – which quickly followed 'Sentimental Journey' to the top of the charts – she had them in the palm of her hand. And when she ended this first recital with Jimmy Van Heusen's 'It Could Happen To You' (which she was due to record the next afternoon) she received a standing ovation.

Yet the reviews for her debut at The Little Club were barely more than backhanded compliments. One journalist called her 'good, but not *that* good'. *Variety* half-enthused, 'Miss Day is a charming young songstress,' only to conclude, 'She'll need a little more zing and change of pace to give her that special distinction that really counts for above-par values.' Even so, she had made the essential break from band to cabaret singer and her struggling husband was green with envy. Just three days later, when Billy Reed had already offered to extend her season by another month, Weidler contacted her by letter, demanding a divorce because he was convinced that his wife's continued success would only end up driving a wedge between them.

Doris had never considered herself a torch singer by any means but when Al Levy and Melcher read the contents of the letter (this had been sent to the Little Club so there was every chance that they got to read it before Doris), they monopolised the situation by changing her programme. Now she was expected to sing numbers such as 'Little Girl Blue', 'Glad To Be Unhappy' and 'You Won't Be Satisfied Until You Break My Heart' to inject a little realism into her repertoire. Unfortunately, unlike her contemporaries Helen Morgan and Ruth Etting, she was unable to contain her misery while performing and at least one show ended prematurely when she fled the stage in floods of tears.

Unable to cope with the situation any longer, Doris walked out on her contract with Billy Reed. Leaving Terry in their hotel room with Alma, she headed for Hollywood to beg Weidler to reconsider divorcing her. When she arrived at the trailer park she discovered he had moved out of their home without even leaving a forwarding address, and contacted his mother: he was eventually located and even agreed to a meeting in Pasadena. Doris called ahead to book a hotel there and arranged to meet him at the railway station but he failed to turn up and left a message with the hotel receptionist for her to meet him back at the trailer park. The couple spent one last night together, wherein Weidler told Doris he had never loved her – though this did not prevent her from having sex with him. 'I could not doubt his strong desire for me,' she later observed, 'But I guess his desire not to be Mr Doris Day was even stronger.' The next morning there was an amicable parting of the ways. The couple had been married less than eight months though their divorce proceedings were to drag on for some time on account of Doris' persistent attempts to be reconciled with him.

In the meantime, she embarked on what would become a six-year 'duets adventure' with a group of singers who appear to have been selected by her, inadvertently or not, with two criteria in mind: they had to be Jewish also like herself, descendants of immigrants. They would include Dinah Shore, Frank Sinatra, Johnnie Ray, Guy Mitchell, Frankie Laine and Donald O'Connor.

Shore was Jewish, likewise Mitchell, who was of Croatian extraction, while Sinatra and Laine were of Italian and Sicilian descent; both had Mafia connections. Donald O'Connor hailed from Irish immigrant stock. And was it merely by chance that some of these men happened to be gay at a time when Doris was starting to develop such a following and when, like Elizabeth Taylor and Judy Garland, she possessed a sixth sense for detecting a man's sexuality? The first was Buddy Clark (1911–49), born Samuel Goldberg in Dorchester, Massachusetts. Clark made his debut with Benny Goodman in 1934 and was later a regular on the *Your Hit Parade* radio show – he had had a Top Twenty hit with 'Spring Is Here'. Another success came in 1947, the year he first worked with Doris. 'Linda' was specially written for 6-year-old Linda Eastman, daughter of a showbusiness lawyer – many years later she was to marry Beatle Paul McCartney. Additionally, Clark worked as a playback singer, dubbing for other actors.

Doris and Buddy Clark entered the recording studio in November 1947 and cut two sides, 'Confess' and 'Love Somebody' (a hit for Patti Page) with George Siravo and his orchestra. The record sold a million copies and topped the American charts. On the strength of this they cut three more tracks the next year including Frank Loesser's 'My Darling'. Despite her hectic love life – at this stage of her career, one more would not have made much difference – Doris found Clark attractive, and was not put off by him being gay, though needless to say they never had an affair. Neither would she forgive him in the spring of 1949 for recording 'Baby It's Cold Outside' with Dinah Shore. To exact her revenge, she persuaded Shore to duet with her on the deprecating, appropriately titled 'You Can Have Him'. Then, in October 1949, she was consumed with guilt when she learned of his death in an air crash. He and four friends were returning from a college football game when their Cessna crash-landed on Beverly Boulevard. Even more tragic from Doris' point of view was that

Clark, thrown from the craft on impact, was the only one killed. His last hit record in his lifetime – dedicated to an unnamed male lover – had been 'I Love You So Much It Hurts'.

While George Weidler continued his tour with Stan Kenton, Doris sent Alma and Terry ahead of her and announced for the umpteenth time that she was giving up showbusiness and returning to Cincinnati. Al Levy, who had developed an unhealthy interest in her, tried to persuade her to stay by arranging for her to be invited as his date to a number of Hollywood parties which often saw her sitting alone in a corner and feeling miserable because she was always there very much against her will. One such event took place at the Beverly Hills' home of the composer Jule Styne, where the guest of honour was Styne's songwriting partner Sammy Cahn. The two had recently completed the score for a musical, *Romance On The High Seas*, which Michael Curtiz was to direct for Warner Brothers. Some time before that Curtiz offered the central role of struggling nightclub chanteuse Georgia Garrett to Judy Garland, who had been forced to reject it, being in the middle of yet another personal crisis. Curtiz next approached Betty Hutton, who signed the contract only to discover that she was pregnant. Styne heard Doris singing the Jane Froman standard, George and Ira Gershwin's 'Embraceable You' on the radio and it was he who contacted Al Levy. At his party she was asked to perform the song to determine whether she should be sent around to Curtiz' bungalow on the Warners' lot the next morning with a view to having him secure her a screen test. She refused, declaring she was not in the mood for entertaining! Such a defeatist attitude in the company of Hollywood's elite might have resulted in any other artiste being shown the door. She was still sent to Curtiz and after hearing her sing – very badly it would appear because the song reminded her of George Weidler and she could not stop crying – he refused to take no for an answer. She was offered the test and shown footage of some of the other actresses Curtiz had tested and rejected just to remind her how privileged she was. 'Literally, the screen exploded,' Sammy Cahn recalled in a BBC interview of 1994. 'All the others were hopelessly inept – there was absolutely no questioning this girl's talent.'

Hungarian-born Michael Curtiz (Mihaly Kertesz 1888–1962) was one of the most respected but feared directors in Hollywood. He began work for Warner Brothers in 1926 and since then he had made over 60 films, many of them timeless classics. These included *The Adventures Of Robin Hood* with Errol Flynn, *The Private Lives Of Elizabeth* with Flynn and Bette Davis, *Casablanca* with Ingrid Bergman and Humphrey Bogart, and most recently *Mildred Pierce* with Joan Crawford – all tetchy individuals who needed firm directorial control but who had only brought out the worst in his volatile temperament.

Despite his many years in America, Curtiz deliberately failed to master the English language other than its profanities from which no one was spared. Depending on their own temperament, various stars had their own ways of dealing with him. Tough-guy actor George O'Brien, denounced as a 'prickless faggot' on the set of *Noah's Ark*, burst into tears. Bette Davis spat in his face during *Cabin In The Sky* when he called her 'a sexless son-of-a-bitch'. When Ross Alexander stripped for a flogging scene in *Captain Blood* and displayed exuberant armpits, which contravened Hays Office censorship regulations, Errol Flynn had grabbed the razor Curtiz just happened to have in his pocket and threatened to cut the director's throat, should he so much as remove one hair of his lover's 'magnificent oxters'.

David Niven recalled in his memoirs, *Bring On The Empty Horses*, another altercation with Flynn while shooting *The Charge Of The Light Brigade* when Flynn returned an insult by calling Curtiz 'a thick-as-pig-shit bowl of goulash', bringing the response, 'You lousy faggot bum! You think I know fuck nothing! Well, let me tell you something, I know fuck *all*!' His attitude to Doris' apparent lethargy was to order her to 'drag her sobbing mother-fucker ass' across to the Warner lot for a screen test. She claimed to have been so shocked that she complied. Even so, her attitude was no less contrary. Not caring whether or not she got the part – this had been toned down to fourth lead now that the role of Georgia Garrett was not going to Judy Garland or Betty Hutton – she called Billy Reed the same morning and agreed to return to the Little Club to complete the second four-week season that she had just walked out on. For Curtiz' benefit she made an effort not to look smart, turning up in clothes she usually wore for lounging around in, with her hair unkempt. When his assistant commented on her lack of enthusiasm she gave as good as she got. She always had her hair done Tuesdays, so why have it done now when it was only Monday?

Jack Carson, the star of the film, decided he did not want to get involved with the screen test and sent a stand-in instead. Therefore, Doris opined, why should she bother? Curtiz admired her spirit and lack of nerves before the camera and asked her to do two songs: 'Embraceable You' and Leo Robin and Arthur Schwartz's livelier, 'What Do We Do On A Rainy Night In Rio', which she hated. Like Peggy Lee, her nearest contemporary, she performed both songs standing stock-still and when Curtiz asked her to swing her hips a little, she replied that she did not want to, which precipitated him grabbing her about the waist and commanding, 'I said *move* that motherfucker ass, darlink!' Her reaction was peppered with more expletives than he had probably heard from a woman, resulting in her becoming one of a mere handful of female stars who not only liked Michael Curtiz, but asked to work with him again. The reason for her fearlessness was uncomplicated: like Greta Garbo she frequently declared that if push came to shove she could always return to her home, Cincinnati, and her roots.

If Doris pretended to be shocked by Curtiz' gruff mannerisms and colourful language, in return he was genuinely surprised by her honesty. This was an age of studio publicist-invented biographies. Back then the general public never found out how Joan Crawford clawed her way to Hollywood by way of the casting couch and a collection of stag-movies. Nor were they aware that Clark Gable had sold himself as a prostitute to other men or indeed that Errol Flynn had come from Tasmania by way of an extremely controversial path and that he was not really an Irish ex-boxer! Doris shared one facet of her character with Crawford in that her motto was, 'I am what I am, and so is a stone – those who don't like me can leave me alone!' Curtiz and the executives at Warner Brothers were told in no uncertain terms that should she become famous (which she herself personally doubted) then she would never hide her light under the proverbial bushel. She was an ordinary girl from Ohio, the daughter of a broken home, and a divorcee who had had a very rough time of things with an abusive husband. There was nothing she had ever done in her life, she added, that she should feel ashamed of and no publicist would ever make up stories about her otherwise she would cry them down at the expense of a movie career she had never been bothered about in the first place!

By sticking up for herself, Doris got the part in *Romance On The High Seas* and Michael Curtiz went out of his way to defend her when Jack Warner tried to add a clause to her contract that she should have a crash course at the studio's acting school before shooting began. In her memoirs she recounted the cleaned-up version of how the director took her to one side and told her in his broken English, 'You have a natural thing in there should no one ever disturb. You listen, Doris! Is very rare thing, do not disturb!' Many years later she would use the latter phrase as the title for one of her films.

Warner Brothers' rivals never expected the film to amount to much and they were proved right. MGM more or less had the monopoly on directors, producers, scriptwriters, costumiers, photographers and stars at this time. Nor was Curtiz experienced in the medium, his own speciality being adventure and drama. As an actress Doris is hopeless in her part and in the light of her later successes it is at times embarrassing to watch, though through no fault of her own. The dialogue she pronounces is corny and she is not allowed enough time to deliver each line, resulting in her speech being gabbled and frequently incomprehensible. She was also the first to confess that much of the time she looks a mess. 'There I was on the screen,' she said, 'a pancaked, lacquered Hollywood purse made out of Cincinnati sow's ear.'

The plot of *Romance On The High Seas* centres around the suspected extramarital exploits of a socialite couple (Janis Paige, Don DeFore). When Elvira Kent thinks her husband is cheating on her rather than cancel the ocean cruise to South America that she is already booked on, she hires dowdy Georgia Garrett and spends a fortune kitting her out so that she can impersonate her and stay in town to spy on her spouse. Not that Doris looks particularly good for all the money lavished on her. When he learns that Elvira is going to be singing during the voyage (she is tone deaf), the husband suspects an ulterior motive and hires a private detective (Jack Carson) to keep an eye on *her*. Carson complicates matters by falling for his quarry who has another secret admirer, played by musician Oscar Levant. (It was Levant who famously quipped, some years later of Doris' so-called 'innocence' status, 'I knew Doris Day *before* she was a virgin!'). Naturally all ends well when it is revealed that no one is cheating at all.

Though *Romance On The High Seas* is today is regarded as far too syrupy, its place in Hollywood history is guaranteed by Doris' stunning interpretation of 'It's Magic', which was used as the title of the movie for the British and European release. We first hear it performed in Spanish by two guitarists until someone hands Doris (sitting at a table with Jack Carson) a sheet containing the English lyrics. This being Hollywood, she already knows the tune without rehearsal and can effect a delivery which is not just spot on but sends shivers down the spine, particularly when the Spaniards join her in the final coda. The recording reached Number Two in the American charts and was nominated for an Academy Award, replacing 'Sentimental Journey' as her signature tune and selling a million copies within a month of its release – impressive for the time. Another then important aspect of the film, promoting the Hollywood dream, was the suggestion that any working-class girl could, with the right combination of circumstances and luck, be transformed into a household name.

Though they were worlds apart, artistically Doris could in this way be compared with Joan Crawford, who a decade earlier proved to her legion of so-called 'shop-girl' fans that a formerly downtrodden, poverty-stricken factory worker could through sheer strength of will triumph over every adversity and end up with the society beau. Though this did not happen to Doris, while making the film she did have an affair with gargantuan wisecracker Jack Carson. Born in Manitoba, Canada, Carson (1910–63) worked as an insurance salesman then progressed to Vaudeville. In 1937 he arrived in Hollywood to work as an extra with RKO Pictures. His Warner Brothers' career began in 1941 when he proved himself a dependable character actor typecast as dumb city slickers and the inarticulate guy-next-door with the heart of gold who invariably lost the girl at the end of the picture, as happened with Joan Crawford in *Mildred Pierce*. Despite his carefree on-screen characterisations, Carson was, like all the other men Doris had loved and lost, not always very nice to know away from the screen.

By now the gossip columnists were sending their spies around to Warner Brothers in search of tidbits – as were the Hays Office, who had just found out about Doris being used as a punch-bag by Al Jorden. The studio therefore elected to take advantage of the resulting publicity by teaming Doris and Jack Carson in *My*

Dream Is Yours, again directed by Michael Curtiz. Warner Brothers hit on the idea of drawing attention to the film by pairing Doris with Frank Sinatra (though he had nothing to do with the production) to record Irving Berlin's 'Let's Take An Old Fashioned Walk'. Sinatra's career had recently taken a nosedive and the studio hoped a hit record with Doris (to be released at the same time as the film) might give him for a much-needed boost. But the song was not a great hit and it would take another six years – and the success of *From Here To Eternity* – for Sinatra to get back on his feet. Both he and Doris loathed the experience of sharing a studio booth. She was far too relaxed and he too full of himself for there to be any follow-ups though they would, with extreme reluctance, work together again in the not-too-distant future.

My Dream Is Yours was an out and out dire production, saved only by Doris' magnificent singing, particularly her crystal-clear delivery of 'I'll String Along With You' to her on-screen son, a song she dedicated to Terry. Despite this, there are moments that make one cringe: the dream sequence after she reads the boy a bedtime story sees Doris and Jack Carson camping it up as oversized rabbits – and Warner Brothers getting a plug in for their *Bugs Bunny* cartoons. As in *Romance On The High Seas*, when delivering dialogue she tends to pop her eyes like Eddie Cantor. Lee Bowman, popular with audiences but regarded by colleagues as a nasty piece of work away from the screen, played alcoholic crooner Garry Mitchell, the biggest draw at a radio station, who is fired for being drunk once too often. Enter his manager and talent-scout (Carson), who replaces him with Martha Gibson (Doris), a young widow with a small son. Such a scenario, particularly when she soothes the boy with a tender song, was orchestrated to mirror Doris' own life. Naturally she proves a huge hit with listeners and having fallen in love with the odious Mitchell, she enables him to get rid of his demons by persuading the radio station boss to give him another chance.

The film featured several past-future Doris Day 'regulars'. Roly-poly Hungarian character actor S. Z. 'Cuddles' Sakall (1884–1955), who plays her radio sponsor, worked with Max Reinhardt in Berlin and like many fled to the US on the eve of World War II to evade Nazi persecution. Arguably his most memorable role was that of the wobbly-jowled German waiter in *Casablanca*. Fast-talking comedienne Eve Arden (1912–90), who plays Jack Carson's partner, was a former Ziegfeld girl who also appeared in *Mildred Pierce* as Mildred's wisecracking restaurateur friend and contributed to some of the film's lighter moments. Later in life, similarly to Doris, she was to enjoy great success on the small screen.

Jack Warner tried to fob off Louella, Hedda et al by putting out the story that Doris was at liberty to love whomsoever she chose because she was now a free woman following her divorce from George Weidler. In fact the decree absolute did not come through until 31 May 1949. What Jack Carson did not know was that Doris was actually 'cheating' on him with her husband – the two enjoyed several reunions when Stan Kenton's band came to Los Angeles. Though he also had a mistress, Weidler apologised to Doris for treating her shabbily so soon after their marriage and swore that he had turned over a new leaf, applying the old chestnut that he had found religion.

Born and raised a Catholic, Doris had always disliked the discipline. The fact that as a child she had been compelled to enter the confessional and confess her sins as a small child always nauseated her; children, she believed, did not have sins. Catholicism, she declared, was an empty ritual without meaning, which makes her next move not too difficult to comprehend and again points to her extreme naivety. When a man asked Doris Day to jump, no matter how despicable he might have been, the question she invariably posed was, 'How high?'

A friend had recently introduced Weidler to the teachings of Mary Baker Eddy (1821–1910) who, though raised as a Congregationalist, rejected the formal teachings of her faith following 'divine intervention' during a series of illnesses and a serious spinal injury brought about by a fall from which she had 'miraculously' recovered without medical help. Three-times married and not the role model she made herself out to be, Eddy's theory – which today would almost surely see her labelled a crank but in 1866 was taken very seriously by gullible believers – was that 'illness was but an illusion which could be healed through a clearer conception of God'. As such, she founded the Christian Science movement, whose edicts as detailed in her *Science With A Key To The Scriptures*, published in 1875, profess that since God is good and is a spirit then matter and evil are ultimately unreal. Suffice to say, when she was unable to find a legitimate publishing company willing to take her on, Eddy financed the publication herself. The original print run sold just 800 copies but most of the 'students' who bought copies had begun to move around the country, thereby spreading the word. This resulted in Eddy having many thousands of followers by the time of her death, by which time she had founded several weekly publications including *The Christian Science Monitor*, which is still published today. As a consequence true followers of the religion still shy away from orthodox medical treatment preferring to rely on healing they believe to be brought about by 'operation of truth within the human conscience'. What makes this laughable – hypocritical even – to non-believers is that one of its laws 'shuns the cult of personality' – not that this has prevented many major stars from joining its ranks just to get noticed. Two prime examples have been Joan Crawford and Elizabeth Taylor, whose religious beliefs have almost cost them their lives, both having refused medical intervention when they fell seriously ill. Doris herself has mocked the movement: 'My Cincinnati upbringing had taught me that [Eddy] was some sort of witch and that Christian Science was some sort of crazy ritual which caused you to end up sick and dying because you were forbidden to see a doctor,' she observed in her memoirs. Ironically, after their divorce Doris would sign up to his beliefs.

George Weidler took Mary Baker Eddy's theories a step further, declaring they also applied to the mind: if Doris took the time to search inside her head she would find, by way of her conscience, a means of forgiving him so that he could re-enter her life. Effectively, it was his way of brainwashing her so that he could continue to have sex with her. Al Jorden's earlier accusation that Doris was an unstoppable flirt, if not an actual nymphomaniac, appears to have had some substance. This was partly due to attention-seeking, or it could have been a way of seeking attention or it could perhaps have been exacerbated by the lack of a father figure during her formative years but she certainly seems to have had an uncontrollable appetite for men who were mean, moody or downright psychotic. The latest man to be added to her list was her agent Al Levy, who since introducing her to Michael Curtiz, had taken it upon himself to be her Svengali. Like Jorden, he appears to have been bisexual: his way of displaying affection towards a woman appears to have been similarly through power and fear. Doris played straight into his hands by allowing him to wine, dine and seduce her. This developed into an unhealthy obsession when all she ever wanted from him was sex. With Weidler back in her life – she believed for good – Levy was now unceremoniously shunted aside and told that although she had enjoyed their fling, from now on he would have to be satisfied with just being her agent.

Levy did not take kindly to being relegated from stud to serf and, like Al Jorden, he began to stalk Doris when she was out on the town with George Weidler or Jack Carson. He also 'perved' on her when she was changing in her dressing room or from the catwalk above the studio soundstage. Matters came to a head when Doris confronted him during a 'friends-only' dinner date. Levy followed her back to her hotel room where he attempted to rape her. A more rational woman would have reported such an incident to the police – if not the regular force, then the one employed by every major studio whose methods of dealing with any problem from shoplifting to murder may have been unorthodox but were certainly effective. Instead, she went to see Levy's partners, Richard Dorso and Marty Melcher at Century Artists.

Though Dorso, Melcher and Levy were equal partners in their franchise, Levy was more or less forced to relocate to New York to run Century Artists' office there – it was either that or run the risk of Doris reporting him for rape. The move would see her jumping out of the frying pan and into the fire, however. No sooner was Levy gone than Melcher moved in on her by way of 'helping' her cope with the series of anonymous cards and letters winging her way. All were written on the same stationery, suggesting they were sent by the same person – a woman who had an affair with Levy and who praised his good points (which in truth were few) – and reminded Doris what a fool she had been for letting such a kind, considerate man go. The correspondence was actually from Levy himself, hoping to woo her back. Melcher knew this and, like his predecessor, he was only too eager to take advantage of her vulnerability.

Chapter 4

Shaking The Blues Away

'I always had a feeling, when Melcher was around, that he wasn't looking out for Doris as much as he was looking out for himself. Needless to say, he wasn't one of my favourite characters.'

Bob Hope

Born in 1915 and formerly a native of North Adams, Massachusetts, and 6 foot 3 inches, Marty Melcher was the current tour manager of the Andrews Sisters, who were phenomenally successful during World War II but were now going through a career hiatus. He was also married to their lead singer Patty yet within days of taking Doris Day under his wing, so to speak, the two were having an affair.

It was Melcher who secured one of the leads for Doris in *It's A Great Feeling*, the last of the trilogy with Jack Carson though even as second lead to Carson's first both were way down the celebrity pecking order. This was the first of Doris' six films directed by David Butler (1894–1979), who very quickly developed an unreciprocated crush on the pretty blonde – not on account of her peaches and cream looks but because of the way she expressed emotion. In those days it was considered inappropriate for actresses to be seen with tears streaming down their cheeks, not to mention a problem for the make-up department. What got to him, Butler said in a BBC radio interview of 1994 (around the time of Doris' seventieth birthday), was her uncanny ability to allow her eyes to well up with tears but never release them. Though her collaborations with Butler would only get better, this one failed in its attempt to follow in the stamp of all-star extravaganzas such as *Stage Door Canteen* (1944), in that the director brought in a veritable Who's Who of Hollywood for the cameo roles: Joan Crawford, Gary Cooper, Sydney Greenstreet, Edward G. Robinson, Danny Kaye and Errol Flynn were but a few. Butler hired Jule Styne and Sammy Cahn to write an excellent score (the only saving grace of the production).

The scenario (a satire on Hollywood) was supposed to be funny – and was anything but. Jack Carson, who had several on-set altercations with Errol Flynn, portrayed the ham movie actor whose behaviour is so abominable no one will work with him, mirroring Carson's own characteristics. Not only does he end up directing his own film, he forces his latest leading lady Judy Adams (Doris), a waitress from Gerkin Corners, Wisconsin who he has discovered working in the studio canteen, to camp things up in a scene which is so bad that it becomes a classic. As French chanteuse Yvonne Amour, she dons a gold lamé dress and black wig, murders a perfectly decent song – the first and only time this would happen in Doris' career – and later appears in yet another dreadful dream sequence as a Parisian prostitute crooning 'There's Nothing Rougher Than Love'. Little wonder she is soon winging it back to Wisconsin to wed former sweetheart Jeffrey Bushdinel! During the ceremony the couple stand with their backs to the camera and it is only when they turn round to kiss in the closing shot that the groom is revealed to be Flynn.

It's A Great Feeling premièred in August 1949, the same week as Doris released her first album, *You're My Thrill*, title-track courtesy of Jay Gorney and Sidney Clare. The 10-inch vinyl album in which she duets on four numbers with The Mellow-tones surprised her by shooting to Number Five in the US charts. Highlights included 'Sometimes I'm Happy', 'When Your Lover Has Gone', a near-definitive rendition of Rodgers and Hart's 'Bewitched, Bothered And Bewildered', and a so-so cover of Marlene Dietrich's 'You Go To My Head'. Six years later the album was re-released as *Day Dreams* featuring four extra tracks including the Kate Smith standard 'Imagination'.

Her next film, technically, was but another typical Hollywood exercise in the rewriting of showbusiness history but one that nevertheless resulted in a prestigious *film noir*. *Young Man With A Horn*, Doris' third outing with Michael Curtiz, was based on Dorothy Baker's best-selling novel of 1938 and purported to be a re-telling of the Bix Beiderbecke story. Later she later described shooting as, 'One of the few utterly joyless experiences I had in films.'

Beiderbecke (1903–31) was an impressive cornet player who also excelled as a jazz and classical pianist. Born in Davenport, Iowa, his influences were Mississippi riverboat bands. Sickly throughout his life, he attended Chicago's Lake Forest Academy but flunked his lectures in favour of the city's speakeasies – subsequently the Dean threw him out and he took up music full-time. Beiderbecke cut his first records with The Wolverines in 1924 and went on to play with numerous outfits, most notably The Paul Whiteman Orchestra. No one knows for sure what ailed him – contemporary reports point to polio and circulatory problems exacerbated by suspect prohibition whisky. His death, at just 28, has always been looked on as suspicious: the death certificate states lobar pneumonia but rumours at the time suggested suicide or even murder.

In *Young Man With A Horn* the music is fabulous and everyone smokes a lot – even the narrator played by Hoagy Carmichael is called Smoke. Twenty-something Beiderbecke becomes Rick Martin, played by 34-year-old Kirk Douglas, who eschews his usual hale and hearty self and carries the burdens of the neurotic, hypersensitive musician with great conviction – though by 1950 even those cinema audiences familiar with Beiderbecke's work knew little about his personal life other than the stories fed to the movie magazines by Warner Brother's publicity department. Doris has said that Douglas was civil towards her and that was about all – he also admits this in his memoirs.

The archetypal loner following the deaths of his parents, Rick wanders into a downtown church and learns how to play the piano in a single day. What really interests him though is the trumpet and with the help of friendly black jazzman Art Hazard (Juano Hernandez), he achieves his ambition and success but because he needs to embellish every piece he plays, he soon earns the enmity of the bandleader who takes him on. The playing was by the legendary Harry James: his and Doris' album of the soundtrack topped the American charts.

Enter nightclub chanteuse Jo Jordan (Doris), who teaches Rick to believe in himself, enabling him to get work with a better band only to do him more damage than good by introducing him to her high-brow flighty friend Amy (Lauren Bacall). Rick marries Amy but the marriage fails because she is not really into men; Art dies in a car crash and Rick sinks into alcoholic decline. At this stage in his life Bix Beiderbecke was dying. Kirk Douglas, however, was a huge name and Warner Brothers deemed it inappropriate that an actor of such renown for portraying tough guys should be incapable of fighting the effects of the bottle and mere pneumonia. Therefore he was allowed to live and according to Smoke's closing narration: to survive, achieve fame and become a better person.

Officially Doris was third lead in the film though the press was told that she had equal billing with Kirk Douglas and Lauren Bacall to bolster publicity for her next project, in which she would play the lead. Upon its release in the UK, *Young Man With A Horn* brought guffaws of hilarity from the closeted gay community –

'horn' being a slang term for an erection. Therefore the title was very quickly changed to *Young Man Of Music*. In Europe and Australasia it was given the less endearing title *Young Man With A Trumpet*.

There was also speculation over Amy's sexuality. 'It must be wonderful to wake up on a morning and know just which door you're going to walk through,' Amy says of Jo: 'She's so terribly normal!' And of her friend, Jo tells Rick, 'Amy isn't a stage-door pick-up. I know her much better than you do. She's a strange girl and you've never known anything about her . . . way inside, she's all mixed up!' Later in the film Amy's lesbianism is further confirmed when she announces she is going to Paris with a girl who 'completely understands' her – and by her frequently frosty attitude towards her husband, one of the contributory factors towards his downfall.

The film kick-started Doris' and Lauren Bacall's secondary careers as gay icons, enabling them to join the ranks of Judy Garland and Marlene Dietrich: Doris, because of her off-screen suffering, Bacall on account of a snatch of silly dialogue. There is a scene in the film when upon meeting Rick, Amy pronounces, 'You can call me Amy,' to which he responds, 'I *bet* I could!' In the bars and clubs around Piccadilly, London, where *palare* or gay slang was the order of the day, these became essential chat-up lines for a while. Some years later the film was parodied on Kenneth Horne's high-camp BBC radio series *Round The Horne* when two of the characters brought Piccadilly *palare* to a national audience. It was then re-titled *Young Horne With A Man* featuring Bix Spiderthrust!

Jo Jordan was Doris' first all-out dramatic role, with Michael Curtiz sardonically getting her to inject Method into the role of the long-suffering singer. Even the name was too close for comfort and it must have reminded her of her traumatic experiences with Al Jorden, which is perhaps why she gave such a sterling performance though most of the critics found the film – at almost two hours – too long. Sadly, the songs are all that is remembered of *Young Man With A Horn* nowadays and even they were plucked from Doris' repertoire as a band singer during those miserable years with her abusive ex-husband: 'I May Be Wrong', 'The Very Thought Of You', 'Too Marvellous For Words', 'I Only Have Eyes For You' and 'With A Song In My Heart', which she sang with Jane Froman's blessing. The soundtrack album, released by Columbia in March 1950, topped the American charts.

Another showstopper in Froman's concerts had always been 'Tea For Two' from Irving Caesar, Otto Harbach and Vincent Youman's *No, No, Nanette!* which opened at London's Palace Theatre in March 1925. With Binnie Hale and George Grossmith Jr playing the leads, the production ran for 665 performances before transferring to Broadway. At the time it was claimed that the producer Harry Frazee, a former owner of the Boston Red Sox baseball team, had sold the legendary Babe Ruth to finance the production. In 1930 *No, No, Nanette!* was made into a film starring Bernice Claire and ZaSu Pitts, who also starred in the 1940 remake alongside Anna Neagle and Victor Mature, directed by Neagle's husband Herbert Wilcox.

Now Doris was signed with Gordon MacRae (1921–86) and Gene Nelson to a second remake to be directed by her friend David Butler. For the first time her name headed the credits and as a matter of course she asked for two of her 'regulars' to be given parts: S. Z. Sakall and Eve Arden, who also appeared in the 1940 version. Arden is said to have been behind Warner Brothers' decision to bring in Harry Clork to write the script. Clork (1888–1978) was best known for his stageplay *The Milky Way*, filmed in 1946 as *The Kid From Brooklyn* with Arden and Danny Kaye.

As was usual in Hollywood, Clork was asked to doctor the original story centring around bible-bashing millionaire Jimmy Smith and his tight-wad wife Sue's attempts to transform their wild-child ward Nanette into a respectable lady. In his far-fetched but hugely entertaining version of events, wealthy heiress and aspiring singer Nanette Carter asks her Uncle Max (Sakall) – who manages her financial affairs – to sub her $25,000 so that she can finance a Broadway extravaganza called *No, No Nanette!* featuring songs by her boyfriend Larry Blair (Billy DeWolfe, who nicknamed Doris 'Clara Bixby', a name that would stick until she was 're-baptised' by Rock Hudson) – with Doris and Jimmy Smith (MacRae) as the stars of the show. What she is unaware of is that her fortune – badly invested by Uncle Max – was wiped out by the 1929 Wall Street Crash and that Larry plans on putting his *other* girlfriend Beatrice (Patrice Wymore) into the show. To avoid handing over the money, Uncle Max wagers Nanette $25,000 that she will be incapable of saying 'No' to every question she is asked over the next 48 hours.

Uncle Max tells the story in flashback to Nanette and Jimmy's children. It opens with Nanette and Jimmy rehearsing 'I Know That You Know' with dancer Tommy Trainer – a superlative performance from Gene Nelson, who could have easily given Fred Astaire a run for his money. Of course the public instinctively knew from the moment they set eyes on the squeaky-clean and wholesome Jimmy – and especially after he and Nanette have duetted on 'I Only Have Eyes For You' – that Gordon MacRae and not the camp and cheesy Billy DeWolfe would walk Doris down the aisle after the closing credits but this did not stop them going along with the charade. Thrown into the mix is Nanette's man-mad assistant-confidante Pauline (Arden), who shadows her to ensure she never forgets to say 'No', even when Jimmy asks her if she loves him. Nanette wins the wager only to discover that Uncle Max no longer has the cash to settle up with her and she is further devastated to learn that Jimmy has left town.

Being a Hollywood musical, a happy ending is obligatory, however. Pauline seduces and marries Uncle Max's lawyer whose own fortune was unaffected by the Crash. He puts up the money and Nanette and Jimmy get to do their show – whose title, *No, No, Nanette!* is mentioned for the first time – and naturally it's a huge success. The film ends on the tackiest note imaginable: a ridiculously aged-up Nanette and Jimmy arrive home from a trip to find their children dressed up in their old Vaudeville clothes, offering the last few couplets of the title-track as the credits roll. Doris later recalled that this reminded her of the sketch that she and Jerry Doherty performed for the Almes & Doepke department store competition all those years ago when they wore cheap garish costumes designed by their mothers.

Tea For Two was a hit on both sides of the Atlantic, with five of the leads – Doris, Gordon MacRae, Gene Nelson, S. Z. Sakall and Eve Arden – receiving equal plaudits. MacRae enjoyed some success as a child actor on radio before moving to the Broadway stage. His film debut was in 1948 in *The Big Punch* and the following year he made his first movie musical: *Look For The Silver Lining*, with June Haver. There would be four more films with Doris, who appears to have shown amorous interest in the hunky baritone. This was unreciprocated – until their divorce in 1967 MacRae would only have eyes for his British actress wife, Sheila MacRae (Sheila Stevens) who he married in 1941.

Gene Nelson (1920–96) would also ask to work with Doris again. Inspired to take up dancing by watching Fred Astaire and Ginger Rogers' movies, Nelson worked with the Sonja Henie Ice Show for three years before serving in World War II. His acting career, which peaked with the role of Will Parker in *Oklahoma!* (1955), ended two years later when a horse fell on top of him, shattering his pelvis. However, he went on to enjoy success behind the camera, directing episodes of television's *I Dream Of Jeannie* and *Star Trek*. With his producer-partner Sam Katzman he also became a supremo of the frequently tacky, ultra-camp and rapidly assembled Hollywood musicals that were hugely reminiscent of the pre-war 'quota-quickies'. Two notable examples starred Elvis Presley: *Kissing Cousins* and *Harem Holiday*.

If Doris was riding on the crest of a wave after the success of *Tea For Two* then she was brought back down to earth with a bump when Marty Melcher informed her that her next film, *The West Point Story*, would see her relegated to third billing after James Cagney and Virginia Mayo. Again applying the adage that she didn't care whether or not she returned to Cincinnati – there would be a place for her in *somebody's* band, she declared – she marched right into Jack Warner's office and for the first and last time in her career gave a studio mogul a piece of her mind. Garbo had done this many times with the equally megalomaniac Louis B. Mayer but with the exception of Garbo, major stars had been fired for less and Warner informed Doris in no uncertain terms that if she wanted to quit the movies, he personally would escort her to the door. She capitulated on learning that Gordon MacRae was to be in the film and when Warner further added that her 'forfeit' for questioning his judgement would be a second film with third billing, she accepted her punishment with dignity. Despite her threat she really did not want to go back to being a band singer.

In *The West Point Story* James Cagney plays Bix Bixby, a washed-out Broadway musical director, who against his will accepts a commission from a producer to stage a show at West Point – written by the producer's nephew Cadet Tom Fletcher (MacRae). Bixby travels to the academy with his girlfriend (Mayo) in the hope of getting Tom to leave West Point and return with him to New York. This being a Cagney film, there are the inevitable resulting fisticuffs with 50-year-old Cagney-Bixby ridiculously becoming a cadet himself. Fifty minutes into the film, enter former chorus girl and now movie star Jan Wilson (Doris), one of the proposed stars of the show, who goes out to West Point to rehearse. Naturally she and Tom fall in love and he asks her to marry him. When Jan receives a studio call and returns to

Hollywood, Tom goes AWOL to be with her; he gets arrested and the production is cancelled. From that point on the story becomes too far-fetched. It just so happens that the French prime minister visits West Point, remembers presenting Bixby with the *Legion d'honneur* for his bravery while fighting with the Resistance and therefore offers him a pardon! The show is allowed to proceed but only with its original all-male cast. Then there's another twist when Tom is about to sing his big production number, Sammy Cahn and Jule Styne's 'You Love Me' to 'princess' Alan Hale when Doris emerges from the scenery and saves the day!

Like *Tea For Two*, *The West Point Story* has more than its share of camp moments, particularly some of the scenes at the academy, where during rehearsals for Tom Fletcher's show, the absence of women results in all the parts being played by men. The 'Kissing Rock' sequence where the cadets dance with each other must be seen to be believed and one wonders how it got past the censor! James Cagney fought against shooting the scene in which he punches a cadet – the young man wolf-whistles at him while he teaches a man how to dance like a lady!

There's no doubt that this is Cagney's film, through and through. 'If everything about *The West Point Story* were anything near as good as Jimmy Cagney,' enthused the *New York Times'* frequently acerbic Bosley Crowther, 'this would be the top musical of the year . . . The measure of Mr Cagney's impact upon the whole tenuous show is patently indicated when he is *not* on the screen. For then the thing sags in woeful fashion, the romance becomes absurd and the patriotic chest thumping becomes so much chorus-boy parade. And this despite some vigorous punching on the part of a bright young thing called Doris Day.'

Fancying a change of pace, Doris tentatively agreed to play the lead in David Butler's *Painting The Clouds With Sunshine*. Her co-stars for this lively romp set against a Tin Pan Alley background were Dennis Morgan and Gene Nelson. Just as quickly she then changed her mind on hearing that Steve Cochran (1917–65) had asked for her to appear in his next film.

Though she had tremendous admiration for her childhood idol Ginger Rogers – even more so once she learned Rogers was a devotee of Christian Science – Doris was very much against being billed beneath her in *Ku-Klux-Klan: Storm Warning*, which for obvious reasons would be abridged to *Storm Warning* during the production stage. She also protested against her character dying, the first and last time this would happen in a Doris Day movie. What angered her most of all, however, was being told that Rogers had only been offered her part because Joan Crawford had turned it down with a curt, 'Who the fuck's gonna believe that somebody like me would have a sister like Doris Day?' In this respect, Doris would have her revenge. Years later she told her friend Rock Hudson, 'Who the fuck would have believed that the sister Joan Crawford never had would have ended up with her fella?'

Joan would always dislike Doris for 'purloining' Steve Cochran, one of the film's two male leads – the other was dull-as-watching-paint-dry Ronald Reagan. The previous year Joan and Cochran sizzled as the gangster and his moll in *The Damned Don't Cry* and they had enjoyed a passionate affair during and after the shooting schedule. The fact that Cochran had been offered his part in *Storm Warning* after Joan turned hers down would always rankle, particularly as he did not end his relationship with Joan before making a play for Doris, who like his other conquests did not take much tempting to fall in love with him.

Steve Cochran was an extremely handsome, virile and famously hirsute actor who oozed heated sexuality and said more with his heavy-lidded eyes than most actors could put into words. A former cowpuncher, he appeared in Mae West's scandalous Broadway revival of *Diamond Lil* and made no secret of the fact that he kept the much older star's bed warm every night after the show. He invariably played the cynical, hard-edged thug whereas away from the set he was regarded as one of the nicest, gentlest men in Hollywood. Cochran also had a fearless reputation as a womaniser: besides Joan Crawford and Mae West his scores of conquests included Jayne Mansfield, Sabrina, Merle Oberon, Ida Lupino – and Mamie Van Doren, in whose memoirs no details about their sex-life are spared especially when discussing his legendary appendage, said to have been one of the largest in Hollywood which had earned him the nickname 'Mr King Size'. The Los Angeles crime writer James Ellroy, who frequently referred to Cochran in his novels, took this one step further by awarding him the moniker 'Steve The Schvantz' . . . *schvantz* being the Yiddish word for penis. Cochran's lovers and friends, Doris included, were devastated when, in June 1965, shortly after his forty-eighth birthday, this fun-loving man died aboard his yacht of an acute lung infection, a tragedy made even worse by the fact that his body lay aboard the craft for 10 days until it drifted into a Guatemalan port because his three-female 'crew' had not known how to navigate or signal for help.

Like *The Damned Don't Cry* and Cochran's earlier gangster classic *White Heat* (1949) which most critics regard as his finest hour, *Storm Warning* is a cracker of a film albeit very disturbing, even now over half a century on, with its graphic scenes of violence and burning crosses.

'I got power – I'm a big guy in this town!' the caption beneath his publicity shot reads, while the trailer proclaimed, 'Here Is A Picture More Tense Than Words Can Describe – As Fresh As The Ink on Tomorrow's Headlines!' The story centres on Marsha Mitchell (Rogers), who is first seen late at night on the rickety bus en-route to Rock Point, a backwoods town where, in this instance and certainly so far as the scriptwriter was concerned, intelligence appears to be on ration and everyone seems to have a secret agenda. Marsha is there to visit her pregnant sister Lucy Rice (Doris), who works as a waitress at the local bowling alley. Unable to find a cab, she sets off walking but while hiding in the shadows, she witnesses a reporter being pursued and shot by members of the Ku Klux Klan. They remove their hoods and she recognises one of the killers as Lucy's husband Hank (Cochran). This leaves her with a predicament: Lucy knows nothing about his criminal activities – to her, he's just a simple mill-worker; should she go to the police and later testify in court to what she has seen subsequently ruining her sister's happiness?

Marsha's mind is made up when the over-sexed Hank gets drunk and tries to rape her after she calls him a 'stupid, vicious ape'. She is subsequently apprehended by the Ku Klux Klan and seems set to be disposed of until the District Attorney (Reagan) arrives with the cops. Neither are the locals interested in opposing these people, it seems. 'We don't *like* these people,' one big-wig opines, 'but this prosecution's *bad* for the town, bad for business!' Even at this stage Lucy refuses to see anything wrong in the man she married, reflecting real life of course. 'He isn't bad,' she screams, 'I don't care what he's done, I'm not gonna leave him!' In the ensuing scuffle after Marsha finally shops him to the authorities, Hank pulls a gun and fires at Marsha, but it's Lucy who catches the bullet, expiring in Marsha's arms. *Storm Warning* remains least favourite of many Doris Day fans simply because she died in it. This is a great pity because like *The Damned Don't Cry*, it is in every sense a *film noir* and as such a mini-masterpiece of the genre.

Around this time Doris was certainly burning the candle at both ends which may explain why Alma did not wish Terry to spend too much time with her. Besides Steve Cochran, Jack Carson, George Weidler *and* one of the bit-parts from *The West Point Story*, she was also seeing Marty Melcher and involved with Ronald Reagan, who many agreed was as dull as Cochran was exciting. Reagan had recently divorced *Johnny Belinda* star Jane Wyman and was also playing the field. With Weidler and Cochran it was rough-and-ready sex; with Carson it was therapeutic – he was helping her to cut down on her three-packs-a-day smoking habit and she in turn was trying to prevent him from drinking himself to death. With the bit part, it was the challenge of having sex with an openly gay man while with Melcher, she claimed they spent most of their time together studying Christian Science – as Weidler had got her hooked, so she had begun initiating Melcher into the religion. She reckoned that two things impressed her about Reagan : his skill on the dancefloor and his intellect and ability to have a decent conversation. The two would sneak off to his apartment high in the Hollywood hills and make love while marvelling at the panoramic view below.

It was back to the glossy ultra-camp world of Broadway musicals for her next venture – *Lullaby Of Broadway* directed by David Butler – and so buzzing with classic songs and spellbinding dance routines that one virtually ignores the trite storyline when the film shows up in television retrospectives. Courtesy of June Haver turning the part down, Doris was topping the bill again – and a first for her friend Gene Nelson, who was cast as her leading man and love interest.

This was the golden age of the Hollywood musical, an entirely Jewish concept that came about as a result of the influx of immigrants arriving in America two decades previously after escaping Nazi persecution. Besides the opportunity to make money, the emphasis was on optimism for this hugely talented bunch of individuals. Throughout the ages the Jewish race had suffered enough and to their way of thinking there really was a pot of gold at the end of the rainbow. For every story beginning with the words 'Once upon a time,' the ending could only be ' . . . and they lived happily ever after'. Added to this was Middle America's wildly over-exaggerated interpretation of what was considered 'normal'. In these films everyone dressed well – even hobos looked clean and just slightly ragged around the edges. Characters had good jobs, lived happily in comfortable houses with their spouses and children (as many as possible). There was no such thing as straying away from family values. If someone committed adultery, this was usually proven to have been as a result of someone else grabbing the wrong end of the stick and the problem was always rectified by the last reel. Stupid people were invariably portrayed by fat and bespectacled actors; gay characters were permitted so long as they adhered to the bumbling, lily-livered stereotype and death was strictly taboo unless the deceased happened to be some unseen long-lost relative who expired, leaving one or more of the other characters even more well-heeled than before. So far as her fans were concerned, Doris slotted well into the requisite pigeonhole of the fun-loving musical comedy star. Few extant of her circle knew about her busy love life, fickle mental state and temper tantrums not to mention her ever-present marital problems. So far as they were concerned, her private life was just as radiant as her smile.

Harry Warren and Al Dubin's 'Lullaby Of Broadway' was composed for Winifred Shaw to sing in *Gold Diggers Of 1935*. It won the Oscar for Best Song and featured in the musical *42nd Street*. In the Hollywood scriptwriter's version of events, it had been created by musicals' legend Jessica Howard (Gladys George), whose career is on the skids after hitting one bad patch too many. Now an alcoholic, Jessica is reduced to singing torch songs such as 'A Shanty In Old Shanty Town' in Greenwich Village clip joints. Even so there's a poignancy in her voice reminiscent of Helen Morgan and Libby Holman.

The film opens with Jessica's songstress daughter Melinda (Doris) sailing back to New York after a British tour – she dons top hat and tails for a nifty 'Just One Of Those Things' immediately attracting the attention of hoofer Tom Farnham (Nelson), who pretends to have two left feet so that she will give him a dance lesson. Later he turns up at the mansion in Beckmam Place, which Melinda thinks still belongs to her mother but is actually now owned by millionaire producer Adolph Bubble (S. Z. Sakall).

'You wouldn't believe I gave him his first lesson!' Melinda quips after watching Tom dance. For the time being she is kept in the dark regarding Jessica's downfall and the fact that her mother is ashamed to see her – Hubble and his ex-Vaudeville servants (Billy DeWolfe, Anne Triola) feed her the story that Jessica is touring with a smash-hit show.

Hubble is so overwhelmed by Melinda's charisma that he puts her up at his house and hires her for his next Broadway revue alongside Tom, who naturally has fallen in love with her though she remains standoffish towards him until the last frame. The producer then sets about arranging a reunion between Melinda and Jessica, who plans on 'breezing into town' and surprising her daughter at a party chez Hubbell – his only problem being to keep her off the bottle long enough to make the reunion look convincing. Unfortunately Jessica has a twinge of conscience, drinks more than ever and ends up in detox. 'Jessica Howard,' she says of herself, 'the voice that even the drunks won't listen to, the beer-singer of Washington Square.' It's only when Hubbell's 'society dragon' wife (the magnificent Florence Bates) suspects him of having an affair with Melinda that Jessica sobers up and comes to her daughter's rescue. 'It's tough being a mother after all these years,' she says. 'I guess I need a couple more rehearsals.'

Then comes the title-song finale, a wonderful evocation of the Busby Berkeley era, minus the overworked schmaltz of show-stoppers such as 'By A Waterfall' and 'A Pretty Girl Is Like A Melody'. Wearing a floor-length gold lamé Milo Anderson gown and mink stole – which with her loathing of cruelty to animals she would subsequently denounce – Doris and a tailed Gene Nelson lip-sync to perfection while dancing up and down a long flight of stairs in one of the most difficult choreographed sequences of any Hollywood musical. What the public did not see were her bruised legs, brought about by countless tumbles while Nelson and his wife Miriam put her through her paces.

'Though she is no Eleanor Powell,' observed the make-or-break Bosley Crowther in his *New York Times* column, 'she has learned to dance effectively and very competently cuts several neat capers with Nelson.' Crowther was less enthusiastic about the film itself. 'All things considered,' he concluded, '*Lullaby Of Broadway* is not likely to cause talk at all.'

As Warner Brothers did not have their own record company there could be no official soundtrack album so Columbia set about making one up – minus Doris' co-stars, with her singing to the Buddy Cole Quartet accompanied by the Norman Luboff Choir. Of the eight songs 'Fine And Dandy' had not been in the film and it has to be said that her version of 'In A Shanty In Old Shanty Town' lacks the cracked quality of voice required for such a torch song that Gladys George possessed in abundance (in Britain the song was later a hit for Max Bygraves). Even so this did not prevent it from rocking to the top of the American charts.

Despite her hectic love life (of which he must have been aware), Marty Melcher was obsessed with walking Doris down the aisle although he was not yet divorced from Patty Andrews. (It later emerged after his death and the subsequent trial of Jerry Rosenthal, Melcher's business partner, that he was also keen to protect his double-dealings and have legal access to Doris' earnings.) Since arriving in Hollywood, Doris lived in a succession of hotels, more often than not leaving Terry with Alma. Melcher had successfully negotiated her Warner Brothers' contract which saw her salary increase in leaps and bounds, from $300 to almost $5,000 a week. He was of course pocketing a healthy percentage – just how much Doris would later learn to her chagrin when it was too late.

Her newfound wealth enabled her to pay out $30,000 for a small house in Toluca Lake, which just happened to be within a stone's throw of Melcher's own home. This brought about a sharpening of quills from Hedda Hopper, who hinted in her column that

Doris and her manager were having an adulterous affair and that he was but a cog in the wheel of her busy personal life. This was absolutely true of course and Patty Andrews reacted badly to the news – according to one press report with a baseball bat, with which, she screamed, she was going to cave in someone's skull. Whether she meant that of her husband or Doris has never been established. Luckily, neither was at the house: they were publicising *Storm Warning* with Steve Cochran, whose own affair with Doris was still going strong.

Patty Andrews immediately filed for divorce and Melcher asked Doris to marry him when he was free. She accepted at once and promised to give up the other half-dozen or so men in her life. Secretly, she did not love him: she later confessed to feeling comfortable around him, no more, appreciative that he and Terry had taken to each other and hoped the affection might come later. The ceremony took place on 3 April 1951, her twenty-seventh birthday. Not a single member of her family turned up at the Burbank City Hall. Melcher was a lapsed Orthodox Jew but despite his leaning towards Christian Science this cut no ice with Alma. Like her other relatives, she regurgitated all the archetypal prejudices about Jews only being interested in money and swindling, though in Melcher's case this would turn out to be true.

Chapter 5

What A Calamity!

'That face that she shows the world – smiling, only talking good, happy, tuned into God – as far as I'm concerned, that's just a mask. Doris is just about the remotest person that I know.'

Kirk Douglas

fter a brief honeymoon at the Grand Canyon, the Melchers returned to Hollywood to settle down to a life of largely wedded non-bliss. Doris and Marty sold their respective houses and she shelled out $40,000 for a family home, still in Toluca Lake, Los Angeles, which had formerly belonged to the comedienne Martha Raye. Eleven years later Raye appeared alongside Doris in *Billy Rose's Jumbo*, and later still Doris was instrumental in Raye replacing Nancy Walker as Rock Hudson's feisty, wise-cracking housekeeper in the *McMillan and Wife* television series. Seven-year-old Terry moved in with them – a terrible wrench for the boy who later said that until then he had no idea who his mother was. '"Mother" was just a word without meaning,' he recalled. 'My grandmother was my total parent.'

Meanwhile, Doris' next film, premièred four months after her marriage and directed by Roy Del Ruth, involved a juxtaposition of two works by Booth Tarkington, the creator of *Monsieur Beaucaire* – regarded by her as a lucky omen because she had been named after Doris Kenyon, who starred with Valentino in the movie adaptation. The main character in *On Moonlight Bay*, set in Indiana on the eve of World War I, was based on Tarkington's *Alice Adams*, previously filmed with Katharine Hepburn though the script itself had as its foundation his *Penrod* series – suitably mangled by scriptwriter Jack Rose who further complicated matters by changing the names of the characters.

At the time Rose was accused of emulating the very similar *Meet Me In St Louis* (1944). Even so, the songs are amazing. Percy Wenrich and Edward Madden's title-track was composed back in 1912 and became popular among barbershop quartets. The other numbers included 'Cuddle Up A Little Closer', 'Tell Me', 'I'm Forever Blowing Bubbles' and a rip-roaring 'Pack Up Your Troubles In Your Old Kit Bag'. In an age when the word had a completely different meaning, the original playbill that proclaimed, 'Everything's Gay On Moonlight Bay!' more or less sums up the attitude towards the film of some modern-day audiences. For lovers of kitsch and pure corn, it is unrivalled – even the actress playing Doris' mother is called Rosemary de Camp.

The role of the roguish Penrod was assigned to child star Billy Gray, though in the rewrite the initial emphasis is on his tomboy elder sister Marjorie Winfield, paving the way for Doris' later Calamity Jane, who would much rather swing a baseball bat than involve herself with more ladylike pastimes. When she meets boy-next-door (literally) Billy Sherman (Gordon MacRae), it is after she has confiscated a gun from her tearaway brother Wesley (Gray); this goes off and for her irascible behaviour Bill gives her a spanking.

University student Bill has a radical way of observing life. He strongly disapproves of marriage, which he calls 'slavery for women, prison for men'. They go to the fair, fall in love and initially First National Bank vice president Mr Winfield (Leon Ames) approves. But he soon changes his mind when Bill declares his loathing of the banking system by tearing up a $5 bill. Bill goes back to university and Winfield fixes up his daughter with local geek Hubert Wakely (Jack Smith). She, however, longs only for the Christmas holidays when Bill will be coming home. But her plans are shattered when she hurts her ankle during a snowball fight with a bunch of roughnecks. Wesley gets into trouble at school and tells the teacher the reason for his recklessness: he cannot sleep because since hitting the bottle his father is knocking his family around hence Marjorie's injured leg.

All ends well, naturally. Bill graduates and goes off to war – but not until we have heard his and Marjorie's stunning duet 'Till We Meet Again' and he has gone against his beliefs by asking her to marry him. Marjorie promises she will wait for him but audiences have to wait a few more years for the sequel to find out if she kept her promise.

The soundtrack album reached Number Two in the American charts and like Doris' last movie album this was something of a mish-mash, albeit a fine one, because Gordon MacRae was not allowed to participate. MacRae was contracted to Capitol Records so the songs on which he duetted with Doris in the film were covered by second lead Jack Smith. Again Columbia brought in the Norman Luboff Choir to fill in for the other members of the cast and Paul Weston was hired to conduct.

It was around this time that Marty Melcher decided to legally adopt Terry and give him his name – his way of reassuring Doris that theirs really was a happy marriage, though nothing could actually have been further from the truth. Neither had ever been faithful to whatever partner they had been with at the time and though everyone connected with Doris seems to have suspected Melcher was robbing her blind, she still refused to listen. Her next three films did little to develop her career and were nothing to write home about. *Starlift* was Warner Brothers' futile attempt to recapture the magic of the *Stage Door Canteen*-type morale-boosting productions of the previous decade, wherein the plot was relegated to the minor key and employed little-known actors to play the major roles while the big stars appeared in cameos as themselves. Mike Nolan and Rick Williams (Dick Wesson, Ron Hagherty) are two US airmen serving as crewmembers on the shuttle to Korea. Making up the story that they are about to go into combat and possibly never return, they put on a USO command performance involving just about every top-liner on Warner's roster: Doris, Gordon MacRae, Randolph Scott, Jane Wyman, Cary Cooper, James Cagney and Gene Nelson were but a few. Particularly disturbing was the scene where MacRae linked up with the US Air Force Choir to perform 'Good Green Acres Of Home' with over one hundred cheesy-grinning soldiers – hardly an inspiration for those unfortunates in the Korean War. As for Doris' contribution, the less said the better. Performing Marlene Dietrich's 'You Do Something To Me', she strolls across to a young soldier and lights his cigarette for him – Marlene did the same thing hundreds of times when she risked her life in Europe during World War II and what she said to me about Doris' scene in the film, though she was only following the director's instructions, remains unprintable.

I'll See You In My Dreams tells the sanitised version of the Gus Kahn story. Cabaret performer Danny Thomas, the most unlikely of her leading men, portrayed the famous lyricist and Doris was his wife, Grace LeBoy, who wrote the story on which this is based and supplied the music for his first big hit. The couple fall out because of Kahn's involvement with a showgirl (Patrice Wymore). They then make up and survive the Wall Street Crash by which time the viewer has listened to some pretty stunning numbers but not given much thought or compassion to the so-called hero because he is so boring – or for his long-suffering wife because she has been stupid enough to get involved with him in the first place. Among the songs were 'It Had To Be You', 'Makin' Whoopee!', 'Ain't We Got Fun', 'The One I Love Belongs To Somebody Else' and 'Love Me Or leave Me' which Doris would return to, much more spectacularly, a few years hence. What gave the film a bigger boost at the box-office than it probably deserved was the announcement towards the end of shooting that Doris had entered the Top Ten Hollywood Stars list. Much better then for enthusiasts to content themselves with the chart-topping album soundtrack, not quite so 'doctored' as its predecessors in that Columbia allowed her to record her two duets with Danny Thomas, the only difference being that Paul Weston conducts the orchestra, as happened with *On Moonlight Bay*.

Weston also accompanied Doris on her cover-version of South African singer Eve Boswell's chart-topper 'Sugar Bush' released shortly afterwards. She had wanted to duet on the song with Johnnie Ray but Columbia teamed her with Frankie Laine, whose most recent hits included 'Jezebel' and 'I Believe'. The two blend well together and the record was a hit on both sides of the Atlantic. Far more interesting, however, was the flipside 'A Guy Is A Guy' – Oscar Brand's much cleaned-up version of a World War II soldier's ditty 'A Gob Is A Slob', more frequently sung in barrack-rooms as 'A Knob In Your Gob Is Worth Two In Your Bush', which certainly *would* have been an innovation had Doris sung those lyrics! After leading us through the narrator's extremely varied and promiscuous sexual adventures, the ditty ends by informing us, once he has made his willing victim pregnant, 'And they found him in the churchyard with his toes turned up!'

Sadly there would be no more quality duets as with Frankie Laine. Her next coupling – with Donald O'Connor on 'No Two People' – was weak by comparison. This was originally sung by Danny Kaye and Zizi Jeanmaire in the film *Hans Christian*

Andersen (1952) and reprised by Kaye and Jane Wyman, giving the *Johnny Belinda* star a surprise hit.

There is no doubt that Doris' marriage to Marty Melcher coincided with, or rather brought about, what we now know to have been a temporary bout of mental illness. Signs of this started to show while she was shooting *I'll See You In My Dreams* with Melcher setting what would be a precedent in his attempt to inject a little Method into the proceedings in the hope of making Doris' dramatic scenes more realistic and hard-hitting. There is a scene in the film where Grace LeBoy goes into hospital to have a baby and is desperate to have her husband by her side. But he is working out of town and gets there too late. To comfort her he sits next to the crib and sings his latest composition 'Pretty Baby'. Doris was expected to cry in the scene but somehow she was unable to do so. Therefore Melcher asked her to imagine that it was Terry that she had just given birth to and to remember how she had felt back then.

He knew only too well that Al Jorden deserted Doris on the eve of her son's birth so the tears flowed liberally, though she would never forgive him for making her relive such a traumatic experience. Realising his ploy had worked and taking some sort of sardonic pleasure in the way she clung to him once the cameras stopped rolling, Melcher milked her emotions for all he was worth. Another precedent had already been set and would continue throughout her career whether she approved or not. If a film did well at the box-office, the leading man would be used again, as would the supports – prime examples being Gordon MacRae, James Garner, Rock Hudson, Gene Nelson, Rod Taylor and S. Z. Sakall. However, she very firmly drew the line at working with Danny Thomas again, even when begged to do so by Michael Curtiz for the remake of Al Jolson's *The Jazz Singer*. Curtiz' reaction was to denounce Doris – as he did anyone who got on the wrong side of him – with a tirade of expletives in his bad English and to promptly hire Peggy Lee, who it has to be said was better suited to the role, not that this made the film any more than instantly forgettable. For her pains, Doris' next two films saw her working opposite two actors who were even more lacking in lustre.

She received top billing in *The Winning Team* though Ronald Reagan was promoted as its star – at 41 playing 20-something baseball legend Grover Cleveland Alexander when the film begins, a portrayal so tepid and unconvincing it vanished without trace. Doris was cast as his wife Aimee, arguably the most boring character she ever played. If we are to believe the dubious storyline, it was she who gently badgered him into becoming a household name, helping him through his battles with epilepsy and double vision until he reaches the zenith of his career, pitching in the World Series. The journalist writing for the *Hollywood Reporter* must have been watching a different production when he or she observed, 'Miss Day gives her finest dramatic performance to date'. Hardly any Doris Day fan has seen the film; it never turns up in television retrospectives and so far as is known it has never been released on video or DVD.

Few would argue that *April In Paris*, directed by David Butler, was similarly one of the worst films Doris ever made. Its saving grace, aside from a couple of otherwise excellent tunes, is the appearance of dapper French actor Claude Dauphin (1903–78), who later claimed Butler only hired him because he had mistaken him for Claude Rains! The story is trite and ridiculous.

Legendary actress Ethel Barrymore has been asked to represent the United States at the International Festival of Arts in Paris but the invitation is mistakenly sent to chorus girl Ethel 'Dynamite' Jackson (Doris), currently appearing in a Broadway revue. The man responsible for the faux-pas is S. Winthrop Putnam, assistant many times removed to the Under Secretary of State played by Ray Bolger and best known as the scarecrow in *The Wizard Of Oz*, a co-star even more dull than Ronald Reagan, if such a thing were possible. Additionally, Bolger – 20 years her senior – is Doris' love interest, leaving critics astonished that she should even look at such a charmless man let alone fall in love with him. One is instinctively reminded of the films of British star George Formby, the apparently gormless comedian who always ends up with the pretty posh girl – a situation unlikely ever to have happened in real life, though Formby was possessed of an innate charisma and charm sorely lacking in Bolger who comes across as stupid and embarrassing to watch. Indeed the Melcher marriage draws parallels with that of the Formbys. Like Marty Melcher, Beryl Formby always kept her husband on a leash, maintained a tight grip on his money, vetted his film contracts, organised his concerts without discussing them with him and was, by and large, an insufferable martinet, though unlike Melcher she was at least honest and would never have thought about robbing him.

Anxious to make good the mix-up, Putnam rushes to New York. Enthralled by her performance he is unable to tell her the truth and in next to no time she becomes a national heroine, 'one of the rank-and-file citizens' given an opportunity until now reserved for the privileged. Putnam capitalises on this: for ten years he has been doing the same mundane job and now promotion is in the offing. En-route to Europe, aided by Parisian nightclub owner Phillipe Fourquet (Dauphin) and posing as a ship's waiter while working his passage home, having been stung by the US government for unpaid taxes, Ethel learns basic French etiquette and table manners. Because waiters are not allowed on the exclusive dancefloor, they and the staff hoof it up in the kitchen to a pretty nifty 'Auprès De Ma Blonde', one of the film's few inspiring moments for it is only at this point that it springs to life. But if one expects Ethel to make a play for the suave womanising Frenchman, there's a surprise in store when she snags Putnam; they are married by the 'captain' (actually, another waiter). Then, upon his arrival in Paris, Putnam gets a shock when his fiancée Marcia shows up – she happens to be the daughter of the US Secretary and has flown ahead to surprise him with a marriage proposal.

Putnam wants to avoid Marcia and her father finding out about the marriage out of fear of damaging his career, therefore Ethel promises to keep quiet until after the Arts Festival. And of course Marcia gets jealous of all the attention her 'fiancé' lavishes on this chorus girl, resulting in the two women having a catfight. Then comes a truly silly scene when Putnam takes Marcia to Phillipe's nightclub, for topping the bill is Ethel. Her showstopper is 'That's What Makes Paris Paree', which sees her emulating a tableau from a 1932 revue featuring French music-hall legend Mistinguett. Wearing a sailor's cap with aigrettes and a see-through skirt, Doris cavorts around chorus girls walking pastel-dyed poodles aimlessly about the stage, that appear just as confused as everyone else. The film ends with Doris singing the title-track, once more in Putnam's arms on the steps of the Sacre Coeur – which, as this has an Eiffel Tower back-drop, would have meant rearranging the Parisian skyline: but a minor slip-up for the artistic director of this meaningless trash!

On and off set, Doris and her co-star Ray Bolger hated each other. Bolger, even more so than Bob Hope, Jack Carson and Ronald Reagan, was the complete megalomaniac. Unlike most actresses in her position – she was now Number Two in the Box-Office Poll – Doris had no say in script, co-star or any other film-related approval. Bolger, though starting to become old hat, had been permitted to hold onto such privileges since *The Wizard of Oz*. Doris wanted her friend Gene Nelson to choreograph the dance routines, which by way of a clause in his contract would have necessitated him being offered a part in the film. But Bolger could not stand him so David Butler brought in Eddie Prinz whose pedigree spoke for itself – among his successes was Joan Crawford's *Dancing Lady, Gone With The Wind* and Doris' own *Tea For Two*. And though she adored Yip Harburg and Vernon Duke's stunning title-track, which they composed back in 1932, she considered the rest of the score penned by Duke and Sammy Cahn to be mediocre.

At the end of 1952 Doris began what she hoped might prove a lengthy partnership with Johnnie Ray. Most of her other duets had been organised by Columbia; the theory being that putting two chart-topping artists on the same record would double the takings. This had not always been the case – the 78rpms with Buddy Clark sold fewer copies than those with Frankie Laine. As happened with Judy Garland and also Rock Hudson towards the end of his life, Doris would look upon Johnnie Ray as a soul in dire need of saving. Born in Oregon in 1927 and of American-Indian extraction, he became deaf in one ear at the age of 12, following a boy-scout blanket-toss when he fell on the ground, hitting the side of his face. A bungled operation subsequently left him almost completely deaf in both ears and he often appeared on stage wearing a mauve hearing-aid – a dead giveaway so far as gay fans were concerned though, like Liberace, he had been long courted by well-heeled matrons hoping to get him to the altar while he was secretly engaged in any number of affairs with men. His first hit record in 1951 was 'Whisky And Gin' but he will be forever associated with Churchill Coleman's 'Cry', his signature tune, which still dominated the charts on both sides of the Atlantic when he worked with Doris.

Marty Melcher intervened with the Columbia chiefs on learning that Doris wanted to record with Johnnie Ray. His homosexuality was pretty much an open secret – additionally, he had taken over where Frank Sinatra left off as the idol of the bobbysoxers and had gone one step further with his manic antics on stage. These involved him stomping on top of his piano, writhing on the floor, ripping his clothes, flinging the microphone stand around and bursting into tears. When Melcher learned that Ray had told one journalist he got so worked up during his performances that he actually ejaculated, he forbade Doris to sing with him, though thankfully for once she pleased herself. Their first single 'Ma Says, Pa Says' – an English adaptation of a French song originally recorded by Patachou at that time touring the United States – was a huge hit. This was followed by catchy 'Let's Walk That-A-Way' – no less successful on both sides of the Atlantic, though the flipside made Melcher see red. Fred Rose's 'Candy Lips' (though over the heads of the general public) was interpreted by Ray as an ode to oral sex; therefore no more duets with Johnnie Ray.

Doris would not be surprised when Johnnie Ray's indiscretions eventually caught up with him a few years later. Like Rock Hudson and many others, he married to protect his image but failed to curb his behaviour. Following his arrest for importuning in Australia in 1959, his career declined rapidly. There was a brief comeback in the 1970s, by which time he had become a chronic alcoholic. In 1990 he died, aged 63, of acute liver failure.

Meanwhile Doris worked with David Butler again, along with most of the cast and crew from *On Moonlight Bay*, on its long-awaited sequel *By The Light Of The Silvery Moon*. At the end of 1952, shortly before shooting began, she received news that she had been voted Most Popular Female Vocalist in the end-of-year Quigley Poll. This prompted Marty Melcher to renegotiate her salary with Warner Brothers. Basically, Jack Warner was told that unless he dipped his hand in his pocket and paid Doris what she was worth, she would break her contract and work elsewhere. Technically this would not have been allowed to happen: Warner would have suspended her and she would have remained unemployed until the end of her contract term. Even so Warner upped her salary to $5,000 a week, still much less than topnotch stars such as Joan Crawford and Bette Davis, but nevertheless a step in the right direction.

By The Light Of The Silvery Moon represents the precognitive dream: the fact that all will turn out well if that is what one wishes.

As such it is a false representation of America immediately after the Great War with the country heading towards the Great Depression with soup kitchens, mass unemployment and far less optimism generally than displayed. One almost gets the impression that people like the Winfields, first seen in *On Moonlight Bay*, never even took the time to reflect on the sacrifices made by their countrymen to ensure that they could sleep soundly in their beds. That said, as an exercise in whimsy it works well. *Screenland* called it 'As harmless as tiddly-winks and as gay as its Tecnicolor lensing' while the *New York Herald Tribune* enthused, 'The movie is a spun-sugar musical, prettily pink to go with the season of bunnies, lilies, and new bonnets.' In other words, almost like every film of this genre it was camp but hugely entertaining.

The film opens with housekeeper Stella (Mary Wickes) introducing us to the Winfields. Since *On Moonlight Bay* the family has been augmented by a noisy dog and Gregory, a pet turkey, who in the first half of the production very nearly runs away with the show. Then there's Chester (Russell Arms), Marjorie's cheesy beau, who has been dating her during Bill's absence and who composes equally squirmy songs such as 'Be My Little Baby Bumble Bee'. Wesley (Billy Gray) is just as troublesome as before, while 18-year-old Marjorie (29-year-old Doris) is still the grease-monkey tomboy. The Winfields are about to celebrate their twentieth wedding anniversary which coincides with 20-year-old Bill Sherman (31-year-old Gordon MacRae) coming home from the Front. Everyone is expecting he and Marjorie to marry but he decides to postpone matters until he has a job and financial security. This upsets her: the event will be a small affair, she says, because she herself will not be there.

Complicating matters is sexy French actress Renee La Rue (Maria Palmer), who breezes into town to put on a revue at the local theatre: as the establishment's trustee Mr Winfield must sanction her script and their private meeting – set to the music of

Edith Piaf's 'La Vie En Rose' – gives everyone, save Mrs Winfield who is kept in the dark, the impression they are having an affair. When Bill lands a job at the bank and takes out a loan so that he can marry Marjorie, she puts off the ceremony on account of her parents' 'troubled' marriage, leaving him to believe she is having an affair with Chester. Of course it's all a huge misunderstanding. The compromising letter Marjorie has found relates to the characters in Mlle La Rue's play. Doris and Bill then prepare a surprise for her parents: they will drive them to a skating-party anniversary bash at Miller's Pond in the very surrey that conveyed them to their wedding all those years ago – cue for the title-track, beautifully performed by Doris and MacRae in what would sadly be their last film together.

Like *Young Man With A Horn* and *On Moonlight Bay*, *By The Light Of The Silvery Moon* very quickly became a favourite of Doris' growing army of lesbian fans. 'Look at her,' Marjorie's father opines of her fondness for male attire, 'No wonder men leave town – a fine picture of grace, beauty and femininity!' There is also a lesbian character named Toby, who works at the local telegraph office and is responsible for spreading the rumours about Mr Winfield and Renee La Rue.

The tension she experienced while working on the film put Doris on the verge of a nervous breakdown, not helped much by the friendship she struck up a little earlier with Johnnie Ray – aside from Judy Garland arguably the most neurotic entertainer of his day, albeit a phenomenally talented one. Luckily for her then that her greatest triumph so far was just around the corner though this would not come without considerable cost to her already-fragile psyche.

Many regard *Calamity Jane* as Doris Day's finest film prior to her teaming up with Rock Hudson. 'It's success is due to its star, a Wild Western shrew magnificently worth the taming,' observed critic Paul Dane in his syndicated column. 'With her dirty face, her cowpoke clothes, and a hairdo like a truss of hay, she takes the script between her perfect teeth and makes off at a graceful gallop for the foothills of real stardom.' The role of Jane was originally played by Louise Dresser opposite Richard Arlen in *Caught* (1931). Five years later Jean Arthur more memorably portrayed her opposite Gary Cooper's Wild Bill Hickok in *The Plainsman*. In *Calamity Jane* (1984), she was resurrected with Jane Alexander in the title role, a remake of which the least said the better.

As per usual, with Hollywood's tendency to gloss over the truth, the real Calamity Jane bears little resemblance to the on-screen interpretation by Doris Day. Martha Jane Burke (1852–1903) was born in Princetown, Missouri, and following the death of her father in 1868, she and her five siblings moved to Fort Bridger, Wyoming where she is thought to have worked as a prostitute for a brief time. Soon afterwards she more or less deserted her charges to head for the Great Plains, working as a scout, teamster and supplies transporter for the US Army. An excellent shot, she acquired her famous nickname by promising 'calamity' to any would-be aggressor.

Prone to gross exaggeration later in life, Jane often claimed that she served directly under General Custer but there is no evidence to support this; the nearest she came to it was when she spent several months at Fort Custer in 1874. Similarly, her claims that she actually married Wild Bill Hickok (1837–76) are pure fabrication. They are known to have first met in July 1876, one month before Hickok was shot dead by Jack McCall during a poker game (Hickok had only recently married Agnes Lake Thatcher). Eight years after his death, Jane moved to El Paso, Texas, where she had met and married Clinton Burke. The marriage lasted less than 10 years and in 1896 she began to travel with various Wild West shows still boasting of her marriage to Hickok and the fact they had had a child; again a figment of an overactive imagination. In 1903 she died of pneumonia and someone must have believed her for she lies next to Hickok in Deadwood's Mount Moriah Cemetery.

Calamity Jane, Doris' last film with David Butler at the helm, was conceived as competition against 20th Century-Fox's predicted blockbuster *Gentlemen Prefer Blondes* (1953), currently shooting with Marilyn Monroe and Jane Russell. For the first time in her career Doris was permitted to choose her own co-star and she plumped for Howard Keel, at 39 the exact same age Hickok had been when he met Jane. Born Howard Leek in Illinois, the navyman-turned-coalminer hit a high note six years earlier when he had received an unprecedented 14 curtain calls before a royal audience at London's Drury Lane Theatre. Since then he had achieved tremendous success on the big screen with *Annie Get Your Gun*, *Showboat* and *Kiss Me Kate*. Lumpish but engaging, his film career petered out during the late-1950s, though his recording and concert career flourished for another 30 years. His swansong would be as Clayton Farrow in the glossy television soap *Dallas*.

When the film opens tough talking, sharp-shooting Jane rides atop the stagecoach with one of the boys in buckskins, red neckerchief and Confederate cap, belting out 'The Deadwood Stage' and introducing us to the rest of the characters as she arrives in town. This was the first song to be written for the film, with Sammy Fain and Paul Francis Webster allegedly donning cowboy costumes to get the ambiance of the piece spot on. Like the real Calamity Jane, the one on screen enjoys telling tall tales and soon has everyone spellbound as she recounts her latest adventure: rescuing Lt. Danny Gillmartin (Philip Cary) from the Sioux. She gives every impression she is sweet on him though she also has an eye for Wild Bill Hickok (Keel), who finds her too tomboyish for his tastes and taunts her persistently. In 'I Can Do Without You' (allegedly composed as an anodine to *Annie Get Your Gun*'s 'Anything You Can Do'), they rain insults upon one another, hoping to disguise their true feelings which emerge as the scenario unfolds.

Tonight the Golden Garter saloon is putting on a special entertainment – actress Frances Fryer (Dick Wesson), who turns out to be a man: Francis. Owner Henry Miller (Paul Harvey) has staked his reputation on the show, therefore the all-male audience must not be disappointed. Francis drags up and causes uproar by singing 'I've Got A Hive Full Of Honey For The Right Kind Of Honey Bee'. To save Miller from ruin, Jane promises to get him the famous actress Adelaid Adams who, as one observer quips, would not be seen dead in this town. Bill goes one step further: if Jane gets Adelaid (currently wowing audiences in Chicago) he will drag up as a Sioux squaw with a papoose.

Jane sets off for the Windy City, subsequently awarded a song of its own, where she catches Adelaid's final performance watched from the back of the gallery. The song is the first of three with homosexual undertones. 'It's Harry I'm Plannin' To Marry' is reminiscent of Al Jolson's 'I'm Just Wild About Harry', which he initially performed as an appreciation of his lover, American-Hungarian dancer Harry Pilcer, some 40 years earlier. This particular Harry is addressed as a 'mate' and we are told he is 'a horse from a different safari' but somewhat shallow and dim. 'Though he's built like a bust of Apollo, just remember a statue is hollow,' Adelaid croons. Striding into her dressing room after the show, by which time Adelaid has left for a European tour, she sees her maid Katie Brown (Allyn McLerie) trying on her dress and jumps to the logical conclusion. Katie initially mistakes her for a man and Jane scarcely conceals her attraction – not so long ago, having seen Adelaid's picture on a cigarette card, she dismissed her as 'a fat, frilled-up side of beef'. 'You're the purdiest thing I ever seen – didn't know a woman could look like that,' she pipes.

Persistently put down by her employer for years, Katie has

always dreamed of going on stage and seizes the opportunity to travel back to Deadwood with her new friend, braving Indian attacks on the way. Danny and Hickok are immediately attracted to her. Good to his word, Bill dresses as a squaw but Katie's opening number at the Golden Garter is a disaster. She is also recognised by Fryer, who once worked with the real Adelaid but to save Miller from humiliation, he keeps this to himself. Things turn out better, however, when Katie admits her fraud and Jane orders the audience to give her a chance. Singing properly this time, she's a hit. The next day Jane moves Katie into her cabin so they may 'chaperone' each other. Doris' legion of lesbian fans would later make much of the ensuing scene where Katie teaches Jane how to be a woman – how to dress, cook and turn her rundown shack into a home. 'We'll batch it here, cosy as two bugs in a blanket,' she chortles. Cue for a song, 'A Woman's Touch'.

For the first time we and the folk of Deadwood see Jane wearing a dress – which she promptly ruins when she falls into the muddy creek on her way home, where Bill and Danny are waiting to invite their girls to a ball at the local fort: Jane's first. En-route, everyone sings 'The Black Hills Of Dakota', the film's second-best number. Transformed from tomboy to beautiful debutante, no one recognises her and the boys queue up to fill her dance-card. Jane still naively believes herself in love with Danny – who loves Katie, who in turn thinks he should love Jane because she thinks she loves Bill! Such complications lead to more jealousy and Jane ordering Katie out of town on the next coach to Chicago. But Bill bawls her out and he and Jane finally admit their true feelings. Next comes the delightful 'Secret Love', the only sequence in the film shot in a single take – the rhythm plodding along to her horse's footsteps as she rides sidesaddle through the beautiful daffodil-carpeted landscape with a violin solo coursing through the piece like a clear mountain stream. Many believe this to be Doris Day's finest moment in a musical film. It is after this that Jane sets out after the stagecoach, enabling the squabbles and confusion to be rectified by a double wedding.

'It's DAY-lightful!' the playbills proclaimed and it was. As with Gordon MacRae, Doris loved working with Howard Keel; there was a great deal of clowning around and just one half-serious argument. This occurred when they were filming the 'I Can Do Without You' sequence, where the pair get mad at each other and Hickok is supposed to rough-handle Jane, his Neanderthal way of displaying that maybe he is attracted to her after all. Doris insisted Keel should not 'pussyfoot around' with her so when he grabs her this is for real. Doris subsequently ended up with a few unexpected bruises and, according to Keel, cursed the air blue afterwards. Director David Butler, witness to her outburst, confessed he had been worried about the scene where Jane turns up at her cabin drenched in mud. Doris demanded she should not be seen actually falling into the creek so it was arranged for a trough to be filled with mud, heated to exactly the same temperature as her morning bath. Gingerly, she prepared to step into this, only to be grabbed by the technicians and flung in – the way (they said) the real Calamity Jane might have appreciated it! She saw the funny side and began flinging handfuls of mud at them; after the scene the same technicians drenched her with buckets of water.

Rightly or wrongly, *Calamity Jane* will go down in movie history, like Joan Crawford's *Johnny Guitar* released the following year, as a lesbian classic. Both films figure in Vitto Russo's celebrated *Celluloid Closet* with Doris' film assigned to the category largely on account of Sammy Hain and Paul Francis Webster's 'Secret Love' (which won an Academy Award), the 'Woman's Touch' sequence, and of course Jane's predilection for crossdressing. Even when looking radiant in an expensive gown, she still walks and behaves like a man. Like many of the 'cowboys-versus-injuns' Westerns of the time, this one also suffers elements of racism then widely accepted as the norm. Terms such as 'painted varmints' and 'redskin naked heathens' would be inappropriate today though in the context of Calamity Jane's colourful vocabulary they come across as reasonably innocuous.

Calamity Jane was arguably Doris' most acclaimed and successful portrayal thus far in her career but physically the most taxing. No sooner had shooting wrapped than the mental breakdown already hovering in the wings for some months earlier hit her with a vengeance. She began suffering panic attacks with frequent episodes of palpitations and breathlessness; she had been prone to heartburn since the days when she wolfed down hamburgers and huge portions of raw onions in the front of Al Jorden's car but now she was convinced she was about to succumb to tuberculosis or a heart attack. On at least two occasions she had an attack in a restaurant and almost choked to death. Matters were exacerbated when she discovered a small lump in her breast. This period of her life and the way she describes it at great length in her memoirs makes for painful reading. It was as if Doris allowed herself to become imprisoned by some weird cult, of which unbeknown to herself, she was founder member. As if brainwashing herself, she quotes endlessly and extensively from Mary Baker Eddy. Neither was she particularly helped by two new friends she made at the time – musical comedy star Charlotte Greenwood and Judy Garland.

Charlotte Greenwood (1890–1977) and her composer husband, Martin Broones (1892–1971) were practitioners of Christian Science but more obsessed with the religion than anyone Doris had ever known. Therefore, to her way of thinking at the time, their word was God. They strongly advised her not to seek medical help for her problems, despite Marty Melcher's spot-on prognosis that clearly she was having a mental breakdown and for once it might be better to bend the rules. Suffice to say, the Broones were paid handsomely for their foolhardy advice. Whether or not they or their friends were behind the malicious telephone calls Doris received at this time, threatening her with rape, or whether it was Marty Melcher compounding her fear by reminding her of the incident with Al Levy – the fact that the more paranoid she became, the more she clung to him – is not known though the Broones also cashed in on this.

Doris was offered 'counselling' to calm her nerves. No matter what the malady, physical or mental, Mary Baker Eddy had the definitive answer, she was told. What made the rape threats even more bizarre was that Doris claimed to recognise the caller as an assistant from a store she visited regularly. 'His voice was clearly manic and he had no sooner identified himself than he began an insane attack on me, threatening me with every conceivable sexual assault,' she recalled in her memoirs. Why then, did she not report the matter to the police and have the man arrested? Almost certainly she was persuaded not to by the Broones and Melcher, which suggests that if they had been behind the scam, they too might have been exposed. The Broones would have lost a temporary but invaluable source of income while Melcher might have been compelled to say goodbye to his wife's fortune, which he was later proved to have been siphoning off at an alarming rate, along with his business partner Jerry Rosenthal.

Melcher therefore brought in a Doctor Hearn, who lived nearby, and he diagnosed nothing more serious than 'acute hyper-ventilation', for which the treatment was no more complicated than breathing in and out of a paper bag to replace the carbon dioxide lost by breathing too quickly. Hearn booked Doris into a private room at St Joseph's Hospital for further examination of the lump in her breast, which fortunately turned out to be benign: it was removed the next day by minor surgery. The specialist at St Joseph's, Doctor Van Hagen, prescribed complete rest and a course of sedatives that Doris took very reluctantly – Mary Baker

Eddy would not have approved. She was also sent to see a psychiatrist (described in her memoirs as a 'neuropsychiatric specialist'), who confirmed what she already knew: her health scare was totally the result of an overworked imagination.

Only days after leaving the clinic, cured but still weak, and having the occasional setback when she was convinced Doctor Van Hagen had made the wrong diagnosis and that she was really dying, Doris reluctantly began work on *Lucky Me* with Bob Cummings and Phil Silvers. It was promoted as the first Hollywood musical to be filmed in the new CinemaScope format, though only just. On an adjacent lot at Warner Brothers Judy Garland was already shooting what many now regard as her greatest triumph, *A Star Is Born* (1954), and Jack Warner had just ordered the first month's footage to be reshot in the process. Two years older than Doris, Judy was an absolute physical and mental wreck. Their childhoods were almost directly opposite: whereas Doris had been loved and protected by her mother, Judy's mother, Ethel Gumm, pushed her beyond endurance. Addicted to uppers and downers from the days when MGM kept her working virtually round the clock to get every last ounce out of her, and bloated by medication, for some time Judy had been dismissed as an insurance risk and, as a consequence, not faced a camera in four years. The fact that her mother had just died and that she was playing an on-screen neurotic with an alcoholic husband (James Mason) only added to her personal insecurities, as did the fact that her third marriage – to producer Sid Luft – was falling apart at the seams.

When Marty Melcher introduced Doris to the Lufts, Sid was cheating on Judy with another man and Judy had been put on a crash diet that made her completely irrational. This was a supreme example of the lame leading the lame. Even so, if Judy was a law unto herself, she did offer Doris some sound advice: 'Ditch the religion bullshit!' – which she, in her under-the-spell state, chose to ignore. A 'cure' was therefore effected by more readings from Mary Baker Eddy and benders with Judy, which, though just as detrimental to Doris' health as her imaginary illnesses, certainly enabled her to forget all about them until the next morning's hangover.

Away from the studio Doris became edgy and antisocial. The success of *Calamity Jane* brought a flood of requests for receptions and interviews, every one of which she turned down, including a request to sing 'Secret Love' at the Oscars ceremony. What made matters infinitely worse was that she was not acting on her own initiative but following the Broones' instructions. She even left it to them whether or not she should continue with *Lucky Me* or walk out on her contract and risk suspension. The Broones advised her to complete the project but suggested she insist on a closed set so that 'outside influences might not affect her constitution and spirit'. They really did have a lot to answer for. On the set the smiles and *joie de vivre* were enforced: Doris made it clear to everyone concerned that she had never wanted to do the film in the first place though she got along with most of her co-stars. An exception was Martha Hyer, who plays her love rival. Naturally blonde, on Doris' 'request' she was compelled to dye her hair brunette – or leave the production.

Doris was attacked for her neurasthenia by a number of religious and women's groups. When she refused an audience with the Hollywood Women's Press Club, they retaliated by giving her a gong of their own: the Sour Apple Award. Founded in 1928 by arch-hack Louella Parsons, in recent years the HWPC's most notorious 'accolade' has been accepted with a large pinch of salt, almost like the modern-day Raspberries. Back in the 1950s even being nominated for a Sour Apple was regarded as the supreme insult because it was awarded not specifically for lack of talent but 'irresponsible personal behaviour'. Frank Sinatra, a recipient in 1951, threatened to 'rip off' Louella's head and 'shove it up her ass' while Elvis Presley, who won in 1966, threatened the HWPC with worse. It was this and not the intervention of Judy Garland and the Broones that brought Doris to her senses. To her way of thinking she had mortally offended the public that had made her a star.

'Cross your fingers! Knock on wood! You and CinemaScope never had it so good!' So ran the publicity for this turkey – for while *Calamity Jane* had been the pick-me-up Doris' fans needed, *Lucky Me* is guaranteed to put all but the die-hard devotee to sleep unless one is prepared to brave the first 20 minutes of absolute nonsense with a gloriously unfunny Phil Silvers attempting to steal what few acting honours there are. As Bosley Crowther aptly observed in his *New York Times*' review, 'This project apparently collided with disillusion before it got to midstream, and at that point began to flounder. It was every man for himself from then on.' Candy Williams, breezing through the streets of Miami, sings 'Superstition' while she avoids walking under ladders, etc. 'This is the worst show I've ever seen,' the theatre manager complains after Candy and Hap (Silvers) have purposely murdered 'Men', in what is thought to have been an attempt to emulate Marlene Dietrich and Rosemary Clooney's sparkling duet 'Men Are Good For Nothing'.

Candy and Hap are two of four hoofers (the others are Eddie Foy Jr and future *McMillan & Wife* housekeeper Nancy Walker), who play to near-empty theatres with their hammy travelling show *Parisian Pretties*) and end up working up in a fancy restaurant kitchen when they can't pay the bill. Candy meets top songwriter Dick Carson (Cummings) by way of making him crash his car while swerving to avoid a lucky black cat and in time-honoured and tiresome Hollywood fashion he pretends to be someone else (a humble garage mechanic) to woo her – though to be fair, from this point on the film improves considerably. There is a tremendous sequence when Doris, Silvers, Walker and Foy Jr sing 'The Bluebells Of Broadway Are Ringing Tonight' – the number was a minor hit in Britain for Joan Regan.

Candy falls for Carson, professes her love and sends shivers down the spine by singing 'I Speak To The Stars' then falls out with him on finding out who he really is – the age-old custard-pie-in-the-face routine. All ends well when he offers to put her into the Broadway revue he is writing though not before the obligatory element of jealousy has been eradicated. Before Candy came along, Carson used to be sweet on Lorraine Thayer (Martha Hyer), whose oil magnate father is backing the new production but once she is out of the picture Candy can sign her contract – on Friday 13th, which no longer perturbs her because love has stopped her from being superstitious.

Once the film was in the can Doris again consulted the Broones and it was agreed that she should give a press conference and apologise for her strange behaviour over the last few months. This took place at her home, with Marty Melcher vetting the questions. Doris admitted she had had a nervous breakdown but revealed nothing about the telephone calls and was admired for her honesty. She ended the interview by declaring she was now back to her old self and looked forward to her next project.

If struggling through *Lucky Me* had been an ordeal, her next film, *Young At Heart,* her last for Warner Brothers, would prove a veritable nightmare. Adapted from the novel by Fannie Hurst, this was originally filmed in 1938 as *Four Daughters,* the first in a quartet starring The Lane Sisters, a popular musical comedy act of the day, though its true star was John Garfield as the young, mixed-up musician. It was nominated for four Oscars. The director then had been Michael Curtiz and when it was rumoured that he might direct the remake, Doris had a fit of pique. She had suffered enough of his bad-English insults while making *Romance On The High Seas* and would not do so again, she said. Obviously she had forgotten that since Curtiz' outburst they had become friends. Jack Warner therefore brought in Hal Roach student Gordon Douglas – by comparison an amateur – and as Doris' leading man, Warner signed Frank Sinatra, who was enjoying a career hiatus since being Oscar-nominated for his portrayal of the doomed Maggio in Fred Zinnemman's *From Here To Eternity*. This time there would only be three sisters played by Doris, Elizabeth Fraser and Dorothy Malone. Seventy-five-year-old legend Ethel Barrymore would have the role played by May Robson in the original film and she effortlessly acted everyone else off the screen. Very frail at the time and confined to a wheelchair, it was rumoured she prophesied she would die before completing the film though in fact she lived on until 1959.

As happened with *Lucky Me*, Doris was inveigled into the production by Marty Melcher, who correctly forecasted the former a box-office flop now that the old-style musicals were waning in popularity. When Melcher parted company with Century Artists, and in order to 'strike a bonanza deal' with the studio and at the same time earn Doris as much money as possible, Melcher and Jerry Rosenthal offered Doris a partnership in their new company Arwin Productions, which would handle her affairs, recording contracts, etc. and Melcher's music publishing emporium, which would look after her recorded output. Of course, this was only to do with gaining control of her rapidly growing fortune now that she was earning in excess of $3 million a year including the revenue from her records which were selling at the rate of 500,000 a month. The happy families scenario was completed when Doris' ailing brother Paul was roped into the proceedings and relocated to Los Angeles with his wife and children.

Doris handed over her earnings to Melcher and Rosenthal without question and swallowed every story they fed her regarding the way it was invested – mostly in oil wells, farming projects and real estate. Almost always, she never knew what she had paid until the deal was signed and never by her, always by her husband who she later said had never given her reason not to trust him implicitly. Even so she must have been extremely naive not to examine the books from time to time to see just how much those investments were bringing in. The only time she actually criticised one of these purchases was when Melcher informed her that 'she' had acquired two hotels: one in Dallas, and another in Palo Alto, then a run-down district south of San Francisco. Doris recalled how her husband inveigled her into attending the opening of the latter. It was, she said, the most hideous place she had ever seen in her life and an insult to her name.

Doris always said she would have liked to follow Elizabeth Taylor's example and to have invested in things that were good to look at – antiques, works of art and paintings as well as a beach house. Melcher, Rosenthal and the Broones deemed otherwise. Christian Science denounced such trappings unnecessary luxury and vain. When Doris paid a few hundred dollars for a Dutch Master, Melcher made her ask for her money back. He was, however, prepared to sacrifice his principles should Doris ever want to buy jewellery for this could always be re-sold at a profit. He even followed Elizabeth Taylor's then-husband Michael Wilding's example by buying her a 5-carat diamond ring, which Doris insisted should go back to the shop. Big rocks, she later declared, left her as cold as the women who wore them. 'When I see Liz Taylor with those Harry Winston boulders hanging from her neck, I get nauseated,' she later said of Taylor's somewhat ostentatious ways. 'All I can think of is how many dog shelters those diamonds can buy.'

For now Melcher allowed Doris to keep the beach house she bought at Lake Arrowhead but she hardly ever visited the place. In the later years of her marriage she would spend odd weekends there with Terry to put some distance between her and Melcher. Neither did her husband allow her to spend much money in renovating the house they had bought from Martha Raye. To his way of thinking, the house had been just fine when they had moved in so why waste cash changing it when this could be put to better use?

'Mad For Each Other & Singing Their Hearts Out For You!' said the posters. Much was made of the fact that Doris and Sinatra had worked together before: on radio's *Your Hit Parade* when she was with Les Brown. The truth was far more sinister. Following years in the wilderness, success had gone to Sinatra's head. From the outset he made it clear that, no matter whose name was heading the credits, this was his film alone. He rarely had a good word to say about Doris despite the fact that she always referred to him with admiration – or, on bad days, with controlled reserve. Yet Sinatra only insulted her behind her back, though what he had to say about Marty Melcher – none of it good – was always said to his face. 'The guy's a heel and a fucking creep!' he observed after their first meeting.

Sinatra also issued a warning to Jack Warner – a cardinal sin, in Hollywood – that if Melcher so much as stepped onto the studio lot, let alone the set, he would walk off the picture. The two had a blazing row when Melcher wanted Doris to sing the title-track over the opening and closing credits. Sinatra already had a hit with 'Young At Heart', which he considered his personal property. Melcher backed down while Doris shrugged her shoulders and announced she did not care who did the song. As a result of all the arguing, though the soundtrack album bore the title *Young At Heart*, the title-track would not be on it. Then, when Sinatra learned Warner had hired Charles Lang on Melcher's recommendation to shoot the picture (most recently he had filmed Joan Crawford in *Sudden Fear*) he demanded he be fired and replaced by the no-less-talented Ted McCord, who won an Oscar for *Johnny Belinda* in 1948. Two years after working on *Young At Heart*, McCord was to film James Dean in *East Of Eden*.

Sinatra next attacked Liam O'Brian's script, which called for his character to die at the end of the film following a suicide bid, as happened with John Garfield in the original. Sinatra declared he had done this once before – in *From Here To Eternity* – and that he had no intention of doing so again. The script was duly amended. What he was unable to argue about, however, was the songs, which turned out to be more memorable than the film itself, with him having the pick of the crop: 'Someone To Watch Over Me', 'Just One Of Those Things' and the superb 'One For My Baby'. There was also an unpleasant altercation in the Green Room when Ethel Barrymore celebrated her birthday and the cast and crew threw her a surprise party. Seeing how weak the old lady looked when being helped out of her wheelchair – though she plays her scenes beautifully, and does not look as if she is in pain – was too much for Doris after her breakdown and she burst into tears. When a technician tossed her a box of tissues and this accidentally hit her in the face, Sinatra laid into him and had to be dragged off by security men. He also caused problems by persistently turning up late for shooting – he was already starting to develop the shady reputation that would overshadow his later career – and sometimes the unit would be kept waiting for hours while he recovered from the previous night's bender with his cronies. Doris swore she would never work with him again.

The Tuttle sisters – Laurie, Amy and Fran (Doris, Fraser and Malone) – live with their widowed father (Robert Keith) and his stalwart sister Jesse (Barrymore). Which of course begs the question: why would three women, average age 30, still be living at home, being bossed around by a domineering aunt unless there was something radically different about them? Amy and Fran have beaux whereas Laurie appears to be a daddy's girl. 'There's one thing I've got to have when I get married – lots of laughs,' she says, something which was not happening for Doris away from the studio. Everything changes when cocky, opinionated composer Alex Burke (Young) comes along: first seen delivering puppies on the front lawn, he is invited to dine then board with the family by Mr Tuttle, who went to school with his father. Alex soon takes over the household. All three girls fall for his smug charms but it is

Laurie who ensnares him after singing 'Ready, Willing And Able' – arguably Doris' only good song in the film (and a chart hit) once Sinatra had been given the monopoly. Sinatra, aka Barney Sloane, himself makes his appearance over half an hour into the proceedings as Alex's pianist and arranger, newly arrived from New York to help out with the Broadway show for which Alex has been commissioned on a restricted timescale, causing him to suffer writer's block.

We first see 'Ol Blue Eyes' wearing a hat with his back to the camera and when he turns round it's not a pretty sight: cadaverous-looking, in an ill-fitting suit. Neither is he initially pleasant towards Laurie, being surly, cynical and full of himself – an extension of the real Sinatra – until she breaks through the cynical interior to discover a lonely, disillusioned young man who has been trying to compose that elusive hit song for as long as he can remember. To help him out financially, Alex finds him a job performing at a downtown bar. 'Suburban drunks, they don't listen either,' he opines. Leaning on Laurie, he opens up about his sorry life so far – she even gets him to smile, something he never does. And she is just starting to feel attracted to him when Alex proposes marriage.

The wedding is about to take place when Laurie elopes with Barney, though married life for the Sloanes is no bed of roses as they struggle to survive on the pittance he earns working at local eateries where the customers ignore him. They return to the Tuttles for Christmas and under the illusion that Laurie is still in love with Alex, Barney switches off the windscreen wipers while driving through the blinding sleet and crashes his car. Lingering between life and death, he recovers when Laurie announces she is pregnant – when we see him again it is spring and, remarkably recovered, he serenades her at the piano while Aunt Jessie cuddles their baby. And he has finally finished his song! It was a very good film but the critics almost unanimously condemned Frank Sinatra for being too sure of himself: by refusing to die and thus give the film a more realistic ending.

Neither Sinatra nor Doris made any effort to promote their film – the nearest she got was referring to it briefly in her very first television appearance as a panelist on the quiz show *What's My Line?* broadcast on 2 June 1954, four months after the première. She later said how she had hated the whole television studio concept and that she would not be making a habit of what her later friend Rock Hudson would scathingly refer to as, 'That fucking oblong box in the corner!' There would be one more *What's My Line?* in September 1957. Prior to this and very much against her will, she appeared on *The Ed Sullivan Show* with Rosemary Clooney, Anthony Newley and Sophie Tucker. True to her word, there would be nothing more until her own television series in the late 1960s. She even turned down a staggering $1 million to make a television diet commercial, snarling at the producer, 'I've never had any problem with my figure, so why should I?'

A regular visitor to the set of *Young At Heart* was Frank Sinatra's wife, Ava Gardner – just as brash, vulgar and demanding as he was and no less friendly towards Doris. When Sinatra learned that Doris was being considered to play torch singer Ruth Etting in the MGM biopic *Love Me Or Leave Me*, he began to throw his weight around, demanding that Ava be given the part, mindless of the fact that she could not sing – she had lip-synched to Gogi Grant in the recent remake of *Showboat*. Doris was 'rescued' by James Cagney, four years after working with him in *The West Point Story*. Cagney was already cast as Etting's gangster husband: here was an actor much respected in the business and with considerably more sway than Sinatra. Not only did he want Doris for the film, he insisted that if she accepted the part, her name would appear above his in the credits – the first time this had happened in 30 years!

Marty Melcher negotiated a five-picture deal with MGM, demanding $1 million per film, only to be told by studio chief

Dore Schary that Doris was not worth this amount. After a great deal of wrangling, Schary agreed on $900,000 and she now signed on the dotted line for what many believe was her finest dramatic role and the turning point in her career.

Chapter 6

Love Me Or Leave Me

'If it's true that men are such beasts, this must account for the fact that most women are animal lovers!'

Doris Day

uth Etting (1896–1978) started out as a costume designer with Chicago's Marigold Gardens in 1913. Soon afterwards she joined the chorus and by 1922 she had become the establishment's resident vocalist and the wife of mobster Marty 'Moe The Gimp' Snyder, an unsavoury character who handled her career – and also mishandled her personally very much in to the way Doris was professionally abused by her husband. Etting made her Broadway debut in the *Ziegfeld Follies Of 1927* and regularly appeared there until 1931. She also made a large number of movie shorts and appeared with Eddie Cantor in *Roman Scandals*. Then in 1937 it all fell apart when she had an affair with her pianist Johnny Alderman. In a fit of rage Snyder shot and wounded him, and with her husband jailed for the attack, Etting divorced him and married Alderman, a union that lasted until his death in 1966. The scandal more or less put paid to her career, barring a brief radio series in the late 1940s.

What is important to remember when watching *Love Me Or Leave Me* is that one sees Doris Day emulating herself and not

Ruth Etting. The closest she gets to the real thing is towards the end of the film: singing Etting's classic 'Ten Cents A Dance', she stands, feet apart and with her hands on her hips, wearing a short black dress and aigrettes. Edith Piaf and Judy Garland would repeat the stance, minus the feathers. Otherwise she does not look nearly as rough, ready and tortured as the real chanteuse though vocally she tries her best, dropping her voice half a tone and slanting her notes in the way that Etting did, which is commendable. Nor does she tackle her more realist repertoire, choosing to stick with the lighter standards while the torchier numbers are glossed over. Comparisons may be made with this film and Barbra Streisand's portrayal of Fanny Brice in *Funny Girl* (1968), wherein the producers (in Doris' case Joe Pasternak, who revived Marlene Dietrich's flagging movie career by putting her into *Destry Rides Again*) were more interested in glamorising their subjects than displaying authentic portraits – though the end results could never be faulted. Better to show their subjects like this, they believed, than to have cinemagoers weeping in the aisles.

As such, while making the film Doris set herself a precedent: she refused to sit in on the rushes declaring this would impair her performance. Though the likes of Constantin Stanislavsky and Lee Strasberg did not interest her in the least, in those roles she was essentially a Method actress, psyching herself up for every part to the extent that once she stepped out in front of the camera, she was no longer Doris Day, movie star, but the character she was portraying. The last thing she wanted was to see herself looking downtrodden or badly done to, otherwise she might have asked for the scene to be shot again. Alternatively, when going back to the role for the next day's filming, she might have been conscious of how she looked, sounded, behaved and even thought on the screen. This, she said, would lead to her no longer liking her character and ultimately result in her giving a second-rate performance.

This is the ultimate in biopics and it does not suffer from the usual 'Hollywoodising' of the truth. Etting, Snyder and Alderman were all still alive when the script was assembled and insisted on being involved with the production so the facts could be presented as precisely as possible. Snyder himself told Pasternak that he would not settle for less than being portrayed as 'a piece of shit'! Indeed, his on-screen characterisation is so vile – ordering Ruth (Doris) where to sing, what to eat, never missing the slightest opportunity to publicly deride her – that with Cagney's superlative acting, almost a precursor of Method, the action sometimes becomes too painful to watch. The harmonica player Larry Adler, who in 1994 presented a seventieth birthday tribute to Doris for the BBC, once shared the bill with Ruth Etting and found out for himself how truly obnoxious Snyder had been. 'Compared to the actual gangster, James Cagney was almost effeminate,' he said. He then recalled how Snyder dragged him and his 'tin sandwich' (mouth organ) into his car and across town to the studio where Ruth had been recording 'If I Could Be With You' and stopped the session so that Adler could play just eight bars in the middle of the song, an exercise which resulted in a complete rewrite of Joe Venutti's complicated arrangement. And when Adler enquired about his fee for his services, Snyder snarled, 'You little bastard, git outta here!' and had not even added his name to the credits on the record.

In *Love Me Or Leave Me* Ruth Etting does not have to audition for shows, radio and theatre engagements: Snyder puts the squeeze on producers and club owners, including the great Ziegfeld, who engage her through fear of reprisal. That said, certain elements of the saga did not get past the censor. The scene where Snyder rapes Etting (with James Cagney preceding this on Doris' insistence with a real slap across the face to make the scene appear more authentic) ended up on the cutting-room floor. Etting also refused to meet Doris though she is said to have enjoyed the finished film.

The only sympathetic character in Ruth's life is her pianist-arranger Johnny Alderman (Cameron Mitchell). When he tries to offer her a shoulder to cry on, Snyder gives him money to pay for a prostitute so that he will leave her alone. When Johnny realises he is falling for her and that he can do more for her professionally now she has made it to the top, he refuses to accompany her to New York, where Snyder has inveigled her into the *Ziegfeld Follies*. This engagement, where she introduced her theme song, 'Shaking The Blues Away', saw Etting reach the peak of her career and hit an all-time personal low by marrying the loathsome Snyder. By now she had turned to drink (though on screen this is kept to a minumum) and just about the best compliment her husband can offer is a snarled, 'You're getting to look like an old bag!' When he tells her she must leave *Ziegfeld* and go into the movies, her only response is a sighed, 'Since when was it any of my business where I worked?' And by coincidence, her musical director in Hollywood is Johnny, who has composed 'I'll Never Stop Loving You' for her – this was *not* a Ruth Etting song.

Snyder does not wield the same power in New York as he did in Chicago but he still has the couple watched. For Ruth this is almost the last straw: she asks him for a divorce and in a desperate bid to have something of his own and also to have his name in lights above hers for once (*Martin Snyder Presents Ruth Etting*), he buys a nightclub. Before opening night, however, he catches Johnny kissing Ruth and shoots him. Johnny recovers and we assume the divorce takes place but Ruth still appears to be under Snyder's spell when he is jailed and faces bankruptcy. While he is still inside, she pays off his debts as a way of thanking him for all he has done for her – in other words for making her life an absolute misery – and on his release he is driven to the club just in time to hear her singing the film's title-track . . . once he has calmed down after threatening to tear the place down with his bare hands!

Not all the critics were enthusiastic about the film. Pauline Kael, whose reviews in her syndicated column ranged from sublime praise to downright vitriol, declared *Love Me Or Leave Me* was better than most biopics, only to add, 'But that's not saying all that much. Doris Day is a little less butch than usual, though you can't tell what makes her Ruth Etting a star. From the evidence of her movie appearances and her records, the young soft and sensual Ruth Etting was just about the opposite of this cold woman.' Doris' response to Kael's attack is said to have been unprintable.

The film's soundtrack album proved her most successful thus far, topping the Billboard chart and remaining on the best-sellers list for 28 weeks. Having successfully portrayed Ruth Etting, Doris (and not Marty Melcher) was approached by Michael Curtiz on behalf of Warner Brothers, who had recently acquired the script for the ominously titled *Why Was I Born?* – a Hollywoodised account of the tempestuous life of torch singer Helen Morgan.

Paul Newman was already signed to play her psychotic lover Larry Maddux. A gangster's favourite, Morgan (1900–41) attracted some very seedy characters to her shows, including a string of mobsters who tried, but failed on account of protesting prohibitionists, to fund a club similar to the one Marty Snyder bought for Ruth Etting. Morgan's problem was that she was incapable of performing unless drunk and between songs she often disappeared into the wings to swallow an emetic so that she could consume more illicit liquor. Signed by Florenz Ziegfeld in 1923, after working in his *Follies* she played what would later be regarded as the definitive Julie Laverne in the original 1927 Broadway production of Jerome Kern's *Showboat*, a role she reprised for the 1936 film alongside Paul Robeson.

The title for the film came from one of Helen Morgan's most celebrated songs and while Doris was deciding, Warners changed the title to *The Helen Morgan Story*. Though she had left the studio and had obviously forgotten her animosity towards Curtiz when informed he might have been directing *Young At Heart*, Doris was tempted. Life had always been much more simplistic, she said, when someone else (i.e. Jack Warner) was there to make all the decisions regarding script, director, roles and co-stars. What she referred to, of course, were the days when her husband had less clout and when, as the star of the show so to speak, the last word should have been hers had she been strong enough to stand up to him. Now she announced that she was turning the part down, claiming she did not want to offend her fans by having them believe she may have shared some of Morgan's more unsavoury habits. The truth was that she received hundreds of letters of complaint from fellow Christian Scientists spurred on by the ubiquitous Broones, who now advised her to reject the part 'so as not to offend God'. As Ruth Etting, Doris had 'sinned by drinking, smoking and behaving like a whore' and there was no way the Broones and their cronies would allow her to humiliate herself further by playing more or less the same role again; even worse, by expiring at 40 from cirrhosis of the liver, though this was not eventually depicted on-screen. The part was subsequently given to Ann Blyth, who mimed to Gogi Grant's singing voice.

It was at this point that the undisputed master of suspense, Alfred Hitchcock, offered Doris the lead in *The Man Who Knew Too Much*, to begin shooting in London in April 1955. She and 'Hitch', as she always addressed him, first met at a wrap-up party for *Storm Warning* when he expressed admiration for the way she handled Steve Cochran in the film and promised they would work together some day. The original film, released in 1934 with Edna Best and a fearfully dull Leslie Banks, told the harrowing story of a doctor and his wife who witness a murder while holidaying in Marrakesh and learn of an assassination bid scheduled to take place in London. To guarantee the couple's silence, their daughter (Nova Pilbeam) is kidnapped and threatened with death.

Hoping to add a touch of Method to her performance in the remake, Marty Melcher told Doris to imagine this was a real-life situation and that Terry had been abducted rather than her 9-year-old on-screen son. To add a touch more realism, like the Melchers she and her character's husband bicker constantly.

There is no denying that this is a good film, though for over 50 years Hitchcock 'purists' have never ceased to voice their opinion that the Best-Banks version was the finest because the drama was not offset against 'the vocal interruptions of a hit-parade singer'. Long before shooting commenced, Hitchcock commissioned Paramount's resident songsmiths Livingston and Evans to come up with a catchy number for Doris to sing to her son in the picture – a lullaby that would appeal to all ages. Little did they know when they gave her 'Que Sera, Sera' that they had provided her with a new signature tune and her most popular recording ever. The credo was also pure Doris Day – one of supreme, almost annoying optimism, the concept of the precognitive dream in that 'whatever will be, will be', especially if that is what one wishes.

When the story opens Doris is retired singer Jo McKenna, accompanying her doctor husband Ben (James Stewart) to Morocco. With them is their small son Hank (Christopher Olsen). There they meet a seemingly normal English couple, the Draytons (Bernard Miles, Brenda de Banzie), and a handsome, mysterious Frenchman (Daniel Gelin). Gelin is an Intelligence Officer and the next day he is stabbed in the market place. Before dying, he tells Ben that an important politician will soon be assassinated in London. Before he can inform the police, Hank is kidnapped. The McKennas follow the abductors back to London. Refusing help from Scotland Yard, they attempt to find him on their own and the film reaches its climax during a concert at the Royal Albert Hall. To say more would only spoil the ending for those who may not have seen it.

Doris did not want to work with James Stewart, a Hitchcock favourite who appeared in *Rope* and in *Rear Window* with Grace

Kelly. Such was her determination to have her way that she over-
rode Melcher on this one and provisionally agreed to do another
film with Howard Keel – a remake of Clare Luce's *The Women*,
which George Cukor directed in 1936 with an all-female cast
headed by Norma Shearer and Joan Crawford. Doris was to have
attempted the Shearer role – that of mild-mannered Mary Haines
whose (unseen in the Cukor film) husband is having an affair with
superbitch Crystal Allen, formerly played by Joan Crawford and
now assigned to Joan Collins. But Melcher would not hear of this.
Taking a leaf out of Marty Snyder's book, he forbade Doris to sign
the contract (the part of Mary went to June Allyson, while Leslie
Nielson took over from Howard Keel), and told her to accept
Hitchcock's offer and 'force' herself to get along with James
Stewart. To a certain extent their antagonism comes across on the
screen and maybe Hitchcock planned this to get better performances out of his stars – the fact that they felt uneasy working
together contributed to their on-screen tension, not knowing
whether their child was going to be killed or not.

Doris would later say of Hitchcock that he was the most
organised, even-tempered director she had ever worked with, a
genius and a lovely man. Yet working with him, she confessed, had
also been very disconcerting at first because he never gave her
direction, preferring to sit behind the camera and let her please
herself. Such was her distress that he might have been displeased
with her that she came close to walking off the picture. When
shooting was over she confronted him and asked what she had
done wrong. His response was that she had done everything right
and in his opinion she was such a natural in front of the camera
and had climbed so far into her character's skin that she needed
virtually no direction at all!

Doris was also unhappy with the proposed location filming in
London and Morocco. She had never travelled overseas and since
a radio tour with Bob Hope she had not been in a plane. Indeed

back then she was so terrified of flying that she swore never to fly again; she also did not wish to place an ocean between herself, Terry and her dogs. Marty Melcher talked her into making a compromise: he booked three luxury-class berths on the Santa Fe Super Chief to Chicago. Judy Garland and Sid Luft were also on the train and in the midst of a marital crisis on account of Judy's drinking and his bullying. The press reported non-stop rows, with Luft locking Judy in their berth whenever she was too drunk to stand so that the other passengers would not see her. Doris loathed him for this and insisted she be allowed to sit with Judy while she sobered up – she was only drinking in the first place, she claimed, because her husband was knocking her around. Leaving the Lufts to sort out their differences in New York, the Melchers boarded the *Queen Elizabeth*. Doris later said that she enjoyed this part of the journey most of all: relaxing on the top deck, sunbathing or wrapped in blankets depending on the weather, dining at the captain's table and being left alone by the other passengers.

London was another matter. Doris had planned on taking Terry sightseeing – she was sufficiently naive to think that if they turned up at Buckingham Palace, the Royal family would want to see them. Indeed, when their taxi pulled up outside Claridge's and she saw the huge crowd, she assumed the Queen must have been in the vicinity. It was only when she tried to get out of the car only to find herself surrounded by police that she realised that they were Doris Day fans and more than a thousand of them! With some difficulty, she and Melcher and Terry were manhandled by police and security men through the hotel side-entrance and up the stairs to their suite. So many flowers had been sent ahead of her that it was like walking into a funeral parlour: 'It was as if someone was laid out in the living room,' she observed.

For three days and nights the more overzealous fans took turns in shifts to maintain the hotel entrances: each time Doris showed her face, she was mobbed. Eventually, the hotel manager received so many complaints from other guests who were finding it impossible to sleep that he had to ask the Melchers to leave. They stayed at a secret location, until the first batch of interiors for the film was complete, then flew to Paris – Doris' idea for she did not wish to get onto the boat-train and be pursued by the paparazzi who were starting to make her life a nightmare. In Paris the Melchers met up with some of the other cast members and Doris was fitted out with her wardrobe. There, she was able to relax and see the sights. Most of the general public knew who she was but the French fans were less intrusive. It was then back to the madness when Marty Melcher decided that, instead of staying in Paris a little longer before heading for Marseilles and eventually North Africa, they would drop in on the Cannes Film Festival. This was the year the event introduced the Palme d'Or and he was tickled to discover that one of the contenders was *Marty*, starring Ernest Borgnine. The film won the award.

In Cannes, the trio stayed at the Carlton Hotel, like most VIPs, but when Melcher tried to acquire Doris and himself an interview, none of the journalists were interested – Brigitte Bardot was in town. Even so they were invited to the première of *The End Of The Affair* starring Deborah Kerr and Doris' friend Van Johnson, who were also staying at the Carlton. Cannes' audiences have always been notoriously hypercritical and this film was so bad that halfway through they began booing, forcing Johnson and Kerr to make a hasty exit. Doris signed autographs in the foyer and made arrangements to meet a group of journalists the next day on the beach. There, she was shocked not just to see the topless bathers but young men wearing the 1950s' equivalent of brief style Speedos – including one, she recalled, in see-through trunks! She made it clear to her mini press conference that this would be her first (and last) trip to the Cannes Film Festival and the next day she, Melcher and Terry boarded the ship for Tangiers, from where they travelled by car to Morocco.

In Morocco Doris became embroiled in a row with the authorities over the local location unit's treatment of the animals hired for the film. She had met Grace Kelly in Cannes and risked Marty Melcher's wrath by calling her to ask if she would replace her in the film – something Grace could not have done for two reasons. First, Doris had no back-out clause in her contract, and second, Grace was about to announce her engagement to Prince Rainier of Monaco and royal protocol declared that once married, she would have to renounce her movie career. Doris therefore confronted Hitchcock: unless he saw to it that the animals were properly housed and fed, she would break her contract and return to America. Within 24 hours, a shelter had been commissioned and for two days Doris embarked on a very uncharacteristic bender – 'I fell off the Christian Science wagon with a Tom Collins,' was how she put it. In fact, she had considerably more than one of them. The French actor Daniel Gelin (1921–2002), who plays the part of the murder victim in the film, was for many years the lover of my godfather Roger Normand, who related second-hand one of Doris' 'adventures' in Morocco, which thankfully never made it to the newspapers. Angry over Hitchcock's (sic) treatment of her four-legged friends, Doris wandered around their pens and paddocks with a bottle of Jack Daniels, toasting each and every one and promising them a better life until she could scarcely stand on her feet all the while, according to Gelin, 'yelling more expletives than a legionnaire on dockside leave'.

She also refused to eat in the commissary with the other actors and crew, particularly when she watched them digging their hands into the couscous pot, complete with fish-heads and tails. Every meal she ate in Morocco she cooked herself on the portable stove in her room. Once the locations were in the can and Melcher had booked their ship and train passages to London, she changed her mind about flying and insisted he buy plane tickets. They checked into the Savoy, where they were once again plagued by fans who camped out on the pavement in front of the establishment and at the back where the lawns bordered the Thames, using some pitched tents and make-shift shelters made of clothes-horses and blankets. Photographers patrolled the grounds night and day. For the hotel's resident 'queen' – viper-tongued actor Clifton Webb, who lived in an apartment at the Savoy with his 90-year-old mother – this was the last straw. Declaring the local 'bobbies' useless, Webb called Scotland Yard. Again and through no fault of their own the Melchers were shown the door. They moved to a hotel in Brixton and once the second stage interiors were complete, they flew back to Los Angeles.

Doris' new film was to be produced by Marty Melcher himself. MGM assigned him a budget of $1.5 million and a whopping 50 per cent of the profits. Without even discussing the project with her, he signed the contract for *Julie* on her behalf and then informed her that she would be reliving her nightmare years with Al Jorden and Al Levy while shooting the harrowing tale of the jealous husband who plots to murder his wife. Naturally Doris tried to get out of it, denouncing the whole idea as 'sick'. Melcher stood his ground, and once he promised her that her next film would be a 'nice easy musical', she submitted. Andrew Stone was brought in to direct and MGM hired French actor Louis Jourdan to play opposite her.

Born in Marseilles in 1921, Jourdan was plucked from the Ecole Dramatique in Paris by Marc Allegret in 1939 and cast in *Le Corsaire*, resulting in him becoming a household name in France. After serving with the Resistance, he was brought to Hollywood by David Selznick, where he had scored an instant hit in *The Paradine Case*. Women went wild over his suave and sophisticated mannerisms – he was almost the French equivalent of David Niven – and he also amassed a sizeable gay fan base. Most recently he had starred in *Three Coins In The Fountain* and after *Julie* he would go on to appear with Maurice Chevalier and Leslie Caron in *Gigi*.

Doris always denied having an affair with Jourdan, who was as charming and compassionate as Marty Melcher was bucolic and unpleasant. 'I think that Frenchmen are much better at conversation than Americans,' she commented of his intellect. 'There's nothing like a guy with bulging muscles and a vocabulary of twelve words. Give me a skinny, chatty Frenchman every time!' For the film's locations, Melcher chose Carmel, the coastal resort south of San Francisco that Doris would later make her home. She and Jourdan spent hours strolling along the beach, discussing life in general, and any other little interests they may have shared. Melcher's topics of conversation, she said, were limited to money, and movie and record details – and of course Christian Science. According to Daniel Gelin, Jourdan confessed they did have a brief, passionate relationship – that from day one of the shooting schedule, Doris leaned on her dashing beau for moral support against her bullying husband and that one thing led to another. Melcher's attitude towards his wife and stepson appears to have taken a turn for the worse by this stage. In her memoirs Doris denies that he was physically violent towards her, claiming the nearest he ever got to this was slamming his fist into the wall or door but friends and acquaintances (such as Rock Hudson) have said that he knocked her about. He certainly did hit Terry and often humiliated him in public, calling him 'sissy' or 'delinquent'. When Doris complained that he was being too hard on the boy, Melcher's response was that as the man of the household, he alone was responsible for disciplining Terry. To prove a point, he consulted the oracle – the Broones – who pointed out to her that it was against the edicts of Christian Science to have parents pulling in opposite directions as far as the wellbeing of their children was concerned. 'When the house is divided, it falls,' Mary Baker Eddy decreed, which Melcher interpreted as not having to spare the rod to spoil the child.

In the film Julie Benton (Doris) learns that her new husband, classical pianist Lyle (Jourdan), killed his first wife to marry her. When she walks out on him, he vows she will be next and so she tries to escape him (so many times that the plot soon becomes dull), finally returning to her former job as an airline hostess. Terrified as she is, she is nevertheless dressed up to the nines and perfectly coiffed in preparation for each new screaming fit. Enter new love interest Cliff Henderson (Barry Sullivan) and a scenario which sees Lyle tracking her down and boarding her plane as a passenger. The story then becomes far-fetched for during the ensuing shoot-out, Lyle and the pilot are killed, leaving Julie to land the plane with a little help from the injured co-pilot! This scene was lampooned some years later by Karen Black in *Airport 1975*. Adding the icing to the decidedly stale cake is the plum line, right at the end, which comes from the detective waiting in the control tower, 'I wouldn't do that again!' 'The action is unreasonable,' observed the *New York Times*' Bosley Crowther, 'but if you are credulous and casual, it makes for a lively show. Let's say the whole thing is contrivance and the acting is in the same vein.'

Claiming this was another Method part for Doris to sink her teeth into, Melcher enrolled her on a three-week airline-hostess training course that she did not mind at all. He delighted in subjecting her film character to a series of malicious, anonymous phone calls, knowing that since her breakdown she was paranoid about picking up the phone at home. More cruelly, he took advantage of her fear of flying, arguing that if she was going to land a plane in a movie, she might as well learn how to do it for real! He therefore arranged for her to have flying lessons without telling her until the last minute. En-route to the first of these, the couple were arguing when their car was struck side-on and written off by a drunken driver who shot through a red light and failed to stop. Melcher and Terry were unhurt, but Doris suffered whiplash injuries and severe bruising. Because the shooting schedule for *Julie* was so tight, Melcher would not allow her to stay in hospital overnight for observation and after an X-ray, she was forced to discharge herself.

A few days later, she began haemorrhaging badly on the set and director Andrew Stone assumed this was as a result of the accident. Stone agreed to close the set for a few days until she was taken back to the hospital and thoroughly checked over by a gynaecologist. But Melcher refused to hear of this: Christian Science, he declared, was virulently opposed to an intimate examination by strangers. *She* had made matters worse, he added, by spending too much of her spare time with Louis Jourdan and not enough hours studying the teachings of Mary Baker Eddy. Therefore if she did not recover from this indisposition, she would have only herself to blame! He then 'solved' the situation by bringing in Martin Broones and Charlotte Greenwood, who agreed the only course of treatment she needed was prayer and a few comforting words from the oracle. This went on for several weeks until Doris was in such agony that she could hardly walk. When she begged Melcher to let her see a doctor, he made her wait until he was certain Louis Jourdan was en-route for France for a vacation with his family – according to Daniel Gelin, 'relieved to be free of these nut-cases at last!'

Doris checked herself into the Glendale Memorial Hospital, where surgeons discovered an intestinal tumour weighing almost two pounds. During the subsequent four-hour operation, it was found necessary to reconstruct her small intestine and perform a hysterectomy. She later said that she would rather have died on the operating table than face the prospect of never being able to conceive again, though she also made it clear that had there been another child, she would not have wanted Marty Melcher to be the father.

While she was incapacitated, Melcher was approached by director Rudolph Mare, who wanted Doris to star opposite diminutive actor Alan Ladd and William Bendix in *The Deep Six*. This centred round a Quaker naval officer (Ladd), who is reluctant to enlist to fight in World War II because of his religious beliefs. Mare was told that Doris would never appear in such a film owing to her own religious beliefs and the part was given to the lesser-known Dianne Foster. Doris, who had always admired and wanted to work with Ladd, was said to have 'mildly' hit the roof.

Shortly after discharging herself from the hospital, Doris renewed her recording contract with Columbia for a staggering $1 million. Melcher negotiated an additional $50,000 for expenses that he promptly pocketed. It was he who suggested they up sticks and they paid $150,000 for a 'modest' home on Beverly Hills' exclusive North Crescent Drive. But the after-effects of her operation sent Doris into another downward spiral of depression and to take her mind off her crumbling marriage, ignoring close friends who advised her that the best course of action would be to leave Melcher once and for all, she worked on the interior designs of the house herself. She had frequently met William Haines, the former silents' star whose brilliant career, second only to that of Valentino, ended abruptly after he was arrested by the vice-squad when he was caught in a clinch with a marine in a downtown Los Angeles YMCA hostel. Haines (1900–73) had taken up interior design, working on the homes of Joan Crawford, Carole Lombard and dozens of others – restyling their interiors and making more money than he ever did from movies. He did not work on Doris' house but suggested she 'go with her personality' and use lots of relaxing pastel shades and uplifting yellows. Doris said that if ever she gave up her career – and immediately after *Julie*, she came very close to considering this – she too would take up interior design. Fortunately for her fans, the nearest she ever got to this was by way of her character in *Lover Come Back*.

In September 1956 she spent just three afternoons in the recording studio making what was unquestionably her best album so far. *Day By Day*, which was not quite so successful as its predecessors (it reached Number Eleven in the US charts), contains 12 fine songs meticulously arranged by Paul Weston – who conducts for her – with scintillating cameos from Barney Kessell on electric guitar, Ted Nash on alto and tenor sax and Frank Flynn on vibes. Eleven months later, with the same set-up, she would record a companion piece *Day By Night* (which did not chart at all though it has more than made up for it since) containing mostly songs from the 1930s and 1940s. Both are so relaxed and polished they are perhaps best suited to evening listening. That summer Doris saw Edith Piaf at the Mocambo and she was bowled over by her interpretation of Jacques Prévert and Joseph Kosma's 'Autumn Leaves', which Piaf had just recorded. Another singer making an impact in the United States at that time was Dorothy Squires, who met Doris at the same Piaf recital. 'One of my big songs at the time was "Don't Take Your Love From Me",' Dorothy told me, 'and when Doris said how much she liked my arrangement, I thought it funny. There was Piaf, offering me *her* arrangement of "If You Love Me, Really Love Me", so I said to Doris, "You'd better take 'Don't Take Your Love From Me.' Of course, if you fuck it up, you'll have to answer to me!" I was only joking of course.' Piaf and Doris Day were the most technically amazing women singers in the world!'

Piaf's closest friend and confidante Marlene Dietrich was also at the Mocambo and Doris subsequently added *two* of her songs – 'You Do Something To Me' and 'Soft As The Starlight' ('*Sch, Kleine Baby*', subsequently and horrendously readapted for Doris' film, *Do Not Disturb*) – to *Day For Night* for good measure. The other gems on *Day By Day* included the little-known 'Hello, My Lover, Goodbye' and 'Gone With The Wind' along with more established standards such as 'The Gypsy In My Soul' and the title-track, a reprise of the song which had started her off on the gilt-edged road to fame with Les Brown.

In the meantime *Julie* premièred on 8 October 1956 and Doris never initially questioned why, of all places, MGM elected for the event to take place at the Albee cinema in Cincinnati. She had never been back to the city since leaving to become a band singer – nor had she had any desire to do so. The whole concept was a publicity stunt organised by Marty Melcher to gain maximum publicity for 'his' film. The studio's founder, the soon-to-retire Louis B. Mayer, strongly adhered to a 'family values' policy – the fact that one's relatives must be respected at all times, whether the star in question got along with them or not. As such Joan Crawford and Judy Garland had had to be seen embracing their mothers in public even though they hated them. Now Mayer was on the verge of retirement and the man tipped to become his successor, Dore Schary, joined forces with Melcher to locate Doris' father, who she had not seen in almost 20 years.

Frederick Kappelhoff was discovered to be still living in Cincinnati, running a German-style bierkeller in the city's black ghetto with his common-law wife Luvenia Williams – who, once a few hundred dollars had exchanged hands, was elevated to the position of fiancée. Doris was told none of this, only that the Governor of Ohio, Frank Lausche, designated this Doris Day Week throughout the state and she would naturally have to attend the première. Why it had taken Cincinnati all this time to recognise her, she never questioned. She certainly fought against going, especially when she was informed that she would also have to attend 20 more functions, including banquets, garden parties and the like. 'Of all things on God's green earth I detest, it's having to participate in mass functions,' she recalled.

It did not take her long to realise she had been conned. Instead of being accompanied by just her husband and son, she found herself travelling with a 40-strong entourage of cameramen, reporters and studio personnel. One of the first to greet her at the Plaza Hotel was her father – Schary had arranged for him to be planted in the crowd within the lobby so she could hardly ignore him, though initially she did not recognise him. Schary's publicity department put Frederick, normally the hard man, through his paces. He hugged his daughter, burst into tears, apologised profusely for the way he had treated her and Alma, and invited her to drop in on them the next day. Frederick had been told not to bring Luvenia to the Plaza – the movie magazines, Schary had decided, would not wish for Doris to be photographed with a black woman. She herself was astonished to find this undisputed racist living among the black community and obviously well respected by the people he had once so openly condemned. In her memoirs she claims to have been deeply touched by his unexpected change of character but her positive attitude towards him was just as much a charade as the trip to Cincinnati: she did not wish her fans to think her disrespectful.

The performance continued when the MGM party arrived at Frederick's place – a fleet of Cadillacs headed by a chauffeured limousine, which must have gone down a treat in the neighbourhood. Hundreds of locals crowded the pavements as the car drew up, most of them genuine fans who appreciated Doris spending an hour or so chatting with them and signing autographs while the all-white MGM party stayed in their cars. Within the bierkeller, outside of which hung a 'Welcome Home Doris!' banner, she was photographed drinking beer – alone – then standing in front of the juke-box which, no real surprise, contained nothing but Doris Day records.

Doris' father was not invited to the *Julie* première – Dore Schary had given instructions that Luvenia Williams should not be permitted to attend and Frederick declared that if she was not welcome, then he too would be staying home, which suggests he genuinely loved her. Eventually they married and some years later, when Doris returned to Cincinnati of her own accord, she asked him to a reunion at the home of her uncle, Frank Welz. Frederick turned up but was told by his still-racist relatives that his wife would have to stay outside in the car. Doris would never see him again and made no public comment when he died. 'I never go to funerals,' she later wrote. 'I mourn the passing of someone dear to me in my own way. I don't approve of public grief.' For her father, there would be no private grief either.

Chapter 7

'Calling Rhett Butler And Eunice Blotter!'

'Nobody knows how difficult comedy is. It's much more difficult than drama because it's unreal!'

Doris Day, 1989

D oris' next film was *The Pajama Game*, the Broadway smash hailed by French director Jean Luc Goddard as 'The first left-wing operetta'. Co-directed by Stanley Donen and George Abbot, it reassembled most of the Broadway cast headed by John Raitt (1917–2005) in his only on-screen musical lead – less charismatic than he is said to have been on the stage though vocally superior to Doris' previous male leads. The choreographer was Bob Fosse (1927–87), and he too was making his screen debut, though unlike Raitt much of his work would be seen in the future. Supporting were Eddie Foy Jr, roly-poly actresss Reta Shaw – and Carol Haney, one of Hollywood's saddest casualties. The same age as Doris she was discovered in 1946 by choreographer Jack Cole. Three years later she was hired by Gene Kelly as his assistant choreographer and they worked together in *An American In Paris* and *Singin' In The Rain,* among other productions. Haney, a bundle of electrified energy whose limbs appeared to be made of rubber, danced with Bob Fosse in *Kiss Me Kate* and it was he who signed her to play Gladys Hodgkiss, the role she reprises in the stage version of *The Pajama Game*. She subsequently won a Tony and two Donaldson awards. A diabetic, she later coped with the pressures of work by hitting the bottle. In 1964, while choreographing *Funny Girl* for Barbra Streisand, she died aged 39 of pneumonia, aggravated by alcoholism.

The production was beautifully filmed by Harry Stradling Jr, nephew of Walter – who had been Mary Pickford's favourite cameramen. British-born Stradling was a genius whose forte was capturing the essence and frequently darker qualities seen in the Dutch masters, for the screen, particularly when the central subject was a beautiful woman. He had filmed Marlene Dietrich in *Knight Without Armour*, Judy Garland in *Till The Clouds Roll By* and *Easter Parade*, and Vivien Leigh in *A Streetcar Named Desire*. Later he would photograph Audrey Hepburn in *My Fair Lady* and Barbra Streisand in her first four films.

As with *Lucky Me*, one has to get through the first 10 minutes of the film to appreciate just how good it is – possibly Doris' best musical after *Calamity Jane*. She plays Babe Williams (Janis Paige played her on stage), shop steward at the Sleep Tite Pajama Factory. Babe is sexy and sassy; she is also popular with the girls, singing 'I'm Not An All In Love' with her cloying sidekicks in a scenario that would not have been out of place in the much-later Australian television series *Prisoner: Cell Block H*.

Babe falls head-over-heels in love with new superintendent Sid Sorokin (Raitt) at the factory's annual July picnic and words defy the feast of fun, superbly choreographed by Bob Fosse which would be part-reprised in Barbra Streisand's *Hello, Dolly!* The song here is 'This Is Our Once-A-Year Day', where the principal player is Gladys Hodgkiss with Carol Haney putting so much zip into her performance that one finds it hard to believe she was already seriously ill. Later in the film she puts on a show with the boys at a trade-union meeting but her greatest moment comes with 'Fernando's Hideaway'. Babe's affection for Sid is short-lived because they are on opposite sides of the factory floor. Even so, they get in a couple of formidable duets – 'Small Talk' and the rip-roaring 'There Was A Man'. There is then a temporary hitch in their relationship when the union demands a pay-rise and the manager is unwilling to pay up. Babe organises a go-slow and Sid has to fire her.

The film's *coup de grâce* is Doris' definitive rendition of 'Hey There', sung to herself while staring at her reflection in the mirror. In 1980 Elizabeth Taylor would parody this in *The Mirror Crack'd*, sighing to Rock Hudson, 'Bags, bags, go away. Come right back on Doris Day!' Doris sang the song in a single take, live on the set, as had happened with 'Secret Love' earlier in the film – Sid has duetted on the song but Babe does not get to finish before collapsing on the bed in tears. We know that Babe is ultimately going to get her man by the end of the picture but this does not deflect from the pleasure of the will-she-won't-she build-up. This happens when Sid discovers the factory manager has been diddling the workforce. The dispute is settled and the film ends with a pajamas fashion parade – Sid and Babe sharing theirs, she wearing the top and he the trousers, sucking in his stomach and flexing his muscles.

Shortly after she completed *The Pajama Game* Doris' brother died suddenly, though not unexpectedly, of a seizure, aged 36. Paul Kappelhoff and his family relocated to Hollywood a few years earlier to work as a music publicist for Doris and Melcher's production company Arwin. He never recovered from his baseball injury and for some time he had been addicted to prescription drugs. Doris never found out until after his death just how badly her husband had treated him: making him work long hours for less than the minimum wage and mocking his affliction. Sam Weiss, Doris' friend and the head of Warner Brothers' music department, knew exactly what had been going on but refrained from telling Doris, knowing how she would have reacted. 'Doris adored Paul,' he wrote in a paragraph that she added to her memoirs, 'and if she had known how Marty was treating him, I think Doris would have pitched Marty out on his ear.'

Her next film, an exercise in casting caution to the wind, saw Hollywood's 'perennial virgin' teamed with its former romantic hero and still loveable lecher, 57-year-old Clark Gable. Paramount's *Teacher's Pet*, produced by William Perlberg and George Seaton, and directed by the latter, was scripted by husband-and-wife team Michael and Fay Kanin, who had written *Woman Of The Year* for Spencer Tracy and Katharine Hepburn. It was a gentle sex comedy, a precursor to the trilogy Doris later made with Rock Hudson. The format is almost the same: Gable the worldly cad, assuming another identity to seduce the gullible Doris, who initially finds him reprehensible, then starts to fall in love with him so that by the time his true identity is revealed, she is willing to forgive him anything. There is also the stooge who provides the protagonists with a friendly shoulder to lean upon: Gig Young, who would subsequently be nominated for an Oscar.

The idea worked well, resulting in a smash hit that would leave fans of both stars clamouring for more. Gable and Doris were perfectly matched – she getting laughs for her dotty antics while he was appreciated for his quirky facial expressions and quick-fire delivery. Gable called her 'screwy and delightful, a pleasure to work with.' In return, she wrote of him, 'He was as masculine as any man I've ever known, and as much a little boy as a grown man could be. It was this combination that had such a devastating effect on women.' Speaking in a BBC interview 20 years later, she would slightly revise her opinion, saying, 'He was anything but macho. He was the gentlest, dearest man and very humble,' adding of his insistence that every take be spot on, 'He would say to the director, "George, are you sure that I gave you what you wanted? I'd be happy to do it again!'" It was Gable's mania for detail that partly contributed towards his death; two years later and soon after completing *The Misfits* with Marilyn Monroe – a film which saw him doing his own stunts, lassooing mustangs in the fierce heat of the Nevada desert while well aware that he had a heart condition. Doris' single of the title-track, penned by Roy Webb and Joe Lubin, stormed into the US charts.

Due to failing health Gable had looked ropey in his last few films, and this one was shot in monochrome to reduce the risk of this happening again. Gable comes across as cosy and affable as the roguish Jim Gannon, editor of the *New York Chronicle*, whose tough exterior is not completely impenetrable. He adopts a fatherly attitude towards his errand boy-cub reporter (Nick Adams), agreeing with the boy's mother that he needs an education and respecting her request to fire him because he knows this is for the best.

Such is Jim's reputation for fairness and for writing good stories that Erica Stone (Doris), eminent lecturer in journalism, wants him as guest speaker at one of her university classes. The two have never met and he is against the idea: not only does he dislike female teachers but he firmly believes that the journalist can only learn his trade via experience and not through books. He sends her a letter, explaining in no uncertain terms why he finds such lessons such a waste of time. When his boss orders him to go, he enrols in the class in the guise of Jim Gallagher, feigning the only knowledge he has of the trade comes from a reporter pal with whom he plays poker on weekends.

Seeing how pretty she is, Jim falls for Erica and repeats what his 'friend' told him: 'He said you'd be a frustrated old biddy who'd read all the text books and never written a line – how someone like that's like betting on a three-legged horse!' Then he squirms as she reads out his letter to her students. Erica gives him his first assignment: he pens a piece about a street killing, purloined from

A rare photograph with bandleader Bob Crosby, on NBC Radio's *Camel Caravan* – minutes before he fired her.

Away from her work, Doris had just two passions: her dogs, and her son Terry, pictured here with her in 1951. After his death in 2004, she became an almost total recluse.

Doris marrying third husband, Marty Melcher. He was a bully who knocked her around, and swindled her out of millions.

With Alfred Hitchcock on the set of *The Man Who Knew Too Much* in 1956. 'Hitch' never gave her directions, claiming that she was such a natural in front of the camera, it was unnecessary.

'Roy Harold' meets 'Eunice Blotter'! Relaxing between takes on the set of *Pillow Talk* (1959). Rock Hudson was a favourite co-star and they remained friends until the end of his life.

Posed for the press whilst promoting her 'warts 'n' all' autobiography in 1976. It lifted the lid on many controversial aspects of her career, though she still held many things back.

Doris with the Golden Globe's Cecil B. DeMille Lifetime Achievement Award in 1989, one of the last occasions she turned up in person to collect such trophies.

A sneak shot of Doris in 2000. Although she has been seen little in public for the last 40 years she remains instantly recognisable.

another writer which impresses and moves her – the best work any student has ever handed in, she says, and she compares what he has written with the headline in that day's newspaper: BLOOD-CRAZED SEX MANIAC STRIKES AGAIN – the kind of journalism she hates:

> ERICA: Journalism is so much more than blood and sex . . .
> JIM: You liked my story about that murder. That's blood, isn't it?
> ERICA: Now, wait a minute. I didn't say that I disapproved of blood. It's just that . . .
> JIM: How do you feel about sex?
> ERICA: Why, I'm all for it! [Shocked by what she has just said.] Goodbye, Mr Gallagher!

Jim is hooked and unable to concentrate on his work. When he should be jotting down notes, he is doodling her picture on his pad. In her office he hears Erica talking on the phone to a mysterious Dr Hugo Pine (Gig Young) and he learns that the two have been spending a lot of time together. Confident he has more to offer her than the (he assumes) boring, elderly academic, he grabs her and kisses her so passionately her knees buckle – exactly how Doris claimed to have reacted when kissed for the first time by Clark Gable. Somehow one doubts this, taken into consideration reports of his acute halitosis!

Cut to the Bongo Club where Jim is with his bimbo girlfriend (Mamie Van Doren), the resident chanteuse and poor man's Mae West, whose novelty number 'The Girl Who Invented Rock 'n' Roll' does not match up to the hype it received at the time. Erica is also there with Pine and because he is youngish and good-looking, Jim realises he has competition: the pair spike each other's drinks but become friends when Jim learns that Pine is only collaborating with Erica on a book. The scene where Gig

Young and Gable are fixing drinks is genuinely sad and would have benefited from a retake – Gable is clearly suffering from the shakes, slopping his drink and dropping the ice on the counter.

Now the way is open for him to pursue her, Jim confides in Pine the effect Erica has on him: 'Before I had contempt for eggheads like her. I was an obstinate, prejudiced, inconsiderate, whole-hearted louse. But at least I was something. Now that I've come to respect your kind, I'm just a big, understanding, remorseful slob – a complete zero!' There is, however, a temporary rupture in their relationship when Erica visits the newspaper office and finds out who Jim really is. He, likewise, has discovered her father was a Pulitzer Prize-winning newspaperman though this does not prevent him from opining Mr Stone's old-fashioned, non-commercial style of journalism stinks! Later, Erica goes through some of her father's features and realises Jim is right. The film ends, a little disappointingly, not with them in each other's arms but with Jim agreeing to guest lecture to Erica's students – which is what she wanted in the first place.

There were on-set problems between Doris and Mamie Van Doren, and between Gable and Nick Adams, whom Doris 'mothered' throughout the production, aware of his personal demons. Van Doren – peeved Doris' reprisal of her 'showstopper' number in *Teacher's Pet* (while she and Gable are in Erica's apartment) was considerably sexier than hers – later remarked that Doris behaved 'unpleasantly' towards her. This is hard to believe. When one reads contemporary reports of the goings-on in most of Doris' films, particularly her trilogy with Rock Hudson, one wonders how the cameraman managed to shoot a frame without cracking up on account of the zaniness and practical jokes. 'Doris failed in take after take to smile radiantly while watching me dance,' Van Doren complained to Doris' biographer, Eric Braun, obviously very sure of herself and missing the point completely – the fact that in the film the two women are supposed to be *rivals* for Jim's affections and therefore hardly likely to be in the mood for exchanging pleasantries.

The dilemma with Nick Adams – or rather Gable's reluctance to work with him until he was talked into it by Doris – stemmed from the young actor's position among Hollywood's so-called 'open-secret' closeted gay community; the fact that Adams appeared aware of all its murky past and present including Gable's own dalliances on the other side of the fence. Adams (1931–68) had been James Dean's last lover and after his death he had an affair with Elvis Presley, which 'Colonel' Tom Parker, Elvis' cash-obsessed manager, shelled out a fortune to prevent tabloid exposés.

Boastful, predatory and promiscuous, Adams supplied Dean lookalike male whores to big-name actors, Hollywood business-men and studio personnel, including several of those working on *Teacher's Pet*. He was also involved with one of the actors. Gable was terrified Adams might have been filled in about his gay past and he was so nasty to the young man that he asked to leave the production. Doris, well aware of Adams' sexual leanings but hardly likely to have known about Gable's involvement with William Haines, Johnny Mack Brown and journalist Ben Maddox back in the 1930s, was asked to persuade him to stay. She became so protective of Adams that she later insisted on him receiving a part in *Pillow Talk*. In February 1968, by then an established household name by way of the television series *Saints And Sinners*, Adams would be found dead of a drugs overdose. Doris sent a wreath to his funeral – and Elvis Presley suffered a nervous breakdown.

Doris had begun recording songs for an album to be titled *Hooray For Hollywood* in October 1957 and by the time *Teacher's Pet* was on general release, there were 15 songs in the can that she was still recording and she had still not been able to narrow them down to the requisite 12. They included Irving Berlin's 'Cheek To

Cheek', Jerome Kern's 'The Way You Look Tonight' and other standards by Dorothy Fields, Rodgers and Hart and Cole Porter. Now a compromise was reached between her record company and Marty Melcher. Doris would up the number of songs and CBS would release a double-album, in those days virtually unheard of. Conducting the orchestra was Frank De Vol, who accompanied her on 'Que Sera, Sera'. It was an ambitious project and one that had its moments: she sings 'You'll Never Know' beautifully in direct contrast to Johnny Mercer's 'Blues In The Night', which is positively awful and even sees her going off-key but it was not her best effort. Even when CBS re-released the albums separately, they did not chart – the first time this had happened with a Doris Day album.

Compared with *Teacher's Pet*, her next film was an undisputed dud. Marty Melcher was right in assuming that, at 35, Doris was too old for tomboy roles though the 'perennial virgin' tag would stick for a while. A great and egocentric fault of his was selecting the kind of roles for her that he believed she should have been playing. *Tunnel Of Love*, co-starring Richard Widmark, Gia Scala and Gig Young, was filmed on a tight budget over a three-week period and this shows. Indeed, considering its subject matter and Doris' apparent yearning for another child, it was unforgivable of Melcher to expect her to enter into such a scenario.

In a situation that today would be considered highly inappropriate, Doris and Widmark play Isolde and Augie Poole, a frustrated couple who attempt to adopt a baby from the Rockabye Adoption Agency – though from the way they go about this, one might think they were visiting the local market to buy some household commodity! And whoever saw a social worker looking like Gia Scala, decked out in a Jean Harlow-style evening gown, let alone one who feels the solution to the would-be mother's problem is seducing her husband? Considering Doris' anguish over being unable to have any more children of her own, the whole idea of the film must have been a sick joke on Melcher's part – the production deserved to be a flop at the box-office! It was the first film to be directed by Gene Kelly not to feature him heading the credits. The *Hollywood Reporter* enthused of Doris' performance, 'She is as wholesome as wheatgerm, bubbly as champagne'. This may have been true but the film was decidedly flat. Widmark was hopeless at attempting comedy and audiences were tired of seeing Gig Young as the booze-addled lecher; he also drank heavily off the screen. In October 1978, three weeks after marrying a young German actress named Kim Schmidt and following one boozing-arguing scenario too many, Young put a bullet through her skull – and a second one through his own.

Doris' next film, *It Happened To Jane*, was even worse: a silly production from start to finish for which the term 'watching paint dry' could not be more appropriate. For reasons known only to themselves the critics loved it and almost unanimously gave it sterling reviews while the fans, who obviously knew best, stayed away from the cinemas in droves. The cast was above average but not exceptional here: Steve Forrest, Ernie Kovacs – who would die three years later in a car crash, aged just 43 – and Jack Lemmon, who Doris said she found 'disarming and charming' and challenging because of his own comedic timing. Hailing from Massachusetts, Lemmon (1925–2001) was the son of the president of a doughnut company – something that tickled Doris, who nicknamed him 'Lemon Doughnut'. Following a stint in the US Navy, he had taken up acting, first on Broadway and then on the radio before turning to the movies. After numerous bit parts he starred opposite Judy Holliday in *It Should Happen To You* (1954) and the next year won the Best Supporting Actor Oscar for *Mister Roberts*. More recently he scored a huge hit in *Some Like It Hot* alongside Tony Curtis and Marilyn Monroe, therefore his film with Doris (he himself blamed its failure solely on the title) must have come as a sore disappointment. Lemmon would subsequently compare the two actresses and praise Doris for her enticing sexual quality. 'She doesn't lay it out there like a Marilyn Monroe,' he said, 'but it's there nevertheless – the difference between a nude and a woman in seductive clothing.'

The Technicolor photography of the sumptuous Maine locations could not have been bettered. Director Richard Quine has frequently been compared to Frank Capra in his ability to capture the essence of the common man or woman who triumphs over adversity, as Capra had done with Clark Gable and Loretta Young in *It Happened One Night*. This certainly happens here, save the storyline is so utterly trite and uninteresting. Later Doris also blamed the failure on the title though had Columbia (who made the Gable film) stuck with the original title, *That Jane From Maine*, one doubts it would have fared better. In the wake of the phenomenally successful Joan Crawford-Bette Davis schlock horror-fest *Whatever Happened To Baby Jane?* it's title was changed to the even sillier *Twinkle and Shine* but by then it had long since passed its sell-by date.

Doris plays Jane Osgood, a widow with two small children, who runs a lobster business in Cape Anne. This hits crisis point when her regular transporter, the Old 97, is re-routed and her cargo returned dead. The railroad has been taken over by the odious Harry Foster Malone (Kovacs), who wants to make more money by replacing the Old 97 with a passenger train, regardless of the locals, who rely on it for their business. Assisted by her friend and lawyer friend George Denham (Lemmon) and supported by journalist Larry Hall (Forrest) – who has a crush on Jane and asks her to marry him – she fights back. She takes Malone to court and wins her case but is awarded no compensation. Therefore she seizes the Old 97 and sets out to ruin Malone, gaining publicity by appearing on television chat and game shows. Subsequently her lobster farm does a roaring trade though this soon hits another snag when Malone cancels all rail services in and out of Saint

Anne. Only at this stage does the film spring to life when the townspeople muck in to supply coal for the Old 97 so that Jane's lobsters may be delivered before they go off. When the coal runs out and the train runs out of steam, Malone shows up in the middle of nowhere – ostensibly to have it out with Jane once and for all – but once his employees start to walk out on him on account of his churlish behaviour, he capitulates, supplies more coal and even joins in with the shovelling. Larry also turns up, expecting an answer to his marriage proposal, but Jane has already agreed to marry George – 27 years after he last asked her when they were children. And the viewer breathes a sigh of relief that it's finally all over!

When shooting wrapped, Doris entered the studio and recorded over the space of a few days *Cuttin' Capers*. Her last album, *Day By Night*, had flopped (the *Hooray For Hollywood* album was yet to be released) but she had a Top Ten hit with the catchy, self-duetting 'Everybody Loves A Lover'. *Cuttin' Capers* was a mish-mash of standards and novelty numbers, with arrangements by Frank DeVol. Some songs she had already done before – 'I'm Sitting On Top Of The World' and 'Makin' Whoopee!' – and others such as the title-track and Arthur Freed's 'Fit As A Fiddle And Ready For Love', she might have been better off not doing at all. Much better was the sexy 'Why Don't We Do This More Often?' and Irving Berlin's 'Steppin' Out With My Baby', which Fred Astaire sang in *Easter Parade*. Even so, few were surprised when the album did not chart.

Doris learned her lesson the hard way with falling box-office receipts. Henceforth the scripts were meticulously vetted. Marty Melcher would discuss scenarios, ideas and contracts with her, at least pretending to no longer treat her like a commodity – though still ripping her off behind her back.

In the autumn of 1958 she was contacted by producer Ross Hunter with a view to teaming up with Rock Hudson for a 'sex comedy' scripted by Stanley Shapiro and Maurice Richlin entitled *Pillow Talk*. Melcher was similarly propositioned by Twentieth Century Fox – Doris had dropped out of the Box-Office Top Ten and the situation must be rectified. The studio was bringing *South Pacific* to the big screen and wanted her for the part of Nellie Forbush, portrayed on the stage by, it has to be said, the far less engaging Mary Martin. Without even telling her, Melcher agreed she would do the film for her regular salary plus 50 per cent of the box-office. Fox appear to have considered this until Doris was approached at a Hollywood party by Richard Rodgers and asked to give an impromptu recital of some of the songs from the soundtrack. But she was starting to fight back against her martinet of a husband and she refused point-blank, declaring she was not into giving charity performances. The studio contacted Melcher and told him in no uncertain terms what to do with his demands and she insisted this time she would do the film that she wanted to do. Melcher therefore 'gave her permission' to do *Pillow Talk* provided that Universal agreed to place her name above Rock Hudson's in the credits.

Regarding *South Pacific*, Doris compromised by recording 'Wonderful Guy' from the soundtrack and this led to her cutting *Show Time*, an album of showstoppers. Accompanied by Axel Stordahl's orchestra, she chose only selections from those musicals that were still doing big business on and off Broadway. From Cole Porter's *Can Can* there was a zippy 'I Love Paris' and from *Oklahoma!* 'The Surrey With The Fringe On Top' and 'People Will Say We're In Love'. There was also a stirring rendition of 'The Sound Of Music', which, as will be seen, would almost lead to better things.

Doris had been a fan of Rock Hudson's for as far back as she could recall – she admitted having the hots for him, not knowing at the time that he was gay. She flung herself heart and soul into the movie, though Rock was yet to prove himself in the comedy field. Back in 1955 Hunter had taken risks with Rock by putting him in *Magnificent Obsession* opposite Jane Wyman. Until then he had almost always been assigned squeaky-clean beefcake roles in adventure movies and Westerns and his first dramatic role proved a massive success; he and Wyman subsequently made *All That Heaven Allows*. As Hunter unearthed Rock's dramatic qualities, so too did he recognise his hitherto untapped, natural humour – the perfect accompaniment, he declared, to Doris' zaniness.

For his part Rock was as sceptical about accepting his role in the film as Universal were about backing a venture for which they only had Ross Hunter's assurance that it would be a success. He also had reservations about working with Doris, having an 'insider's knowledge' that her off-screen reputation as a tough taskmaster did not match up to the sweetness-and-light image projected in her films. He did, however, suspect there was a good reason for this, later telling *Films Illustrated*'s David Castell in 1976, 'It's true that Doris can come on strong but like most people who come on strong, what she's really saying is, "Help me." And if you help her, everything's just fine.'

The film reunited Doris and Rock with Nick Adams – he had first met the actor with James Dean while shooting *Giant* during the autumn of 1955. At that time he had shown no interest in him on account of Adams' trouble-causing reputation so why he should join forces with Doris now and insist that he be given a part in the film when virtually none of the cast and production cast could stand him is unknown. Certainly, they were never amorously involved.

Rock was informed that he would have to sing in the film, something that terrified him because he had always considered himself tone-deaf. Doris auditioned him at her home and convinced him otherwise. And though renowned in his circle for his ribald and perverse sense of humour and a fondness for playing practical jokes, Rock was unsure whether he would ever be capable of making audiences laugh. Additionally, despite Ross Hunter's much publicised comment that she was possessed of 'one of the wildest asses in Hollywood', Doris refused to believe anyone could perceive her as sexy.

Within days of accepting *Pillow Talk*, Doris was convinced Rock Hudson was gay. This came about by way of an argument with Marty Melcher, who, not satisfied with pocketing $50,000 for co-producing the film – virtually in name only – cornered Rock and suggested that if he knew what was good for him, he would ditch his long-term agent Henry Willson and engage him as his manager. Rock's off-the-cuff response – 'Henry only screwed me for fun, not professionally' – not only let the cat out of the bag but also suggested that he knew, long before Doris found out, that Melcher was a crook. Doris visited Rock several times at his rented stilt-house overlooking the gay section of Malibu beach – he had moved here with his long-term Italian actor lover, Massimo, after his divorce from Phyllis Gates whom he had only married in the first place to stop the tabloids speculating over his sexuality.

Over the years until his death in 1985 when the truth finally came out, journalists would pester Rock's friends – usually offering huge handouts for them to drop a few hints regarding his love life. 'Many, many people would ask me, is Rock Hudson really gay, and I said it's something I will not discuss,' said Doris in a BBC interview of 1989, adding that if she did know, she would still not have discussed it. The mere fact that she said such a thing of course and the way Rock's gay friends went out of their way to defend him – boasting of his insatiable libido where women were concerned – only made matters worse.

Throughout shooting, which began early in February 1959, Rock fought hard to conceal his hatred of Melcher from Doris – who unbeknown to him was beginning to find life with her husband unbearable on account of his near-psychotic treatment of their son. Convinced Terry would grow up to be gay, delinquent – or both – and without even discussing this with his wife, he dragged him away from the Christian Science school that Doris had put him into and installed him at the Harvard Military Academy, declaring this would make a responsible man of him. But he only succeeded in making the boy hate him. Commenting in Doris' memoirs on Melcher's double-standards and his inability to cope with his son being a normal teenager, Terry observed, 'He became hell-bent on making me feel guilty and in trying to run my life like a drill sergeant. He was all holier-than-thou in his Christian Science uniform, ushering on Sundays, and proverbs came out of him at me like machine-gun bullets. "Do as I say, not as I do," which means I get my ass kicked for something he also does but he doesn't get his ass kicked because he told me not to do it.' Terry would have a tough time at military school just because he was a movie star's son. This made Rock angry: his own father had treated him badly and he could not bear this in others. He advised Doris to bring Terry home but as usual she listened only to her Christian Science advisers – Melcher and the Broones. What Hudson was also unaware of was that, after a heated row with Ross Hunter over Melcher's appointment, Henry Willson enforced a deal with Universal wherein he would pocket $25,000 – to be deducted from his client's salary – for his role as Rock's 'adviser'.

Pillow Talk launched the most popular, perfectly matched, credible comedy partnership of the 1960s: the dotty, standoffish perennial virgin, who wears a succession of daft hats but only the finest Jean-Louis gowns and the randy, loquacious but loveable rogue, only interested in getting inside her pants. 'Rock was sexy in the part but not lascivious,' Doris later observed. 'Bemused but not overbearing – tough, but not rough.' During her career she would work with some very tall men – Jack Carson, Clark Gable,

Errol Flynn and James Garner were all over 6 feet – but at a good 6 feet 4 inches in his stockinged feet, Rock was the tallest apart from Clint Walker. Doris too, at 5 feet 7 inches, was among the tallest of his leading ladies, so together they do not look quite as ridiculous as Rock would have with pint-sized Debbie Reynolds, said to have been pencilled-in for the role before Rock insisted on Doris. The film opens with a close-up of New York interior designer Jan Morrow's shapely legs – dismissing at once Doris' theory that she was unsexy. Then the screen divides into three segments: Jan is compelled to share a party line with Brad Allen – whom she has never seen – and hears him serenading his latest squeeze with the song he claims to have written just for her. This is 'Inspiration', whose lyrics he amends time and time again throughout the scenario so that they include the name of whichever easy lay he is hoping to get into bed. At one stage he even croons in French while reaching for the control box next to the couch: one switch automatically locks the door on his conquests, dims the lights and operates the record player; another converts the couch into a bed. Jan butts in and bawls him out. He is hogging the line and this is hindering the running of her business. Brad accuses her of being a bore to which she yells, 'If I could get a call through every once in a while, my life wouldn't be so drab!'

Jan complains to the telephone company and is told that she can only have a private line in the event of an emergency such as her becoming pregnant. All the same, an inspector calls on Brad, only to succumb to his charms. Brad discovers who has reported him and calls Jan to give her a piece of his mind: 'Get off my back, lady! Stop living vicariously on what you think I do. There are plenty of warm rolls in the bakery. Stop pressing your nose against the window!'

Next to enter the fiasco is Jonathan Forbes (Tony Randall), Jan's client and Brad's thrice-married millionaire sponsor, who hopes that Jan will become wife number four, regardless of the fact that she does not love him and finds him intolerably dull. Neither Jan nor Brad are aware that Jonathan knows them both and when each tells him of her/his telephone antagoniser, he does not suspect what is going on between them. Brad is sceptical, however, when Jonathan expostulates the joys of wedlock:

> Before a man gets married he's like a tree in a forest. He stands there independent, an entity unto himself. And he's chopped down. His branches are cut off, he's stripped of his bark and thrown into the river with the rest of the logs. Then this tree is taken to the mill, and when it comes to he's no longer a tree. He's a vanity table, the breakfast nook, the baby crib, then the newspaper that lines the family garbage can!

Having fallen for Jan, still unaware of his true identity and becoming aware of how much she loathes him, Brad invents an alter-ego –Texas magnate Rex Stetson, a home-loving country boy who owns a mountain. They meet and as they ride in the back of a cab on their first date, we hear aloud their respective thoughts – the well-raised girl who is interested in marriage and the totally unscrupulous playboy who only has sex on his mind:

> SHE: What a gorgeous-looking man! I wonder if he's single?
> HE: I don't know how long I can get away with this act, but she's sure worth a try!

Rex sweeps Jan off her feet after rescuing her from the attentions of a client's drunken son (Nick Adams). 'We have a saying back in Texas,' he reprimands him, 'never drink anything stronger than you are – or older!' During their next party line spat Brad warns Jan what a scoundrel Tex is; claiming he accidentally overheard them talking on the phone. 'Don't let that yokel act fool you! This ranch-hand Romeo's just trying to lure you to the nearest barn!' On their next date, aware that his gentlemanly behaviour is the characteristic that attracts Jan the most, Rex of course proves the model of respectability. 'I'm not one for making fancy speeches,' he says, 'but I get a nice warm feeling being near you, ma'am. It's like being round a pot-bellied stove on a frosty morning.'

Now Jan is really hooked and the next time we see them chatting on the party line they are in their respective baths, suggestively touching toes where the vertical line divides the screen. Later, in a tableau where he almost bumps into her at the hospital and blows his cover, Brad dashes into the nearest room – an obstetrics clinic – where he demands an examination. 'I haven't been feeling too well,' he tells the nurse. 'Probably just an upset stomach but a fellow can't be too careful!' The doc thinks he is pregnant, especially when a few minutes later he sees him dashing into the ladies' room. Then Brad calls Jan again and attempts to put her off Rex by suggesting the Texan might be gay – Rock Hudson playing dangerously close to home as he drawls, 'There are some men who are very devoted to their mothers. You know, the type that like to collect cooking recipes and exchange bits of gossip?'

On their next date Rex follows this up with archetypal 'lavender' gestures but bottles out and devours Jan with kisses, almost bringing her to the point of orgasm. That same evening he asks her to spend the weekend with him in the country and she complies because she trusts him. They canoodle in front of the hearth and he declares she is no longer a pot-bellied stove but an out-of-control forest fire. A little later she sings her thoughts aloud – 'Possess Me' – and is on the verge of giving in to him when she stumbles across a copy of the sheet music of his seduction piece, 'Inspiration', which she has heard many times when eaves-dropping on Brad's conversations. 'Bedroom problems,' she scathes at a photograph of the fake Texan. 'At least mine can be solved in one bedroom – yours couldn't be solved in a thousand!'

Having packed her bags, she is about to leave when Jonathan Forbes turns up. He drives her back to New York and she cries all the way, including in a roadside diner where an angry customer mistakes him for a cad and punches him. 'I never knew a woman who had so much water in her!' he gripes. Brad's machinations to keep Jan to himself have backfired, however. Jonathan has paid him a small fortune for a batch of new songs but Brad feels so guilty over the way he has duped Jan that he suffers writer's block. And Jonathan, who now knows the true identities of the protagonists, realises that for the first time in his life Brad Allen is genuinely in love:

> The mighty tree has been toppled. For years I've been
> waiting to hear them yell 'Timber!' over you. You love her
> and she can't stand the sight of you. What a beautiful sight
> – the great Brad Allen, chopped down to size, floating down
> the river with the rest of us guys!

Jonathan urges Brad to rectify the situation but Jan wants nothing to do with him. He tries to worm himself into her affections via Alma, her alcoholic maid (Thelma Ritter), who suggests Brad should get Jan to refurbish his apartment then promptly drinks him under the table. Jan only takes the job because she thinks she can handle him. 'Once I had the mumps,' she says. 'It wasn't very pleasant but I got over it. I look over Brad Allen like any other disease: I've had him, it's over – I'm immune to him!'

Jan turns up at Brad's place and discovers his control box. 'He's like a spider,' she tells herself. 'He wants me to decorate his web!' Brad gives her carte-blanche to turn his apartment into a place she would feel comfortable in, and moves out while she sets to work: as he spends the interim ringing around old girlfriends to say goodbye, Jan transforms the apartment into a harem, even installing an ancient fertility symbol.

Brad gets mad. Bursting into Jan's apartment he drags her out of bed, carries her kicking and screaming through the streets to his boudoir, flings her onto the bed and announces he wants to get married. At first she seems shocked and he is about to leave when she flicks the switch on the re-adapted control box. The door locks and instead of smoochy gramophone music it operates a whorehouse pianola – her way of saying yes. The action then jumps forward three months and we see Brad bumping into the same doctor and nurse, who earlier thought he was pregnant. 'I'm going to have a baby!' he yells before they whisk him off to the examination room and the credits roll.

Within days of starting work on *Pillow Talk*, Doris and Rock Hudson baptised each other 'Roy Harold' and 'Eunice Blotter', nicknames they would use for the rest of Rock's life. In this, and their subsequent films together, so many supposed-to-be-serious scenes ran way over schedule because of their clowning around. Their love scenes were provocative for the day but never over-the-top. As *Time* magazine observed:

> When these two magnificent objects go into a clinch –
> aglow from the sun lamp, agleam with hair lacquer – they
> look less like creatures of the flesh than a couple of
> Cadillacs parked in a suggestive position.

In the trade, the Day-Hudson comedies quickly acquired the nickname 'DFMs' – Delayed-Fuck Movies – on account of the protagonists not being permitted to sleep together until they were married. Their regular foil, Tony Randall, told Rock's biographer Sara Davidson that he was supreme at playing romantic leads because he truly believed in romance. His friend Armistead Maupin, who later based one of his *Tales Of The City* characters on him, opined that Rock was actually indirectly expressing his homosexuality:

> Most of the guys I knew really like to see the old Doris Day films, and I think one of the reasons we laughed at them so hard was that there was a real gay 'in-joke' occurring in almost all of those light comedies – because at some point or other, the character that Rock Hudson played posed as gay in order to get the woman into bed. It was tremendously ironic because here was a gay man, impersonating a straight man, impersonating a gay man!

Pillow Talk and its genre of film was a concept which worked only with the on-screen innocence of Doris Day and the non-graphic, priapic machinations of Rock Hudson – largely because both were playing out of character. In fact Doris was anything but, and she therefore had to try that little bit harder to present herself as an authentic virgin; likewise Rock, because by his own admittance that whenever he pursued a woman on the screen, he was almost always thinking about a man. The film has had more than its fair share of imitators over the years – notably *Down With Love* (2003), with Renée Zellweger and Ewan McGregor – which in the new age of bad language, gratuitous nudity, full-on sex and by-and-large uncharismatic acting – remain worthless when compared to the original.

Chapter 8

'Some of My Best Friends Are Gay'

'So many people write to me and they say that when they're depressed and are feeling really low they go to see one of my films and they feel better.'

Doris Day, 1994

The viewer instinctively knows just by hearing the music over the opening credits for *Please Don't Eat The Daisies* that is they are in for a treat. Add to this the talents of producer Joe Pasternak and the directorial genius of Charles Walters and we are almost guaranteed a sure-fire winner – not to mention a wealth of gay 'in-jokes' which, when the film was released in 1960, would have sailed over the heads of general family audiences. On the negative side there is not much of a storyline – the emphasis is on the sparkling banter between the leads – and a couple more songs might not have gone amiss. Besides a reprise of 'Que Sera, Sera' sung to an accordion accompaniment, there's a catchy rendition of 'Any Way The Wind Blows' – and the title-track that sees Doris and a bunch of children dancing around the school playground.

Based on the best-selling novel by Jean Kerr with a crisp screenplay by Isobel Lennart, who scripted *Love Me Or Leave Me*, the film had David Niven as Doris' leading man – the suave and sophisticated anodine to her dotty Kate, wife of former college professor Larry Mackay. Throughout the scenario Kate struggles to keep control of her four unruly children. The youngest drops water-bombs out of the apartment window onto the heads of unsuspecting passers-by (inspired by Doris' recollections of her son Terry's own 'delinquency phase' when, at 3 years of age, he did exactly the same thing) – which explains why Kate keeps him locked in a cage, where he makes animal noises, bringing the comment from one visitor, 'What's with him – queer?' Later the toddler stomps around in Mommie's shoes. Adding to the never-ending hysteria is Hobo, the Mackays' neurotic dog.

When the film opens Larry is writing a novel and starting out on a new career as one of New York's 'Holy Seven' – one of those critics who, frequently drawing attention to themselves at some-one else's expense, can turn a Broadway play into an overnight sensation or close it after a single performance with a scathing review. Larry's first commission is reviewing *Mlle Fantan*, written by his best friend Alfred North (Richard Haydn) and starring talentless sexpot Deborah Vaughn – aka Janis Paige who played Babe in the original stage version of *The Pajama Game*. When Larry writes the truth – the play is dire – Deborah slugs him in a society restaurant. This makes the front pages of the newspapers, enabling the show to become more successful than it would have done and allowing Larry to exact his revenge by criticising Deborah further, drawing particular attention to her 'fanny'. In Great Britain this has a completely different meaning to its American counterpart, leaving the censors in a stew as they deliberated over whether to allow Janis Paige to repeat the word a dozen times! The plum line, however, adopted that season by London's closeted gay community, came from Kate's pet shop owner mother (Spring Byington), who tells her grandson, 'Gabriel, don't get too close to that monkey – he squirts!'

There is disruption for the family when the Mackays forget to renew the lease on their apartment and have just three weeks to find a new abode. Larry wanted a place in the country until he embarked on his new career but now he wants to stay close to theatreland. Kate gets her own way, however, and they buy a run-down property in Hooten, 70 miles out of New York – a huge, Addams family-type mansion. 'How come it's so big?' asks one of the kids, bringing the response from Kate, 'Because we couldn't afford anything smaller.' Then another of her brood questions one of the local welcoming committee, 'Excuse me are you a lady or a man?' The visitor affirms that she's 'in between'.

With Larry returning to New York, everyone pitches in to make the place habitable but Hobo dislikes country life as much as his master and is so terrified of cats and frogs that he ends up on tranquilisers. Then, when the local school asks Kate to help out by finding them a play for their drama group, she contacts Alfred, who exacts his revenge on Larry for the panning he gave him by loaning her Irving O'Reilly's *Ghostly Music* from his 'Drop-Dead File' – actually a turkey called *So Passion Dies*, which Larry wrote some years ago. In the meantime, suspecting him of having an affair with Deborah Vaughn, Kate bawls him out, and when Larry thinks she's up to no good because she's not home when he calls, she levels, 'I was having a rendezvous with Rock Hudson!' At first Larry will not let her use his play, even when Alfred forgives him his past misdemeanour and convinces him the work is so bad, it's actually good. Larry relents when Kate tells him he has become almost as mean as his reviews though to save face he still pans it, applying the maxim, 'I'll go on yelling tripe whenever tripe is served!' Then the film ends as it began, with the baby dropping a water-bomb out of the window – this time onto his parents' heads.

Please Don't Eat The Daisies was a huge hit with the box-office and seven years after its release spawned a 58-episode television series of the same name starring Patricia Crowley as newspaper columnist Joan Nash with Marl Miller playing Jim, her college professor husband. Shortly after the première Columbia released *What Every Girl Should Know*, a tremendous work resplendent with echoes of Doris' big band days. Under the baton of Harry Zimmerman she interprets a dozen 'mood songs' – indeed, cream of the crop was her superb reading of Duke Ellington's 'Mood Indigo'. From the Rodgers & Hammerstein stable are the gentle, rarely-heard 'A Fellow Needs A Girl' and 'What's The Use Of Wond'rin', followed by a stirring 'Something Wonderful', second only to the version recorded by Peggy Lee (with Frank Sinatra conducting the orchestra!) two years earlier. She ups the tempo with 'When You're Smiling' then rounds the whole thing off with 'The Everlasting Arms'. This last song came about following her previously mentioned meeting with Edith Piaf at the Mocambo. Yul Brynner, putting together his *All Star Festival* album to raise money for the World Refugees Project, had already persuaded Bing Crosby, Nat King Cole, Mahalia Jackson and Piaf to contribute but so far the other stars he had approached proved too tight-fisted to donate their services for free. Piaf would suggest Doris, and Doris in turn suggested Ella Fitzgerald and Caterina Valente. 'The Everlasting Arms' was commissioned from her 'spiritual adviser' Martin Broones and a fine piece it is with a beautiful violin weaving its way through a highly emotive tapestry of faith – not in the religious sense but faith in love itself for at the last minute Doris wisely got Broones to change the opening line from 'When you walk with God' to 'When you walk with love'. Cynics have suggested the Broones might have been better composing more songs of this quality and intensity than filling Doris' head with nonsense.

If David Niven had been a model of English sophistication in *Please Don't Eat the Daisies* then Rex Harrison's character in *Midnight Lace* could not have been creepier even when he was trying to be pleasant – an exercise in miscasting that gives the game away the moment he appears on the screen. Far more engaging are Hollywood legend Myrna Loy and Mexican-American heart-throb John Gavin, who, a few years later, would miss out on playing James Bond by the skin of his teeth. The film also contains a wealth of British character actors including Roddy McDowall, Hermione Baddley and Natasha Parry.

Scripted by Ivan Goff and Ben Roberts, the production was based on Janet Green's *Matilda Shouted Fire* and suitably camped up by Ross Hunter, who co-produced with Marty Melcher. As usual Hunter slips in a number of gay 'in-jokes' including a scene in which Nelson's column is painted by hooligans. 'Horatio Nelson, mind you – pink!' quips a taxi driver. Also, as frequently happens with such films, the powers-that-be in Hollywood feel obliged to remind us, as if we might not know, that we are in London, England: helmeted bobbies, double-decker buses, dodgy accents – and 'pea-souper' fogs which are supposed to be synonymous with crime.

In a succession of Irene Gibbons' gowns Doris played newly married, wealthy heiress Kit Preston, who while wandering in the fog, hears a disembodied voice threatening to strangle her. Her husband Tony (Harrison) dismisses this as a practical joke and of course the menacing continues: shadowy shapes outside the window, creaking stairs, malicious phone calls, falling girders, an attempt to shove her in front of a bus, bungling police officers and red herrings galore as each freshly introduced character seems shiftier than the last – until Kit, about to fling herself to death from her hotel terrace, is finally rescued in a fire-escape scenario by hunky construction engineer John Gavin. For this scene Marty Melcher instructed Doris to imagine she was being menaced by Al Jorden all over again – she later said that she just closed her eyes and imagined him about to give her the beating she had received towards the end of her pregnancy. Indeed, she injected so much Method into the sequence that it became all too much for her and she fainted. Had it not been for

Gavin catching her on the fire escape, she would have suffered serious injury. Director David Miller was sufficiently concerned to close the set and announced shooting would be suspended until Doris had been taken to hospital and thoroughly checked over. But Melcher would not hear of this: once again a 'cure' was effected by Mary Baker Eddy via the Broones by way of a long-distance telephone call.

It was speculated at the time that Doris and 29-year-old John Gavin may have been amorously involved though there was little proof of this – only that while they were shooting the film he was seen escorting her around Hollywood after one of her rows with her husband, which were steadily becoming more aggressive on his part. Gavin is also said to have stayed at her Lake Arrowhead beach house, where she would retreat with Terry when he was on vacation from the military academy. When Melcher read Doris' comments in a newspaper article stating this was her favourite place on earth he made her sell it, unable to cope with her being happy.

The critics viewing the rushes for *Midnight Lace* were confident Doris would be nominated for an Oscar – her only competition, they believed, was Jean Simmons in *Elmer Gantry*. What no one figured was that Elizabeth Taylor would win the award; not that her performance as a callgirl in *Butterfield 8* was more exemplary than that of Doris or Simmons but because the Academy had taken pity on her after her near-fatal illness in London while shooting *Cleopatra*. 'Elizabeth Taylor got an Oscar for almost dying,' Marlene Dietrich quipped when we spoke about this. 'The truth is, that woman died a death every time she stepped in front of a camera!'

Shortly after completing the film Doris went into the studio to record an album which, she said, contained her deepest optimistic thoughts – *Bright And Shiny* was conceived around her favourite word – 'happy' – though during this period of her life she was anything but. It was common practice in those days for record companies to assume DJs and fans might be fooled into thinking that any song could be regarded as happy-go-lucky if the 'g' was missing from the end of a word in its title; there are five examples here, and they were not. The album received little airplay and unfortunately went in the same direction as *Cuttin' Capers*. Its successor, *I Have Dreamed*, recorded at around the same time and released five months later, only just managed to scrape into the Billboard Top 100, though quality-wise it was far superior. For the first and only time in her career Doris performed a Kurt Weill song – 'My Ship' – that is nothing short of amazing as are Oscar Hammerstein and Sigmund Romberg's 'When I Grow Too Old To Dream' and Noel Coward's 'Someday I'll Find You'.

Meanwhile, early in 1961 Doris began shooting her second film with Rock Hudson. *Box Office*, a publication which had been generally dismissive of Rock's work over the years, hypocritically observed of his performance in *Pillow Talk*, 'Hudson is as suave, self-possessed and convincing as though he had been delineating lighter roles all through his distinguished career.' Since then he had had a comedy smash alongside Gina Lollobrigida and Nick Adams in *Come September*, another romp awash with gay 'in-jokes'. *Lover Come Back*, which would again see him heading the credits with Doris' blessing, proved even more successful than *Pillow Talk* and propelled him into the same privileged $1 million-plus-per-film earnings as Marlon Brando, Spencer Tracy and Cary Grant.

The rivals-cum-lovers in the film, Carol Templeton and Jerry Webster, work for enemy advertising agencies and their methods of winning over prospective clients could not be more diverse. 'In all beehives there are the workers and there are drones,' the voice-over proclaims. Carol represents the former: a conscientious, hardworking decent girl who (like Jan in *Pillow Talk*) wears a succession of silly hats. Then the camera cuts to the drone: Jerry, half-sozzled in the back of a cab, a pretty girl clinging to his arm. Wealthy entrepreneur J. Paxton Miller (Jack Oakie) has recently arrived in New York and is anxious to spend $5 million advertising floor wax. Carol's gay assistant helps her assemble a suitable package and when he shows her his colour chart she asks, 'Leonard, who has a lilac floor in their kitchen?' – to which he replies with a flourish, 'I do!' Jerry, meanwhile, gets the upper hand when he learns that Miller hails from Virginia. He reads up on the role the state and Miller's ancestors played in the Civil War then whisks him off to a burlesque and while the band plays Dixie tunes, he spins Miller a yarn about their grandfathers fighting for the same side in the same battle. Finally, he fixes 'his' client up with an orgy in his hotel suite.

When Carol arrives for her meeting early the next morning, she finds Miller roaring drunk in his wrecked hotel suite. Horrified, she urges her boss to have Jerry charged with unethical conduct, only to be told this would be a waste of time:

BOSS: He's like a common cold. You know you're going to get it twice a year . . .
CAROL: There are two ways to handle a cold. You can fight it, or you can give in and go to bed with it. I intend to fight it!

Next we see Jerry's neurotic, wimpish employer Peter Ramsay (Tony Randall), who, having received Carol's complaint, turns up at Jerry's pad intent on sorting him out. Jerry retaliates by boasting how good he is at his job – 'Give me a well-stacked dame in a bathing suit and I'll sell aftershave lotion to beatniks!' Then, when Ramsay orders him to call Carol to reassure her of his company's 'high moral character', Jerry offers an 'apology' that only makes matters worse:

JERRY: I'd like to ask you a favour. Will you kindly keep
your big fat nose out of my business? If the competition's
too tough, get out of the advertising profession!

CAROL: You aren't even *in* the advertising profession,
and if I weren't a lady I'd tell you what profession you *are*
in. . . . Let me put it this way, I don't use sex to land an
account.

JERRY: When *do* you use it?

CAROL: I don't . . .

JERRY: My condolences to your husband!

CAROL: I'm not married . . .

JERRY: That figures. A husband would be competition.
There's only room for one man in a family.

CAROL: [clenching her fist] Let me tell you something,
Mr Webster. I wish I were a man right now . . .

JERRY: Keep trying, I think you'll make it!

Carol is really mad now. She calls the burlesque and lets off steam
with Jerry's favourite good-time girl Rebel Davis (Edie Adams),
who in turn threatens to report the philanderer to the Advertising
Council: Jerry swore to Rebel two years ago that he would make
her the Miller Wax Girl and now she realises that all this time he
has been stringing her along with empty promises of television
stardom to get her into bed. Jerry gets himself off the hook by
confessing it has taken him this long to find the perfect product for
her to plug – 'The key which will open the golden gate to
Hollywood'. Rebel is ashamed of ever doubting him and begs him
to give her another chance. She will do anything, she emphasises.
Jerry nods, checks his watch and they head for the boudoir.

On the table is a newspaper with the headline 'VIPs Arrive For
Convention' and this gives him a brainwave: Rebel will henceforth be known as 'The VIP Girl' and the scene changes to show
her posing for the camera in skimpy outfits, promoting a non-

existent product. Confident his career – and neck – has been saved, Jerry tells his producer to file the film and forget about it. He then dispatches Rebel to the Advertising Council meeting, where Carol has arranged to discredit him. As a token of appreciation he has given her his Army good-conduct medal, which he has asked her to wear next to her heart. Rebel shows this off, giving the all-male committee an eyeful of her ample cleavage, and offers Jerry's apology for not being there. 'He's with the Red Cross, donating blood,' she says. Carol cannot resist the quip, 'They wouldn't take *his* blood – it's 86 proof!'

Having been made aware of the non-existent VIP account, Carol now decides to play her rival at his own game by putting in a bid for it herself – while Peter Ramsay, advised by his shrink to adopt a positive attitude towards his life and career, makes his first-ever executive decision, releasing the VIP film of Rebel to a television station, resulting in a massive demand for a product which must now be invented to save his company from financial ruin. He and Jerry attempt to remedy this by enlisting the services of Linus Tyler, an eccentric chemist, who Jerry impersonates when Carol –who, in a repeat of the scenario from *Pillow Talk,* has never seen her rival not even in photographs – turns up at his laboratory in the hope of wooing Tyler into duping Webster and giving her his account. The ensuing mayhem is hilarious as the shy, old-fashioned and inexperienced-with-women 'scientist' berates Carol for attacking Jerry:

JERRY: As my uncle, the missionary, used to say, 'If thou canst not speak well of a man, speak not at all!'

CAROL: You make me feel ashamed of myself . . .

JERRY: It's just that I cannot presume to judge my fellow man. I am but a humble chemist.

CAROL: Oh no, you're a genius and a great humanitarian and I want to know you better. Doctor, there's so much I could learn from you.

JERRY: As my father, the philosopher, used to say, 'Knock
   at my door, and I shall take you in!'
CAROL: Doctor Tyler, I'm knocking.
JERRY: Miss Templeton, I'm taking you in . . .

The phoney academic's ploy – to get this teetotal virgin between
the sheets – almost succeeds when Carol meets Jerry again, this
time as himself, and she lavishes him with attention courtesy of
her expense account. 'A woman instinctively senses when a man
can be trusted,' she overconfidently confides just as the puffer-
fish in the aquarium behind them gulps down its live prey. Then
she takes him dancing, looking like a million dollars while he
turns up in a grotesquely outdated suit. They visit the burlesque
where Jerry takes all his clients, though Carol keeps her eyes
tightly closed while the stripper is performing. Then they go
golfing, cycling, sailing and swimming; when Carol urges him
not to be bashful, he looks truly wonderful in his bathing trunks,
sucking in his stomach and flexing his biceps. And finally she
teaches him how to kiss, cooing, 'I think this may be your best
subject!'

Carol is so infatuated with her beau and so sure he can be
trusted that she allows him to sleep in her guest room. Jerry
maintains the charade by camping things up, confiding that he
will never marry because he is not possessed of Jerry Webster's
finer qualities. Carol reminds him that he knows how to kiss, to
which he gruffly replies, 'A kiss – what does that prove? It's like
finding out you can light a stove. It still doesn't make you a cook.
Forget me, Carol. You need a man, not a mess of neurotic doubts!'
He then flings himself face down on the bed and sulks. Just as she's
about to surrender, the phone rings: it's her boss, warning her that
she is entertaining an impostor.

Carol does not let on to Jerry that he has been rumbled.
She invites him to go for a midnight dip – he has no trunks but

she replies that they will not be necessary. Then she drives off, leaving him naked on the beach where they first kissed. He is picked up by a furs van and dropped back at his hotel, wearing nothing but a mink coat. 'Hey, Fred,' cracks one of the two old men who have turned up everywhere Jerry has been with his womanising capers, 'He's the last guy in the world I would have figured!' Not a sensible line, considering how Universal had fought for over a decade to prevent Rock's 'other life' from becoming public knowledge.

Carol next instructs the Advertising Council to prosecute Jerry because he has conned the public by promoting a non-existent product. He then proves her wrong by turning up at his 'trial' with a box of VIP – sweets that the real Doctor Tyler has eaten, which when consumed enter the bloodstream as pure alcohol. The committee, along with Carol and Jerry, scoff the lot and end up drunk whence the scene cuts to the former protagonists in bed with a marriage certificate affixed to the mirror to placate the moralists in the audience! Unaware of how this has happened, Carol has a fit of hysterics and demands an annulment.

The action then jumps forward to where Jerry is visited by representatives from the liquor industry claiming that they are losing money because one VIP biscuit, retailing at 10 cents, equates to three martinis! Jerry is offered a huge payoff to take his product off the market – which he requests should go to Carol. He then receives a call from the hospital. Nine months after their wedding, his now ex-wife has gone into labour. Jerry therefore acquires a special licence and he and Carol remarry as she is being wheeled into the delivery room!

Rock Hudson always maintained that of all his comedy films *Lover Come Back* was his favourite. In 1976 he would boost his macho image (and evade the outing brigade once more), by telling *Films & Filming*'s Gordon Gow:

The advertising man in *Lover Come Back*, like the composer in *Pillow Talk*, was a ne'er-do-well. And playing a ne'er-do-well is terrific. I guess it's because it's what we all wish we were but don't have the guts to be, the advertising executive who plays around all the time, who was bored until he met Miss Day and said to himself, 'That would be rather interesting to toss in the hay – but I think I'll see if I can get her to go on the make for me!' Now, that's fun and it's very playable!

To coincide with the film's release – and to back a promotional campaign for of all things, Imperial margarine! – Columbia released a 'concept' album, *Wonderful Day* in the US. This was a compilation of Doris' movie hits, centring around the film's title-track and its other song, 'Should I Surrender?' In 2003 this would be released, with Doris' *With A Smile And A Song* album on a double-CD, the bonus being that Sony Music included several alternative versions of these songs along with bonus tracks.

Though Doris had a 'rip-roaring' time working with Rock on *Lover Come Back*, away from the set she quickly lapsed into periods of the blackest depression. Her marriage to Marty Melcher was sinking fast and she took great comfort in her friendship with costumier Irene Gibbons (née Lenz), who had dressed her for *Midnight Lace* and was requested especially for this particular movie. As had happened with Judy Garland, theirs was a relationship founded on misery. Doris admired the way Irene fought her way to the very top of her profession, opening a tiny dress shop in Los Angeles back in the early 1930s and quickly gathering a celebrity clientèle. In 1936 she married scriptwriter Eliot Gibbons and five years later she had taken over from Adrian as MGM's top costume designer, dressing the likes of Marlene Dietrich, Greta Garbo and Carole Lombard. By the time she began work with Doris, Irene's own marriage was on the rocks – Gibbons was away from home most of the time playing the field, leaving her to drink herself into near oblivion once she left the studio. Doris is said to have shared with Irene all the very worst aspects of life with Marty Melcher. Similarly, Irene confided in her what she had never told anyone before – how she was mourning the great but almost certainly unrequited love of her life, Gary Cooper, who died of cancer in May 1961.

At the beginning of 1962 Doris recorded *Duet*, without doubt her most intimate, not to say classiest album. She met singer-songwriter Dory Previn, one year her senior, at a party and the two women had an instant rapport, bonding of all things over a mutual fear of flying. Dory also had a troubled relationship with her father and, like Doris, she had had a severe nervous breakdown. Also, there was the German connection: being orthodox Jews, the Previns had fled their native Berlin to escape Nazi persecution. Within minutes of meeting, and without discussing the matter with Marty Melcher, Doris had had an idea for an album, with Dory sharing in the songwriting and arrangement credits and roping in her pianist-arranger younger brother Andre to accompany her on the 12 tracks. The result, though it never charted and has not sold as well as her other albums, is a veritable treat. Throughout the album the voice is almost tiny – when Doris sings Alec Wilder's 'Give Me Time', for example, one is reminded of the fragility of Marilyn Monroe. There is the same quiver at the end of each extended note. Though never a vamp, she comes across as pretty sexy while crooning Marlene Dietrich's signature song 'Falling In Love Again', a brave choice which made Marlene chuckle when we discussed it. 'Did I mind Doris Day singing my song?' she posed. 'I was sick of singing the accursed thing so she was welcome to it! But doesn't she do it *well*?' The other numbers included Bernice Petkere's 1933 standard 'Close Your Eyes' and Jerome Kern and Dorothy Field's 'Remind Me', and a delectable reading of Brook Benton's showstopper 'Fools Rush In', which includes the rarely heard verse. Perhaps less engaging are the Previns' own compositions though the bouncy 'Control Yourself' would not have been out of place in one of her sex comedies.

Inasmuch as Doris worshipped Rock Hudson for years before working with him, so too had she admired Cary Grant, her co-star in *That Touch Of Mink*, sufficiently to insist his name should appear above hers in the credits. The difference between them was that while she found Rock genuinely engaging and an absolute hoot, someone who would remain a close friend for the rest of his life, she dismissed Grant as distant and egotistical, albeit a consummate professional. Their problems arose over one of the first scenes to be filmed – the one where Doris and Grant are seen riding in the back of a taxi. Doris insisted she should only be photographed from the left, unaware that Grant had demanded the same thing. When the director Delbert Mann tried to point out that both stars photographed inordinately well from any angle, Doris threw a fit and stormed off to her dressing room while Grant vowed to walk off the picture. Marty Melcher brought him to his senses by threatening to go to the press with a matter concerning his private life – almost certainly one of his homosexual escapades – and the scene, along with the film, was completed with as little off-screen contact between the two leads as possible. Remarkably, as with Doris' earlier antagonism towards Kirk Douglas, this does not show. Neither were the critics fair in denouncing Grant as being too old, at 58, to be playing her love interest. Clark Gable had been the same age and Grant is just as credible here as Gable was in *Teacher's Pet*. And what the critics did not know at the time was that, in some of their scenes, it was *Doris* who was filmed through filters! The co-stars too are fascinating to watch: Gig Young is his usual self, John Astin almost as creepy as he would be some years later as Gomez Addams in television's *The Addams Family* and Audrey Meadows equally deadpan as Doris' roommate as she had been in *The Honeymooners*, another 1950s' television stalwart.

As had happened with Rock Hudson, Cary Grant's career had been on a slide for the last few years; he was considered too old to be playing the romantic lead yet not long enough in the tooth for more mature parts. Here he is Philip Shayne, a millionaire New York playboy, who finds the love of his life – unemployed computer operator Cathy Timberlake (Doris) – when his car ploughs through a puddle and drenches her. Gig Young, aka Shayne's sidekick-assistant Roger more or less reprises his role from *Teacher's Pet* while Audrey Meadows steps into Eve Arden's shoes as the roommate who warns her against the perils of this bluestocking. What's astonishing, as with the female characters in *Young At Heart*, is how two women in their late-thirties have so far failed to find a man – even less credible, how they can afford a designer wardrobe and such an opulent apartment when one works in an automat and the other draws welfare! The scriptwriter even risks a lesbian joke when Meadows searches for her friend through the various apertures in the automat. 'Where are you?' she yells, bringing the quirky response: 'In the cucumbers!'

As the film opens Cathy is being chatted up by greasy welfare benefits clerk Beasley (Astin) and is therefore in a foul mood when the cowardly Shayne sends Roger to apologise on his behalf for giving her a soaking. She storms into his office ostensibly to give him a piece of her mind but is mistaken for an unmarried mother by a pair of snooty matrons to whom Shayne has just given a donation and she immediately goes into a trance when she sees how suave and handsome he is. Within hours he whisks her off to a United Nations' conference in Philadelphia and invites her to go on vacation with him to Bermuda.

Cathy acquiesces, naively mistaking this for a marriage proposal, until she realises he plans on them sharing a bed. 'Like watching Joan of Arc going to the fire,' someone quips as she boards the plane. Desperate to remain pure until the ring is on her finger – one aspect of the film which makes it laughable when the virgin is 38 – her abject terror of having sex causes her to break out in spots, which of course means that Shayne does not get to have his way with her . . . and also caused cynics to draw the conclusion that there was something radically wrong with her. Later when she finally decides to yield, 'it' still does not happen because she gets drunk and falls out of her hotel window. Disappointed and frustrated, Shayne encourages her to find another man and so having rejected Rock Hudson, another of scriptwriter Stanley Shapiro's 'in-jokes', she makes a play for the only one who has apparently ever shown any interest in her: social security geek Beasley.

When Beasley elects to drive Cathy in a rickety poultry van to a sleazy motel to have his way with her – making him morally no less reprehensible than Shayne – Shayne gets jealous and sets off to rescue her. This he does, enabling his caveman instincts to surge to the fore as he slings her over his shoulder and carts her off to be married. Then comes the honeymoon, a disaster because it emerges he is not as experienced with women as he lets on. This time *he* is the one who comes out in spots. We are, however, assured – for the benefit of Cary Grant's fans who, heeding the rumours that he was gay, were wondering why his four marriages all proved childless – that there is nothing wrong with him in this respect when in the last scene he, Cathy and Roger are seen pushing a pram through Central Park. Even then, Stanley Shapiro as per usual has the last laugh by intimating Shayne and Roger were once an item when Roger's shrink, Dr Gruber (Alan Hewitt), to whom he has opened up his heart about his non-existent love life, just happens to be strolling through the park. Doris would later condemn the scriptwriter for including such a blatantly homophobic scene. On the couch, upset because he has lost Cathy to Shayne, he fantasises aloud about what might happen if a rich, good-looking man invited *him* on a trip to Bermuda. Assuming Roger is in love with Shayne, he grabs the phone and tells his stockbroker, 'Cancel my order. My patient has developed some instabilities which make his judgement questionable!' When Shayne and Cathy rush off to have their photographs taken, Gruber asks Roger how things worked out between himself and his wealthy gentleman friend. Roger shocks him by plucking the baby from the pram and explains how the wedding took place last summer.

A few weeks after the première of *That Touch Of Mink*, CBS released Doris' *You'll Never Walk Alone* album, a work of extraordinary brilliance and simplicity. Jane Froman recorded an album of spiritual songs with gratitude for surviving her plane crash, similarly to Elvis Presley after the death of his mother. Some may have found Doris' 'quiet Bible-bashing' tedious but far from being 'in-your-face' this collection of mostly hymns is a remarkable body of work. The accompaniment is kept to an absolute minimum – much of the time a simple church organ – and her delivery so heartfelt and sincere that at times one finds it hard to sit the whole thing out. The title-track, first performed in the stage production of *Carousel* by Christine Johnson, provided Frank Sinatra, Judy Garland and Jane Froman with chart hits, and it is rather sad that today it is largely recognised as a pop song and football anthem. Doris latterly admired Barbra Streisand for performing 'You'll Never Walk Alone' at the Emmys ceremony in the wake of the September 11 bombings. It is, however, but one of a dozen spellbinding tracks on the album. Highlights include an arrangement by Martin Broones of 'The Lord's Prayer', along with his moving 'The Prodigal Son', a semi-spoken 'Scarlet Ribbons' and a reading of 'Bless This House' that one would find hard to surpass. The album did not sell particularly well but it did lead to Doris being offered – no doubt with more than a little influence from Martin Broones and Charlotte Greenwood – the opportunity to sing them on the concert platform with the possibility of a nationwide tour. She was almost tempted but Marty Melcher had long since assigned her to her next film – which of course would bring in much more money.

Her next leading man, Stephen Boyd – he of the smouldering looks, deeply-cleft chin and sexy Irish-American drawl – was arguably, with the exception of Rock Hudson, the most handsome she ever worked with. Born William Millar in Whitehouse, County Antrim, in 1931 he began his career in British films but made a name for himself in 1957 starring opposite Brigitte Bardot in *Les Bijoutiers Du Clair De Lune*. This resulted in him relocating to Hollywood to play second leads in numerous films until 1959 when he hit the jackpot being cast as Massala, Charlton Heston's on-screen rival in *Ben Hur*. Rumours of his sexuality had risen during shooting, particularly when he asked for a homosexual subtext to his interpretation – a move opposed by the virulently homophobic Heston. Boyd even attempted to placate Heston and 'normalise' himself by marrying one of the film's executives, Mariella di Sarzana – a union which not surprisingly lasted just two weeks. The fact that Boyd was more or less openly gay also meant that he was by-passed for the Oscar nominations. The role led to the usual typecasting in 'breastplate and toga' movies and the opportunity to star opposite Elizabeth Taylor in *Cleopatra* (1963).

Because of its multitude of on-set problems, exacerbated by Taylor's illnesses, real and invented, Boyd withdrew from the production and was assigned to *The Fall Of The Roman Empire* with Italian sex-bomb Sophia Loren. This enabled him to breathe a huge sigh of relief. While in England the press got a whiff of his relationships with Michael Redgrave, boxer Freddie Mills and crooner Michael Holliday. As shooting on the Roman epic was not scheduled to begin for several months, he was put into *Billy Rose's Jumbo* with Doris.

Doris and Boyd became great friends – like many of her gay friends in the know he borrowed from Rock Hudson and called her 'Eunice' after Eunice Blotter. Boyd was also very close to the film's fourth lead, Martha Raye. Like Doris, secretly admired for her 'gaydar', which would see her supporting friends such as Rock Hudson through their greatest trials. Both she and Doris would be devastated in June 1977 when the recently remarried Boyd, a fitness fanatic who had never been ill, died of a heart-attack while playing golf, aged just 45.

Possessed of a large letterbox mouth, vocalist-comedienne Martha Raye (1916–94) had taken advantage of what some critics regarded as a disability by having the knack of taking the mickey out of herself, notably appearing in a series of toothpaste commercials. In a lengthy radio, television and stage career she worked with every single American comic worth their salt, including Jimmy Durante, who plays Doris' father in the film. In what was to be his penultimate film, Durante (1893–1980) was also a master of self-mockery, arguably the greatest American comic actor of his generation. Self-baptised 'Schnozzle' on account of his large trademark nose, he appeared in the original 1935 Rodgers and Hart stage show that ran for 233 performances. *Billy Rose* was added to the title because producer Joe Pasternak assumed no one would remember Rose, the great entrepreneur who had once been married to Fanny Brice. Some years later their story would be filmed as *Funny Lady* with Barbra Streisand and James Caan. The original production had been more of a circus show than an actual revue, with leads Durante, Mickey Considine and Matt Mulligan Jr secondary to the animals and Barbette, the French-American *travesti* whose speciality had been stripping near-naked while crossing the high-wire, then at the end of his act whipping off his Jean Harlow platinum wig to prove the beautiful 'she' was actually a bald-headed 'he'.

Boasting the legendary Busby Berkeley as its secondary unit director, the film opens like the 1935 stage show with Sam Rawlins (Stephen Boyd) leading the full cast into 'The Circus Is On

Parade' in front of a Jumbo backdrop before this rises on the roustabouts chorus, erecting the marquee and sideshow tents for The Wonder Circus headed by Pops Wonder (Durante), long-term fiancée and phony palmist Lulu (Raye) and Pops' pretty daughter Kitty (Doris). First, she grooms her horse, then introduces us to Jumbo, the main attraction: 'Stolen from the Maharajah of Rangoon – 8,000 pounds of pulchritudinous pachyderm,' Pops proclaims, with Jimmy Durante adding a joke of his own, 'He's like a son to me – you can even see the resemblance!'

Because of Pops' gambling, The Wonder Circus is heading towards bankruptcy with the creditors breathing down his neck and acts working without pay. One by one, they defect to the rival John Noble Circus. Noble (Dean Jagger) has plans to take over The Wonder Circus by poaching the acts and paying off Pops' creditors. Therefore he plants his son Sam among the troupe. When Sam initially shows up looking for work, Kitty sends him on his way but he returns and masquerades as the recently departed Great Martino, the high-wire speciality who has left Pops in the lurch. He is now suddenly flavour of the month: 'I like that boy,' Pops enthuses, bringing the response from Kitty, '*I* saw him first!'

Naturally, Sam and Kitty fall for each other. She sings 'This Can't Be Love' while riding bareback, diving through fiery hoops and swinging from the trapeze. He serenades her on the merry-go-round with 'The Most Beautiful Girl In The World'. In 1935 this had begun 'The most beautiful girl in the world isn't Garbo, isn't Dietrich . . . ' but times had changed and the names had been amended to 'Juno and Venus'. This pleasant little episode ends with Kitty face down in the mud. Later she proposes to him, sings 'My Romance' and when the Big Top is wrecked by a storm and Pops is pinned down by a post and thinks he is dying, he asks Lulu to marry him –14 years to the day since they became engaged. 'Get that girl,' he says of his gurning bride, who not so long before he had shot out of a canon, 'A vision. And all this time I thought she looked like George Washington!'

The wedding ceremony, however, is interrupted when Noble arrives with the town marshall; he has paid off Pops' debts and now owns The Wonder Circus. He also reveals Sam's identity, breaking Kitty's heart, and worse still, is there to collect Jumbo. A hilarious moment occurs when Pops stands in front of the huge beast and a cop yells, 'Hold it! Where are you going with that elephant?' to which he replies, 'What elephant?' Devastated, Kitty sings 'Little Girl Blue'. Then she, Pops and Lulu set off on the open road, putting on a paltry sideshow until Sam catches up with them. Unable to forgive his father for what he has done, he has walked out on him and brought Jumbo back! The film ends with The Wonder Circus back in business, the four leads alternating as clowns and trapeze artistes for the final production number 'Sawdust, Spangles And Dreams' – with Jimmy Durante (and to a certain extent Stephen Boyd, in view of the rumours) a sight to behold in pink tights! And if that's not enough, there's a double wedding!

Billy Rose's Jumbo premièred in New York at the Radio City Music Hall in November 1962 – a bad time for just about every film which had the misfortune to be released then, for America was locked in a newspaper strike which meant all the leading publications virtually ignored it. As a result it flopped at the box-office and was Doris' first failure since *It Happened To Jane* – though it has since more than made up for it with television rental and video sales.

Doris so loved working with Stephen Boyd there was talk of the two pairing up again once he had finished shooting *The Fall Of The Roman Empire* with her next production, yet to be decided on. One proposed joint project was *The Unsinkable Molly Brown*, though Harve Presnell was already signed for the male lead following his Broadway triumph with the role. Eventually the part of Molly would go to Debbie Reynolds. Next, Doris and Boyd were approached with the roles of Maria and Captain von Trapp in *The Sound Of Music:* she had recorded the title-track in 1959 and included it on her *Show Time* album. Doris may have been in favour though in retrospect the part would not have suited her – she was the first to admit she was too American to be playing an Austrian nun! As for Melcher, he hated any man showing the least interest in his wife even platonically. Boyd, he declared, had begun to pose a threat to his marriage insomuch as Doris had taken to confiding in him – the sort of 'girl talk' she had enjoyed with Judy Garland, Rock Hudson and Irene Gibbons.

With Rock heavily involved in the narration of *Marilyn*, a documentary about the life and career of Marilyn Monroe, who had been found dead on 5 August 1962 – suicide, accidental overdose, murder, no one would ever be sure what happened – Doris had spent a lot of time with Irene Gibbons of late. Suffering from depression, Irene was still drinking heavily and at first Doris matched her glass for glass, her own way of coping with an increasingly psychotic husband. She had just found out that Marty Melcher had been beating her son Terry for years. Friends – and in particular, Rosenthal, Melcher's business associate – who had suspected refrained from telling her. In Rosenthal's case this was for financial reasons while the others were afraid of making a mistake and being kicked out of her inner circle; worse still, of being sued. Similarly, several of her closest allies were terrified to tell her that Melcher and Rosenthal were almost certainly embezzling money from her bank accounts and transferring this to tax-free accounts in Switzerland, just in case they happened to be wrong. Gradually Doris tried to get Irene to cut down on her alcohol consumption and on 14 November 1962 they spoke on the phone and made arrangements to have lunch the following week. The next day Irene booked into Los Angeles' Knickerbocker Hotel under an assumed name and cut her wrists. When this did not work, she calmly took the escalator to the top floor and flung herself out of the window. Her suicide note simply read, 'I'm sorry. This is the best way. Get someone very good to design and be happy. I love you all'.

Doris was devastated. Comforted by Stephen Boyd, she refused to attend Irene's funeral, setting a precedent for her never to be seen publicly mourning a friend or loved one. Two weeks after Irene's death and following one argument too many that had resulted in Terry being knocked unconscious, Marty Melcher stormed out of their North Crescent Drive home to take up residence at the Sunset Towers complex on Sunset Boulevard. But if her mother and son were crossing their fingers that he would never come back, Doris would soon have other ideas . . .

Chapter 9

From Bad to Worse

'Marty liked to bust people, humiliate them in front of their co-workers, show what a big shot he was by loudly nailing some poor little bastard for some insignificant mistake he made.'

Terry Melcher, 1975

*L*ike Marty Snyder in *Love Me Or Leave Me*, for years Marty Melcher was desperate to become involved in something not connected to his meal ticket (Doris) and as far as the press were concerned, the Melcher's marriage was solid as ever and he was merely about to hit the road with a play that he was producing: *The Perfect Setup*. Doris is on record as describing the work as 'a piece of shit' and she cannot have been far wrong. After a lightning tour of the provinces it opened on Broadway, only to be savaged by one of the 'Holy Seven', as portrayed by David Niven in *Please Don't Eat The Daisies*, and closed after only a couple of performances.

Terry, now 20, begged his mother to slam the door in Melcher's face when he returned to North Crescent Drive with his tail firmly between his legs. What made matters infinitely worse was that he was less interested in making amends for his abominable behaviour than warning Doris that if she divorced him, she would effectively be shooting herself in the foot because their finances were so inextricably linked that should they part permanently, the only outcome would be the bankruptcy court. She was naive enough to swallow the story and so Melcher moved back into their home. The brief separation, however, had enabled her to at last gather her senses and now she laid the law down. She was the breadwinner in the family and, as such, entitled to some respect. From now on, she would make all the decisions about her movies and recording career.

So far as their personal life was concerned, the outside world would be told nothing but from now on they would 'live separate lives whilst living together'. Melcher no longer shared their marital bed but was relegated to the spare room. Their love life had apparently been disintegrating for some time – Doris referred to this as 'Saturday night sex' – so she would not miss that side of their relationship. If Melcher wanted to take a mistress, she added, it was fine by her so long as she never found out her identity. As for herself, there was no one else in her life right now; in any case, she was not looking for sex, being too involved with her work to even think about it. It all sounds like a plot from one of her films and such statements were carefully rehearsed and delivered to stay in keeping with her girl-next-door image. Doris was 38 and still attractive so of course there would be other men in her life.

As Melcher moved back into their home, and with his stepfather pressurising him to attend Principia College, St Louis with a view to becoming a fully fledged Christian Science Practitioner, Terry threw in the towel and moved out – but not before giving Melcher a taste of his own medicine the next time his stepfather attacked him by getting in the first punch. 'I only wish I'd killed the bastard,' he told his friend Gram Parsons.

A few years later, he put Melcher in his place once and for all at a Christmas party organised by Doris at the home on Cielo Drive

– soon to become notorious – which her son shared with Candice Bergen. Guests of honour were The Byrds, who got Doris to join them in an impromptu performance of 'Turn, Turn, Turn' in front of the Christmas tree. What seems strange is that though most of those around her suspected Doris' husband was up to no good with her money, Terry appears to have trusted him enough to publish some of his compositions through his and Jerry Rosenthal's company. At the party Terry claimed that he and Melcher had got into an argument over something and that Melcher had turned on him with, 'Why don't you take your fucking copyrights and get the hell out of here?' He subsequently handed him a cheque for $345,000 – which the young man had ripped to shreds and flung back in his face – declaring 'This is for all the time you've given me and for all the years you've boarded with me!' It seemed like a noble sacrifice but Terry was simply making the point that he would not be knocked around any more and assumed the royalties would be assigned to him by the correct procedure at a later date. Little did he know that when that time came by not taking the cash and cashing it while the funds were there he would end up with egg on his face.

Despite the mental trauma inflicted on his stepson, Melcher's cruelty would effect a positive move in Terry's blossoming career in that, in moving out of the family home, he was forced to stand on his own two feet. Initially he moved in with his grandmother Alma, of whom he had seen more while growing up than his own mother. He would then get a place of his own. Terry cut his first record in 1961 (as Terry Day) and as an aficionado of the surf-rock craze, he formed a partnership with his best friend and future Beach Boy Bruce Johnson: as Terry and Bruce they would score a minor hit in 1963 with 'Be A Soldier' and Terry went on to co-write songs with Randy Newman and Bobby Darin. By the end of 1963 – not without Doris' influence, though he would be much more appreciative of her help than his stepfather had been – he was taken on by Columbia as a record producer earning in excess of $250,000 a year. He would work with Paul Revere and The Raiders and guest perform on The Beach Boys' album *Pet Sounds*. Most notably he was to produce The Byrds' 'Mr Tambourine Man' and 'Turn, Turn, Turn' though his tenancy with the group proved acrimonious. One critic would label his involvement with their album *Byrdmaniax* as 'Melcher's Folly' and, as will be seen, this would lead – again by way of Doris – to his involvement with the greatest country-rock artist of them all, Gram Parsons.

Doris, meanwhile, announced to close friends such as Rock Hudson and Stephen Boyd, as well as her mother, that for some time she had been locked in a marriage that was in name only. They and other friends attempted to convince her that without her, Marty Melcher would be absolutely nothing while without him, she would still be Doris Day, still America's Number One Female Box-Office Star, still earning upwards of $1 million a movie and so more than capable of survival. Her lawyer further advised her that if she showed him the door, she most definitely would not end up bankrupt yet she still chose to stay with him. Like Joan Crawford, Billie Holliday and Edith Piaf, she seems to have derived a kind of masochistic pleasure from being treated like a doormat by some of the men in her life. This really was a classic case of the clown hiding the tears behind a façade of mock happiness.

While suffering from depression, she entered the recording studio to record her most boisterous album since the soundtrack to *Calamity Jane* and with a similar theme. For years she had wanted to play Ohio sharpshooter Annie Oakley on the big screen, though there was little chance of this as the definitive version had already been filmed back in 1950 with Betty Hutton in the title-role and Howard Keel as her marksman husband Frank Butler. Doris had been touched by the couple's devotion towards each other – the fact that Butler stopped eating after Annie's death and followed her to the grave just 20 days later. For a while there had been talk of her recreating the role on Broadway (motormouth chanteuse Ethel Merman first played her on Broadway in 1946) but given her intense stage fright, this was soon nipped in the bud. Now Columbia approached her and asked if she would be interested in recording the soundtrack and she immediately agreed – it was only after Marty Melcher signed the contract that she realised she would not be making the record with Howard Keel but with Robert Goulet, currently the talk of Broadway with his interpretation of Lancelot opposite Richard Burton and Julie Andrews in Lerner and Lowe's *Camelot*. The album was cut quickly as per usual and released in February 1963. Doris exonerates herself well, throwing herself into raunchy showstoppers such as 'Doin' What Comes Naturally' and 'You Can't Get A Man With A Gun'. On the other hand and though a fine singer, Goulet lacks the chutzpah of Keel and as such he lets the side down, particularly when duetting with Doris on 'Anything You Can Do, I Can Do Better'.

Inasmuch as later in life she would collect waifs and strays from the animal world, Doris had, by way of personal experience, developed herself into an authority on the human condition – a trait she would share with Elizabeth Taylor so far as helping so-called 'lost causes' was concerned, with Rock Hudson being the prime example for whom they shared responsibilities when he fell ill with AIDS many years later. Her next co-star, James Garner, was likewise no stranger to family upheaval and Doris is reputed to have asked for him as her leading man in *The Thrill Of It All* on account of a press report she had read regarding his childhood. He was certainly very impressed by her, later telling a press conference, 'She was the Fred Astaire of comedy. Making a movie with Doris was a piece of cake – a sexy ride on her coat-tails all the way.' Garner even confessed that such was his attraction that, had he not been married, he would almost certainly have had an affair with Doris. He also said that he loathed Marty Melcher more than any man on earth and that the safest place to keep one's hands when in his company was on one's wallet.

Born James Scott Baumgarner in Oklahoma in 1928, he had lost his mother when very young and had subsequently been subjected, along with his two brothers, to a tyrannical stepmother who beat him black and blue on the slightest whim. A big, manly man in the stamp of Rock Hudson and Stephen Boyd, like them he was never afraid of expressing his emotional side – including a potentially (at the time) career-damaging admission that this dreadful woman had punished him by making him wear a dress in public. At 16 he joined the US Marines and after World War II he worked for a time modelling swimwear in Hollywood. With his superb physique this naturally got him noticed: Broadway beckoned and his first experience of treading the boards had been as a bit-part in *The Caine Mutiny Court Marshall* starring Henry Fonda. By 1957 he had appeared in several movies and had shortened his surname to Garner. Then came his most famous role, that of Bret Maverick in the *Maverick* television series, which topped the ratings for three years. By the time he worked with Doris he had left the series following a dispute with Warner Brothers and was replaced by Roger Moore. Later of course he would triumph as Jim Rockford in *The Rockford Files*.

These were serious times for America. In every major city there were protest marches against the threatened war in Vietnam: Bob Dylan sang 'Blowin' In The Wind' on the radio while Marlene Dietrich made audiences weep with Pete Seeger's 'Where Have All The Flowers Gone?' And less than three months after the film's première President Kennedy was to be assassinated. On a lighter note The Beatles released their first recordings with Beatlemania erupting on both sides of the Atlantic – and Doris and Garner gave a disenchanted public something to smile about with *The Thrill Of It All* and *Move Over, Darling*.

Still playing on Doris' 'virginal' reputation, the playbills read,

'She's Hoping He's Ready – He's Wishing She's Willing!' –
misleading because in this instance she is married with two
children. She and Garner played Beverly and Gerald Boyer,
himself a top New York gynaecologist who, as the story opens, has
been treating soap heirs: the Fraleighs (Arlene Francis, Edward
Andrews). When Mrs Fraleigh falls pregnant, the Boyers are asked
round for dinner where Beverly impresses Mr Fraleigh Sr
(Reginald Owen) with her enthusiasm for the company's product,
Happy Soap. She is subsequently offered an $80,000-a-year salary
to appear in a television commercial to promote the product, very
much against her husband's wishes. Shooting proves a disaster –
Beverly fluffs her words and bawls the director out live on air.
While this infuriates the television company, the public clamour
for more of the bumbling, would-be actress, who for her part has
vowed never to appear on TV again. She does, of course, when
Fraleigh Sr ups her salary and as the 'Happy Girl' she becomes a
household name. It is all piffle, but very enjoyable as fame goes to
her head and her marriage starts to disintegrate with art reflecting
life in Doris' case. One gets the impression, though, that her bust-
ups with Marty Melcher would not have had everyone choking
with laughter, as happens when James Garner comes home in a
huff and drives his car into the swimming pool – which was not
there that morning when he left! He retaliates by trying to make his
wife think he's having an affair – lipstick stains on his shirt,
mysterious phone calls, etc. in the hope of getting her to give up
showbusiness, which of course she does in the days when the
average American husband believed the wife's place was at home,
looking after the house and children. It is also interesting to note
two of the bit-parts: in what would be her penultimate film former
silents' 'spinster' specialist ZaSu Pitts (1898–1963) and Kym Karath,
who as one of the Boyer's children made such an impression on
director Robert Wise that soon afterwards she was signed to play
one of the Von Trapp children in *The Sound Of Music*.

Doris' next film, Twentieth Century-Fox's *Move Over, Darling*, featured a recurrent if not by now tiresome theme: one partner planning to remarry, thinking the other is dead only to have them return and cause chaos just as the other is getting his or her life back together again. This particular story was first filmed in 1911 by the legendary D. W. Griffith as *Enoch Arden* with Lillian Gish. The 1940 remake *My Favourite Wife* starred Cary Grant and Irene Dunne with Grant's long-term lover Randolph Scott as the musclebound show-off protagonist Stephen Burkett. The production with Doris was originally intended as a 'comeback vehicle' for Marilyn Monroe. Titled *Something's Got To Give*, shooting began in April 1962, with Marilyn as Ellen Wagstaff Arden and Dean Martin as her husband Nick. At the helm was George Cukor, a director famed for taming temperamental actresses though he soon lost patience with this one. Shortly before his death in November 1960, Doris had learned from Clark Gable how unreliable Marilyn proved on the set of his last film *The Misfits*. Indeed, many blamed her for Gable's death because she kept him (with a diagnosed heart condition) and everyone else waiting for hours, sometimes days, in the scorching Nevada desert because it was too much trouble to get out of bed. Pretty much the same happened during *Something's Got To Give* and Fox had already had enough of tetchy stars pulling sick-leave stunts – *Cleopatra* had cost a fortune on account of Elizabeth Taylor's indispositions. Therefore, after canning just 32 minutes of film (subsequently included in the documentary *Marilyn: The Final Days*, aired on 1 June 2001, which would have been her 75th birthday), Cukor fired the finicky star. Initially, he engaged Lee Remick to replace her but Dean Martin refused to work without her and so the project was shelved until the October, by which time the studio hoped Marilyn might have woken her ideas up. Then in the August of 1962 she died and the film was abandoned altogether.

As soon as Doris had agreed to make the film, Dean Martin and George Cukor were contacted. Neither wanted anything to do with Marty Melcher, who in turn did not want the original Stephen Burkett – Tom Tryon – in the production because, like Stephen Boyd, he was more or less openly gay and Melcher was afraid Doris and he might 'gang up on him' as had happened with Boyd, her first choice for Nick Arden, and Rock Hudson. Therefore the part went to the far less personable Chuck Connors, while James Garner was signed up to play Nick, and for Nick Arden's fiancée (originally to have been Cyd Charisse) everyone finally agreed upon Polly Bergen. And to play Nick's mother, director Michael Gordon brought in Thelma Ritter, who Doris had admired for years after seeing her as Jane Froman's companion in *With A Song In My Heart*.

The phrase that springs to mind after watching *Move Over, Darling* is 'too daft to laugh at'. Even the acting is second rate, not a patch on the remaining footage of Marilyn Monroe and Tom Tryon. James Garner fails in his attempts to obviously step into Rock Hudson's shoes: he tries too hard to be over-masculine and only ends up coming across as camp whereas Tryon, unashamedly gay at a time when gay men were regarded as effeminate, appears twice as butch. Throughout the film Doris emulates Marilyn Monroe – the way she walks, pouts and whimpers; how she wears her hair, like every other female in the production courtesy of a 10-cents wig that keeps changing shape. As the neurotic new wife Bianca, Polly Bergen is positively dreadful, alternately shrieking, preening and bellowing her neuroses like a poor man's Elizabeth Taylor. 'You're just like all the others!' she bawls during one of their rows. 'Every husband I've ever had only thinking of himself!' As for Ellen's children they are so awful that one wonders why she wants to see them again. 'Are you a lady or a man?' pipes up one, purloining a line that sounded much funnier in *Please Don't Eat The Daisies*.

As in the earlier version of the film, the Ardens' plane went down in the Pacific and while Nick and the children were rescued, Ellen was pronounced drowned and the first prolonged scene sees Nick petitioning the judge (Edgar Buchanan) five years on to have her declared legally dead so that he can marry Bianca. Cut to Ellen, rescued by the US Navy and returned home on the very same day, hardly catching her breath before pursuing the happy couple to the same Monterey hotel where she and Nick spent their own honeymoon in the hope of preventing the union from being consummated. Then, for the next hour or so, she tries to win him back. He wants her back, but is too much of a weakling to tell Bianca the truth.

When Ellen returns to the house she shared with Nick and his mother and he arrives with Bianca, having faked a back injury so the sham marriage will not be consummated, Ellen poses as a Swedish masseuse telling Bianca that dead wives can return from the grave, an example being Irene Dunne returning to Cary Grant in *My Favourite Wife*! (This scene led to a four-day delay in the shooting schedule when, dragging Doris off Polly Bergen, James Garner accidentally broke one of her ribs. Incredibly she was able to complete the take without him knowing this.) Then Stephen Burkett is reported to be in town and about to publish his memoirs of life on the desert island with Ellen – save that they then called each other Adam and Eve. Ellen tries to fool Nick by passing off a geeky shoe-clerk as the mysterious Burkett, unaware he has seen the muscle-bound original showing off to dozens of female admirers at the poolside. 'Man, she sure looks great in clothes!' he drawls, climbing out of the water and flexing his pecs. Then comes a car chase like something from the closing seqence of *The Benny Hill Show* which ends with the film's only funny moment when Ellen gets stuck in a carwash in her convertible with the top down. Meanwhile, tired of the arguments, Bianca falls for her analyst so that by the time the truth emerges she is more than willing to have her marriage annulled while Grace, eager to sort out this tiresome matter once and for all, shops her son to the authorities for bigamy. Cut to where the film opened and the same judge doing exactly this – just before Ellen bashes Burkett, the way she has been doing these last five years each time he tries to seduce her.

The reviewer for *Motion Picture Magazine* who praised this as 'one of the funniest, brightest marital adventures of the year' surely must have been watching something else according to the majority of Doris' fans. Bosley Crowther, the *New York Times* no-nonsense critic, dismissed it as a feeble frolic and concluded, 'At one point, when some of Miss Day's gambits to recapture her spouse have failed, Miss Ritter acidly suggests, "better think of something else." That advice could apply to *Move Over, Darling*, too.'

Through no fault of anyone involved in it, the film was released at a very bad time: December 1963 when America was still in shock after the Kennedy assassination and not in the mood to laugh at *anything*. Additionally, the snooty Hollywood Women's Press Club bestowed on Doris a second annual Sour Apple Award and this time she was intent on having her say, accusing those 'suffering sick ladies' of having nothing better to do than 'fuck with people's lives when there were so many dreadful things happening in the world'. On the positive side, the film gave her one of her biggest hits. The title-song, penned by Joe Lubin, Hal Kanter – and Terry Melcher – on which she sounded sexier than ever, stormed into the Top Ten in Britain, though it was not quite so successful in the US. Terry produced the single for Columbia, along with 'Rainbow's End', 'Let The Little Girl Limbo' and the theme song for 'Send Me No Flowers', rarities fans would have to wait until 2000 to hear when they were released on a box-set on the Bear Family label (see Appendix II).

That same month Doris more than compensated for her 'movie shortcomings' by releasing a superb studio album. *Love Him* barely scraped into the *Billboard* chart, but has more than made up for it since. Recorded at the Columbia Studios in just two sessions in the October and November under the baton of Tommy Oliver and produced by Terry, each of the 12 songs was presented as a *symphonie en miniature*. As would later happen with Gram Parsons, Terry persuaded his mother to ditch her sweetness-and-light movie image and experiment outside her somewhat limited range. The title-track was by Barry Mann and Cynthia Weil, arguably the most successful songwriting partnership since Lieber and Stoller. Sung as a bolero, it tells of a woman advising her friend on the man she has just yielded up to her – a subject with which Doris was familiar. Following in the footsteps of Billie Holiday and Ruth Etting were the torchy heartfelt 'Since I Fell For You' and 'Losing You'. By way of Terry, Doris met Elvis Presley and though this was completely unnecessary, she asked The King's permission to record two of his greatest hits: 'A Fool Such As I' and 'Can't Help Falling In Love With You', which in the opinion of many is the definitive version of the *Blue Hawaii* anthem. From the soundtrack of Lionel Bart's *Oliver!* came a sultry version of 'As Long As He Needs Me' which builds up to the most tremendous crescendo and at the other end of the scale a rip-roaring 'Lollipops And Roses', previously a hit for Jack Jones, and from the pen of Willie Nelson a very noisy 'Night Life', the latter perhaps out of place on a 'mood' album. There were also cover versions of Matt Monroe's 'Softly As I Leave You' and 'More', an Italian ballad with which Caterina Valente had had a big hit. The other songs were 'Funny', 'Moonlight Lover' and the moving 'A Whisper Away'.

Early in 1964 Doris was thrown a lifeline of sorts when she was asked to make another film with Rock Hudson. Since working with her in *Lover Come Back*, Rock had made another comedy film, *Man's Favourite Sport?* with Paula Prentiss. Directed by Howard Hawks, equally at home working with intense drama (*Scarface*) as he was screwball comedy (*Bringing Up Baby*), this one had been decidedly second rate. Unlike Doris and Gina

Lollobrigida, with whom Rock had made *Come September*, Prentiss had not 'clicked' with him and this was reflected at the box office.

Inasmuch as he disliked Rock, Marty Melcher did not balk when Harry Keller of Universal contacted him with a view to Doris appearing with him in *Send Me No Flowers* – again, she would be billed beneath him and for a third time the foil would be Tony Randall. Melcher had no objection to Randall but he did put forward a lame argument to the studio that James Garner would be a better choice for leading man despite his hopeless performance in *Move Over, Darling*. Rock had already been assigned to the part, however, and had script, director and co-star approval. What he had no control over was the producer and naturally one of Melcher's terms was that he would have to co-produce with his customary $50,000 bonus on top of his usual salary and percentage. In Rock's opinion Melcher was a 'conniving, thieving little shit', but he was so eager to work with Doris again that for the duration of the shooting schedule he agreed to 'set aside' his hatred for her husband provided personal contact between them was kept to an absolute minimum.

In the film he plays hypochondriac George Kimball, who is too wrapped up in his imaginary ailments to know much about the outside world: he takes his temperature under the shower and for breakfast devours a plate of pills from his bathroom pharmacy. 'Men of my age are dropping like flies,' he tells Judy (Doris), his scatty, long-suffering wife – who aids his habit by grinding sugar to make fake 'Seconal' sleeping pills – 'Do you ever read the obituary page? It's enough to scare you to death!' George consults his doctor about his chest pains and the doctor assures him that he is suffering from indigestion, adding he only wishes that all his patients were as healthy. He then overhears his doctor discussing another patient over the phone. 'Bad news,' he says. 'Not much you can do when the old ticker goes.' Thinking he may only have a few weeks to live, George confides in his best friend Arnold (Randall), who promises to write the eulogy and handle the funeral arrangements – and promptly copes with his grief by hitting the bottle. He then becomes concerned for his widow-to-be. Not wishing Judy to run off with the first man she sees, he sets about finding her a new husband and buys a burial plot for the three of them.

Several candidates are considered but fate lends a helping hand when Judy is swept off her feet literally when he rescues her from a runaway golf cart by expert horseman Bert Power (Clint Walker), who is also her former college sweetheart. He is a super-smooth charmer who says he is in town for his latest swindle. Bert looks George in the eye and adds, just in case cinemagoers are wondering why he is still a bachelor at 37, that since being dumped by Judy all those years ago he has never been able to settle for second best. Arnold considers Bert ideal husband material and George does his utmost to push the pair together though secretly he despises his smarmy rival – as Rock is thought to have loathed Walker away from the screen. This leads Judy to believe George is cheating on her until he informs her that he is dying and then she pampers him. In the next scene he is ensconced in a wheelchair, talking to his favourite tree! Judy is about to check him into an expensive private clinic when his doctor turns up at the house and she learns of the mix-up. The doctor tells her, 'George Kimball will outlive us all – unless he worries himself to death!'

Judy plots her revenge, certain George is having an affair and that he has invented his terminal illness to cover his tracks. She locks him out of the house, empties his beloved pills out the window and bursts a hot-water bottle over his head. George moves in with Arnold. The spare room is being redecorated and they share a bed and bicker like a long-married couple. Arnold is peeved because his pal is no longer dying: he has spent three days getting drunk and penning the eulogy, all for nothing. The story ends happily when Judy learns about the proposed plot in the cemetery. Realising there never was another woman, she forgives him and Bert is sent packing.

Though Doris and Rock had tremendous fun making *Send Me No Flowers*, he later denounced it, telling *Films & Filming*'s Gordon Gow in June 1976:

> Right from the start I hated the script. I just didn't believe
> in that man for one minute. Making fun of death is
> difficult and dangerous. That scene where I went out and
> bought a plot for myself in the cemetery – to me it was
> completely distasteful.

Coinciding with the release was Doris' *With A Smile And A Song* album, an anthology of children's songs – one of these, Frank Sinatra's 'High Hopes', would be used on the soundtrack of the animated film *Antz* some years later. Also included was 'Nick Nack Paddywack' featured in the Gladys Aylward biopic *Inn Of The Sixth Happiness*, and 'Zip-A-Dee-Doo-Dah' from Disney's *Song Of The South*. The title-track came from his *Snow White* and a real treat for fans was a new arrangement of 'Que Sera, Sera', which many considered superior to the original.

To monopolise on the success of *Send Me No Flowers*, in the space of nine months Columbia put out three more Doris Day albums – it had to happen of course. After the inspirational songs and coinciding with the children's songs, Doris was bound to follow in the recent footsteps of Elvis Presley and Peggy Lee and record an album of Christmas songs. Columbia originally contracted her to do this back in the summer of 1959 when, under the baton of Frank De Vol, she recorded two songs for a single 'I've Got My Love To Keep Me Warm' and 'Deck The Halls' for an album which never saw the light of day. The first was added to her *Hooray For Hollywood* album, while the other was assigned to a

Columbia vault. She also taped 'It Came Upon The Midnight Clear' and 'The First Noel', which to date have never emerged.

Now Columbia brought in Dudley C. 'Pete' King, who had most recently written arrangements for Dean Martin and Julie London, and in just two sessions (17 and 18 June) Doris laid down 12 tracks. Most were standard fare though her cover of Elvis' 'I'll Be Home For Christmas' remains definitive and only Doris could make 'Let It Snow! Let It Snow! Let It Snow!' sound blatantly erotic! Not included on the album this time around was Martin Broones' extraordinarily beautiful and moving hymn 'Let No Walls Divide', which Doris recorded in May 1961 – as with Broones' 'The Everlasting Arms', this was commissioned for a charity album *An All-Star Christmas: We Wish You The Merriest*. This, and the two songs from the aborted single, would be tagged onto the end of the CD release in 2003.

Next to hit the shelves was *Latin For Lovers*, a collection of standards set to bossa nova rhythms by Mort Garson. Four of the songs were composed by that master of the genre Antonio Carlos Jobim, with Garson's arrangement of his 'How Insensitive' almost identical to the one on Peggy Lee's *In Love Again!* album released to great acclaim the previous year with some Lee fans accusing Doris of emulating her. Absolutely first-class are Doris' readings of 'Fly Me To The Moon' and Garson's 'Our Day Will Come', the French version of which had just been a hit in Europe for Edith Piaf's widower Theo Sarapo. In fact there are shades of Piaf herself in 'Be Mine Tonight', Sunny Skylar's adaptation of a Spanish song which 'borrows' the refrain from Piaf's 1957 million-seller 'Comme Moi'. Doris also performs part of 'Be True To Me' in almost flawless Spanish – the only time she ever sang anything in a foreign language.

The album's *coup de grâce* is unquestionably 'Perhaps, Perhaps, Perhaps'. This started out in 1949 as 'Quizas, Quizas, Quizas', written by Cuban musician Osvaldo Farres for Gordon Jenkins' vocalist Tony Bavaar. Like the later 'Que Sera, Sera', the song would be adopted by the gay community as an unofficial anthem. Doris' version was used in 1992 on the soundtrack of the Australian film *Strictly Ballroom* and in 2004 Mexican heart-throb actor Gael Garcia Bernal lip-synched to it in Pedro Almodovar's sublime *Bad Education* . . . two years before the Spanish version was used in another gay-themed classic, arguably the most famous film of this genre, *Brokeback Mountain*. In Britain it would also be less effectively sung by Mari Wilson over the opening credits of the television sitcom *Coupling*.

Columbia's next release was Doris' first concept album *Doris Day's Sentimental Journey*. Re-arranged by Mort Garson, the theme was her signature tune with Les Brown, presented with 10 other numbers either associated with his, or his big band rivals, between 1940 and 1945. By 1965 most people in America had forgotten which girl vocalists originally introduced these songs. Helen Forest had had hits with 'I Remember You' and 'I Don't Want To Walk Without You'. Kitty Kallen sang 'It's Been A Long, Long Time' while Jo Stafford was the first to perform 'It Could Happen To You'. Doris had sung them too, but here – inadvertently and definitively – she makes them her personal property.

Her movie career might have been salvaged at this point had it not been for Marty Melcher's paranoia over her working with gay men and with Rock Hudson in particular. Rock had just been handed the script for *Strange Bedfellows*, a sparkling comedy to be directed by Melvin Frank, for which Gig Young had already been contracted as stooge. Universal begged Melcher to let Doris play love interest Toni Vincente but this time he refused to be swayed and instead the part went to Gina Lollobrigida, his co-star from *Come September*.

In his wisdom Melcher put Doris into *Do Not Disturb*. Her co-star this time was 35-year-old Australian beefcake actor Rod Taylor, who had enjoyed modest success on the stage and on radio back home before moving in Hollywood in 1954. Since then he had appeared in a series of science fiction films, notably *The Time Machine* (1960). Three years later Rock Hudson asked for him to star in A *Gathering Of Eagles* and it was he who suggested Universal cast him opposite Doris in the new film. This was a big mistake. Taylor lacked charisma, and was not adept at comedy, and so it was left to Doris to carry the film from beginning to end. Taylor plays Mike Harper, the head of a wool company who relocates to London with his dotty wife, Janet (Doris). As with *Please Don't Eat The Daisies*, and this being Hollywood, no mere apartment will suffice, so they rent a mansion in the Kent country-side, owned by eccentric Vanessa Courtwright (the equally eccentric Hermione Baddeley). Here, boredom quickly sets in. With her husband away from home much of the time, Janet quickly adopts a family of animals which includes a fox she rescues from the hunt, and a goat named Wellington. She then decides that all she needs to make her 'house' complete in time for their forthcoming wedding anniversary is a Georgian dining suite: enter French Lothario antiques dealer Paul Belassi (Sergio Fantoni), who just happens to have what she is looking for – in his Parisian showroom.

Belassi whisks Janet across the Channel and, with just one thing in mind, he introduces her to his friends, and she gets to sing a risqué *chanson*. 'Connaissez-vous Rock Hudson?' a boy asks, providing the production with its only in-joke. In his shop, Janet quaffs too much champagne and passes out, though it soon becomes obvious that nothing has taken place. Mike does not know this and, when he catches them 'at it', punches Belassi on the nose. Then it is Janet's turn to be suspicious when she follows Mike to a wool convention where every executive has a mistress, and concludes that he must be sleeping with his personal assistant, Claire (Maura McGiveney). This leads up to a rather silly neo-Faydeau scenario which sees Janet pursued around the hotel corridors by an elderly admirer, from whence all ends well. Janet gets her dining suite, at a higher price than she expected because Belassi never got a chance to remove his trousers. It had all been done before, countless times, and much better.

Critics who viewed the rushes for *Do Not Disturb* were enthusiastic that the film would prove a hit and weeks before it was completed, Marty Melcher had already decided that Doris would work with Rod Taylor again, despite being offered the part of Mrs Robinson in *The Graduate*. On this occasion, it was Doris who rejected the role, claiming that after years of playing the hard-to-get virgin she would never get away with being the older sexually liberated woman, even though it is what she had always been since joining Les Brown. What Melcher was too blinkered to observe was that the syrupy comedies that had become her trademark were now going out of fashion; along with the slapstick Dean Martin and Jerry Lewis vehicles, they had had their day. Playing Mrs Robinson would have given her movie career the lift it needed while turning the part down eventually lead to its destruction.

Again, Doris wanted to work with Rock Hudson or Stephen Boyd, with James Garner standing in the reserve. But once again, Melcher brandished the invisible whip – she would work with Rod Taylor again and like it or lump it. Neither did she approve of Melcher's choice of film. In the wake of the Cold War which brought about the James Bond films and the *Man From U.N.C.L.E.* television series, she would play her first and last role as a spy in *The Glass Bottom Boat*, directed by Frank Tashlin, who worked on four of Jerry Lewis' early films. Also roped into the production were John McGiver and Eric Fleming, the sharp-featured neurotic actor who starred as cattle-trail boss Gil Favor in television's *Rawhide* series. In the opinion of many, Doris was once more taking a gamble in the 'too daft to laugh at' category. Indeed this is so painful to watch – even a reprise of 'Que Sera, Sera', which her character sings as her father accompanies her on the ukulele fails to raise it to an acceptable level – therefore the less said, the better. At least with *It Happened To Jane* one makes it to the end without cringing. And even the title song is purloined – set to the music of Marlene Dietrich's '*Shh, Kleine Baby*' and played with such annoying persistence that after half an hour one tires of hearing it.

Rod Taylor played Bruce Templeton, director of a space laboratory, who fakes developing a rocket to Venus while apparently trying to hoodwink a variety of spies – there are appearances by James Bond and *The Man From U.N.C.L.E.'s* Napoleon Solo. Woven into a silly plot is Jenny Nelson (Doris), who is suspected of espionage when she phones her dog Vladimir several times a day – the purpose being that she is too busy to take him for walkies and therefore every time the phone rings he goes berserk and races around her apartment, getting his exercise that way. Jenny works for Templeton, doubling as his PA and biographer while moonlighting for her father, dressing as a mermaid for the benefit of tourists who ride his glass-bottomed boat on trips around Catalina Island. When she realises everyone is spying on her, assuming she must have 'Red' connections, she turns the tables on the numerous intelligents, enabling this pointless mish-mash to come to a conclusion – not before time – wherein she marries the boss.

Despite being dire *The Glass Bottom Boat* was a box-office success though some fans found it hard to watch the scenes with Eric Fleming. After pulling out of *Rawhide* after seven years (to be replaced by Clint Eastwood), Fleming bought a ranch in Hawaii and he was enjoying what he hoped would be a lengthy break when the call came from Marty Melcher. On 28 September 1966, a few weeks after the première and just two days before he was due to marry his longtime companion Lynne Garber, 41-year-old Fleming was filming the locations for his new television series *High Jungle* when his boat capsized on the Amazon and he drowned.

Things couldn't possibly get any worse when Doris made *Caprice* with Irish hellraiser Richard Harris, once more with Frank Tashlin at the helm. The scenario opens well enough: a top Interpol agent shot dead on the Swiss ski slopes, James Bond-style music, spies peering over newspapers and from behind flowerbeds in Paris. Then Doris, aka Patricia Foster, the agent's daughter, makes her entrance in the guise (at 43) of a 1960s dollybird: short skirt, checked coat, huge hat and dark glasses and a platinum wig which makes her resemble a drag-queen. For some reason she meets her contact in the Tour d'Argent restaurant halfway up the Eiffel Tower and is subsequently apprehended by the French police for handing over the secret ingredients of her cosmetics company's under-arm deodorant.

Next, she is pursued by Christopher White, head of May Fortune Cosmetics, who poses as a taxi driver. Later it emerges that he is a double agent who is searching for her father's killer and for information about an international drugs ring. For the moment, he accuses her of 'sabotaging the natural armpit' and hauls her off to his apartment, where he intends to have his way with her but instead of sex he entertains her with his Laurence Olivier impressions and injects her with a truth drug to acquire privileged information regarding a new wig she is developing. Suffice to say, Patricia works out who the villain is and ends up marrying White – though long before this the viewer has thrown in the towel.

The critics loathed it. 'Oh, well,' groaned the *New York Morning Telegraph*, 'to paraphrase the old saying, another Day, another Doris. Only trouble is, it's the same Day and the same Doris.' New York's *Village Voice* denounced it as 'A long Day's journey into naught.' Others were much less kind – in her syndicated column Judith Crist called Doris 'an aging transvestite.' Many of her gay fans also took offence at the scene in the film where her character takes a homophobic stance by pushing cross-dresser Dr Clancy (Ray Walston) to his death from a balcony. Vito Russo, in his celebrated *The Celluloid Closet*, observed, 'Sissies were now cured, killed or rendered impotent in suitably nasty ways. Ray Walston's psychotic killer reflects an unnatural fear that the world is about to become homosexual. Walston's Dr Clancy, a cosmetologist, rationalises that if women are made more beautiful, their husbands "won't want to kiss the bus driver in the morning" – something he sees as a widespread danger.'

The Ballad Of Josie directed by Andrew McLaglen (son of actor Victor) and superbly photographed was very much a return to Doris' glory years though sadly it came too late for her to salvage what was left of her movie career. As so often occurs when a great star takes a step down the ladder – it had happened to everyone, from Garbo to Dietrich, from Hepburn to Bergman – this was not a question of fighting one's way back to the top but someone else had filled the void, ensuring there was no going back, though all of these women with the exception of Garbo would move on to better things. What is astonishing is that Doris, who appears to have submitted to her husband's every whim, actually fought him on this one – without doubt her best film since *Send Me No Flowers*. Her leading man was Peter Graves, prematurely greying star of television's *Mission: Impossible* and brother of *Gunsmoke*'s James Arness, who is almost devoid of charisma, while third lead George Kennedy is his usual aggressive self. The supports too are unremarkable with the exception of Audrey Christie, who plays ladies' boarding house landlady Annabelle Pettijohn; she would have supported Doris earlier had she been given *The Unsinkable Molly Brown*. As such, Doris is left to carry the picture from start to finish, which until the dross of recent years she had been doing inordinately well.

The film opens with Josie Minick (Doris) adding the finishing touches to a *God Bless Our Happy Home* sign, though hers is anything but. Her abusive husband has just been turfed out of the Arapaho saloon for brawling and her small son Luther (Teddy Quinn) rushes home to warn her that he's on the warpath again. During their subsequent set-to she grabs a billiard cue but before she can hit him, he takes a fatal fall down the stairs. Arrested for murder, the judge (Andy Devine) tells her the trial can go either way – she could end up in jail or with a bounty payment for ridding the town of its biggest louse. What happens is that she is acquitted, provided she hands Luther over to Minick's father for safekeeping until she is able to provide for him.

The Minicks had a long-forgotten run-down place at Willow Creek and Josie decides to turn this into a sheep-farm, defying tradition in an area which has always been exclusively cattle country, by renovating the place for herself, her pet owl and a family of skunks, earning the enmity of local ranchers, headed by chauvinistic Arch Ogden (George Kennedy), who believes a woman's place is in the home and that to keep her under control, she needs a sound beating every now and then. Add to this a political sub-plot wherein Wyoming Territory is hoping for State status and will only be granted this, he believes, if women are prevented from becoming too independent by being given the vote. Therefore Josie's enterprise must be nipped in the bud.

Enter Jason Meredith (Peter Graves), who has had his eye on Josie for years and initially supports Ogden's idealogy as far as females are concerned. To dissuade her, he finds her a job in a local restaurant where she becomes the butt of men's jokes until she douses them with coffee. She then hits the local store for a change of wardrobe: Levis, cowboy boots and a man's shirt. 'If the Presbyterians hear about this, I'm through,' the shopkeeper protests before she walks out into the street and causes any number of accidents as the people stare, falling off horses and tumbling into horse-troughs. Opposition to her plans escalates when her men drive the huge flock of sheep through the town and one can almost envisage Doris trying to lay the law down with Marty Melcher as she bawls out the bigwigs at a council meeting when they tell her the sheep will have to go:

> Forget I'm a woman: I'm a human being and I can take
> care of myself and my son without anybody's charity! I can
> think and I can work, and I'm not gonna sit at Annabelle
> Pettijohn's and wait for some nice man to rescue me. I
> don't want a man and I don't need a man and nobody, not
> a damn one of you, is gonna get in my way!

When Jason and his men turn up at Josie's ranch and tell her to leave she almost gives up on her dream but when Ogden's henchmen threaten to club her sheep, Jason has a change of heart. Armed with billiard cues, Annabelle Pettijohn and her ladies lead the insurrection against their men folk and when Ogden tries to burn Josie out, he and Jason slug it out among the sheep. The villain then sees sense when Jason drags him from the burning barn and saves his life – he will buy the sheep from Josie, rebuild her barn and sell her all the cattle she needs at knockdown prices so she can become one of the men! The film ends with her burning her rancher's clothes and donning a Jean-Louis dress so that she and Jason can fetch Luther back, and with Wyoming finally becoming a state *without* its women losing the vote.

Just as *Billy Rose's Jumbo* lost out by being released in the midst of a national newspaper strike so *The Ballad Of Josie* failed when it was released as part of a double bill with Charlston Heston's *Counterpoint* – an 'act of treason' resulting in Doris loathing the *Ben Hur* star even more than she had when informed of his virulent homophobia towards her friend Stephen Boyd . . . and loathing the film still more.

Doris may have laid the law down with her husband over his contracting her to a production and *then* telling her, but this made no difference. Melcher still ensured she would be the last to know details of her latest role and therefore it was back to the dross for her penultimate movie. 'These poor men were the pearls before the swine of these scripts,' she said of her last few co-stars. *Where Were You When The Lights Went Out?* was directed by Hy Averback, best known as the voice over the loudspeaker in the *M.A.S.H.* television series. Prior to this he had made *Chamber Of Horrors* with lacklustre B-movies actor Patrick O'Neal, who is Doris' leading man here. The film has as its scenario the power blackout that paralysed New York in November 1965. It saw her working with her most inept cast ever but what made her a laughing stock with the critics was her character, Broadway star Margaret Garrison is appearing in a comedy titled *The Constant Virgin*. Even more woeful was the inclusion of the so-called Oscar Levant quip when Margaret's husband says of her, 'I knew her before she was a virgin!' Margaret plans to retire after this and have a baby until jealousy raises its head when she finds husband Peter (O'Neal) in a compromising position with flighty journalist Lola Albright. Driving out to her cottage in Bridgeport, Connecticut, in her confused state Margaret stakes an accidental overdose of sleeping draught and flakes out on her bed. What she does not realise is that she has an unwelcome visitor – investment banker (Robert Morse) who has absconded with his firm's takings and hailed a cab; the driver has got lost in the dark and brought him there. And if that was not too ridiculous for audiences to swallow, he has taken the same potion and is sleeping in the same bed! Naturally Peter finds them together and suspects the worst, as do the couple on the bed. Unsure whether or not they have had sex, Peter may be willing to forgive her but Margaret's slimy Peeping Tom manager (Terry Thomas) wants her to keep on working, therefore he tries to convince Peter that she is a scarlet woman. All ends well of course when the sparring couple is reconciled, enabling the increasingly nonsensical scenario to skip nine months to the birth of their child.

Doris hated every moment spent shooting the film – not that this was anything out of the ordinary of late. Matters were only exacerbated by an on-set injury incurred during the scene when Patrick O'Neal gathers her up from the sofa after her 'overdose'. She wriggled when he was moving her and trapped a nerve in her spine, which meant that for the rest of the shoot she had to be put into traction between takes.

Then came her swansong with the absurdly titled *With Six You Get Eggroll* – a non-event she actually *wanted* to make, while Marty Melcher was the one who did not. It was directed by former actor Howard Morris whose debut on the other side of the camera *Who's Minding The Mint* was released the previous year. Doris played widow and lumberyard boss Abby McClure, whose matchmaking sister (Pat Carroll) fixes her up with Jake Iverson (Brian Keith), a widower whose teenage daughter (Barbara Hershey) is no less unruly than Abby's three teenage sons when opposing their forthcoming marriage. Equally troublesome, yet infinitely more endearing is Abby's sheepdog Calico. The quickie marriage takes place in Las Vegas but the bickering continues as the families refuse to get along – and that just about sums up the plot. The title comes courtesy of a fairground scene when what starts out as a fun-loving ride on the dodgems turns into all-out war and Abby's youngest son chirps, 'I'm glad we're a family – 'cos with six you get egg roll!'

Doris had no way of knowing at the time that *Eggroll* would prove to be her last film. During the final week of shooting Marty Melcher fell ill. Over the last three months his weight had dropped considerably and he also developed a severe case of what would today be diagnosed as Irritable Bowel Syndrome. Everyone around him initially suspected he had nothing more than a bad dose of the 'flu. Despite the fact that for some time he had been her husband in name only, Doris insisted on nursing him herself and somehow managed to persuade Terry to start visiting the house again – though later he said he had obliged only because he had wanted to be there when his stepfather died to make sure he was dead and out of the way.

Even when he became desperately ill, Melcher refused to see a doctor, preferring to consult the 'oracle' – Martin Broones and Charlotte Greenwood, who were in the midst of a lecture-recruitment tour of the country. The Broones informed him it was especially crucial that he should not allow Doris to 'endanger' his health with medical intervention though by now he was bedridden much of the time and almost dying. Over the next two weeks, they called twice a day to instruct her which lines from Mary Baker Eddy should be read aloud at his bedside. For his part Terry urged his mother to burn her copy of *Science & Health* – if not, he would burn it for her. While he didn't care two hoots for Melcher, he was concerned that if Doris fell ill, she would certainly deserve more sensible advice than those 'charlatans' were offering.

During this final illness Melcher exercised the same control over Doris as he had throughout their 17-year marriage. She was not permitted to go out alone – he played hell if she so much as left the room. If she talked to male friends on the phone, he suspected her of having an affair. She is said to have *wanted* to have a relationship with Stephen Boyd, seen on the town most nights with a pretty girl on his arm – then seeing her to her cab before rushing home to his boyfriend. There was also talk of an involvement with black baseball star Maury Wills and the tabloids made much of a 'romance' with country singer Glen Campbell. Doris fervently denied both.

Why Terry should have taken the initiative to bring in a doctor to treat his stepfather when for as long as he could remember he had wanted him dead, if only for his mother's sake, cannot be explained. Whatever the reason, Melcher agreed to see a specialist at the Mount Sinai Hospital, though he refused to travel by ambulance – apparently Mary Baker Eddy disapproved of them in their then primitive form – so Doris drove him there. For two weeks she stayed with him throughout the day, returning each night to Terry's house. Hospital staff were instructed that Melcher's business partner Jerry Rosenthal should not be allowed into the sickroom nor should any calls be put through to him, which suggests Doris must have already suspected their dealings may not have been strictly legitimate.

Very early during the morning of 19 April 1968 Doris was contacted by the hospital director: Melcher had fallen out of bed – quite possibly he had suffered a stroke – and she was urged to go there at once. By the time she and Terry arrived he had lapsed into a coma with all hope abandoned. He was rumoured to have undergone surgery for an enlarged heart, though under the circumstances this would seem unlikely. At three o'clock the next morning, Marty Melcher died in his sleep of a heart-attack, aged 52.

Chapter 10

In the Wake of the Crescent Drive Bully

'The really frightening thing about middle age is that you know you'll grow out of it. . . . Wrinkles are heriditary. Parents get them from their children.'

Doris Day

Looking back, by bowing out of the movie scene at 44 and subsequently rejecting every role that came her way, Doris was effectively putting herself in the same reclusive category as Greta Garbo who walked out on MGM after her last film, *Two-Faced Woman* (1941), was slated by the critics. Television series may come and go, while movies last forever; Doris will therefore be eternally remembered as an attractive, charismatic and personable actress who never took the *schlock* horror route of Bette Davis and Joan Crawford or ended up looking like the once-beautiful Simone Signoret or Diana Dors. Much as she had loathed Marty Melcher organising contracts without her knowledge so it would appear that she also disliked the responsibility of making her own decisions and this may have been why her film career suddenly ground to a halt.

Retrospectively, friends, colleagues and fans would agree that having Melcher out of her life once and for all was an immense release though the needless pangs of guilt might have been less intense had she divorced him years ago. Terry pulled no punches when he observed of his stepfather's untimely death: 'It wasn't going to ruin my Christmas,' adding of Melcher's mania for making money, 'but I had figured he wouldn't *allow* himself to die until he had at least a hundred million stashed under the bed someplace.' Though Terry hated him for the way he had bullied his family he did not consider him a crook. 'Although I figured Marty was rather fucked up,' he observed in Doris' memoirs, 'I always rated him as honest. Because how else was he able to live up to all those lofty Christian Science goals?'

What no one could comprehend was the fact that, in allowing her husband to be whitewashed by the Broones, Doris held herself at least partly responsible for what happened to him. This guilt is not hard to comprehend; one only has to study the many cases of domestic abuse against women where, despite attempts to persuade the victim to ditch the thug and press charges, she only returns for more, the maxim always being, 'You make your bed, therefore you must lie on it'. For at least 10 of their 17 years together, Melcher treated Doris like a chattel-cum-meal-ticket but she herself had admittedly been a more than willing victim, institutionalised by past experience. Like the dutiful country widow, she mourned her husband, donning the proverbial hair shirt and telling the world how much she had genuinely loved him. Perhaps she was kidding herself but those around her were unconvinced once they learned the truth about his treachery. Three days after Melcher's death and doubtless following a severe talking to by Alma and Terry who had always seen Melcher as the 'archetypal shit' – Terry's words – reality set in.

Because she did not wish to be reminded of him by having a grave or crypt to visit, Doris had Melcher cremated without ceremony, neither prayers nor words of comfort from Mary Baker Eddy. She had had enough of Christian Science, she said, and the last thing she wanted to hear was that death did not exist and grieving was therefore useless. Once she stopped blaming herself, she held the Broones responsible for her husband's death for a time; the fact that he would have lived longer had they not filled his head with so much nonsense. Yet rumour persists that Melcher deliberately refused medical help towards the end of his life because he wanted to die so that he would not be around to face Doris when she eventually found out that for at least 15 years he had been stealing her money now that Terry was onto him.

Even in death Melcher was still able to exercise an iron grip over Doris' life and career not to mention her fragile mental state. Though she often discussed with him the possibility of having her own television series, she always shelved the idea because she had been against the proposed taping principle; the fact that one programme had to be completed in a matter of days before moving onto the next one without a break to recharge her batteries. Melcher promised a way around this, if a television series ever materialised, otherwise nothing definite had ever been decided on. Now she learned that some months before he had actually signed the contract for *The Doris Day Show* although he must have been well aware that she would have opposed this. He had even commissioned the scripts for the first two episodes and it was he who had had the last laugh in casting her as a young widow. Moreover, several of her co-stars had already signed up eagerly, unaware that Doris had no idea they had been approached!

Of course she could have refused to do the series since she had not committed her own signature to paper. She maintained that she embarked on the new venture to honour her husband's memory, though goodness knows why but this was but the first of many shocks to hit her during the month after his death. First, she discovered that Melcher's Will had disappeared and then she received an irate call from Terry, who had been given the job of handling his stepfather's estate. Several cheques endorsed by Terry and handed over to Jerry Rosenthal (Melcher's business partner of whom Doris had expressed her doubts many times) never ended up in her bank account; similarly cheques issued by Rosenthal had bounced. When Doris received an unexpected tax demand for over $500,000, a further investigation revealed the coffers were empty: aside from personal possessions, her husband had left her broke.

In the ensuing trial it subsequently emerged that Rosenthal had been in on a scam that is thought to have gone on for 15 years. Whenever Doris questioned his motives or business tactics Melcher always came up with some excuse – usually telling her that if she distrusted Rosenthal then it figured she must feel the same way about him. Now it emerged that Marty had also duped his own stepson, urging Terry to hand over royalties from his own compositions and production deals to Rosenthal for safe investment. Doris first learned of the scam when she dropped in at Melcher's office to collect some of his effects – every file, cupboard and drawer had been cleared. Her initial reaction was to attempt to settle her debts before the matter became public knowledge. She contacted Columbia and asked to borrow money from her recording contract account only to be told that this had already been spent and that Melcher had borrowed heavily against her future earnings. As if that was not enough, she was approached by her husband's former partner Richard Dorso and his co-producer Bob Sweeney, acting on behalf of CBS, who wanted to know what had happened to the $500,000 the company had advanced Melcher and Jerry Rosenthal as part of her fee for the television series because this too had also disappeared.

Doris asked Terry to sort out the mess as best he could. Consequently he fired Rosenthal and instigated proceedings against him. Initial findings via the courts revealed that Rosenthal had similarly fleeced Kirk Douglas and Gordon MacRae – the latter by way of a federal land-grant scam that Rosenthal had convinced him would permit him to buy bonds and shares to the tune of almost $400,000 from tax concessions. MacRae would spend the better part of his remaining career paying the money back to the US government. Producer Ross Hunter had also been conned, as had the actress Dorothy Dandridge with tragic consequences. Faced with such a huge mountain of debts and feeling deeply ashamed of herself, though of course she had nothing to reproach herself for, Doris put her house on the market and decided her only solution would be to proceed with the CBS series.

With just six weeks to prepare for her first show – shooting was set to begin on 15 June 1968 – Doris moved into a rented property in Palm Springs. Alma went with her to offer moral support. When she started rehearsals, Doris was in pretty bad shape: addicted to sleeping pills, forcing herself to laugh and act in an amusing way when, as she told one reporter, all she really wanted to do was to go to sleep and never wake up. The television series was promoted as an anodyne against the then new wave in the movies – sex, gratuitous violence, political drama and so on. They tended to use the same syrupy story lines that had occured in Doris' films, though interest in this sort of plot line was waning. Today, productions such as *The Doris Day Show* and *The Mary Tyler Moore Show* would be of little interest to the audiences of *Will And Grace*, *Frazier*, *Ugly Betty*, etc.

The first show went out on 24 September 1968 and followed along the lines of her previous movie *It Happened To Jane*. Each episode was introduced with her singing 'Que Sera, Sera' over the credits. Doris, aka widowed singer Doris Martin, turns her back on city life and relocates to her father's farm in Mill Valley, California, with her oversized dog and two sons – played in the first series by Philip Brown and Todd Starke; her father, Buck Webb, was played by Denver Pyle. As the series progresses the situation becomes more confusing, however. Missing the city, Doris becomes a working mother, commuting back and forth to San Francisco where she works as a secretary on *Today's World* magazine. This leads to her promotion, whence she decides to take her family back to the city.

Then, in Series Four the dog and children inexplicably disappear and she falls in love with dishy Doctor Lawrence – aka British-born hellraiser Peter Lawford. In Britain the series was picked up late by ITV: they screened 26 episodes from the final series between 1972 and 1974, around the same time that the series ended in America.

Today, these shows with their canned laughter, might not always seem funny compared to modern-day humour. Indeed, some episodes follow in the 'too daft to laugh at' tradition of some of Doris' later films. That the humour was mostly contrived, certainly on Doris' part, probably goes without saying. She was very reluctant to work on the series and no matter how amusing the situation most of the time all that was in the back of her mind was how to earn enough money to pay off her debts. Nor was the show broadcast at a sensible time; whereas other sitcoms usually went out during the early evening, this one initially aired at 9.30pm on Tuesdays (Doris had wanted Friday or Saturday) when her younger fans were already in bed. In some episodes she makes a valiant attempt to redress issues of prejudice such as in the show where her sons have to choose classmates to portray their sisters in a television commercial for milk: Toby insists on a little black girl much to the dismay of the milk company.

A major topic throughout the series is of course her love of animals. In one episode an escaped tiger ends up in her kitchen; she feeds it milk from a saucer and when it escapes, she beats the hunters who want to kill it by lassoing it and murmuring pussycat endearments. Several of her co-stars turn up in the series, notably Billy DeWolfe, who plays semi-regular character Mr Jarvis, a camp-as-Christmas efficiency expert. There is even an episode where Doris almost becomes royalty. She meets a prince, takes him home for dinner (homemade stew) and after he learns that he has been deposed by a revolution back in Europe, she gets him to open a restaurant, where an accordionist serenades the customers with 'Que Sera, Sera'. It was all very silly but harmless fun.

Terry Melcher divided his time between acting as executive producer on *The Doris Day Show* and helping his mother through her darkest depression since her time with Al Jorden. He was also on the board of the Monterey Pop Festival, which he had helped organise back in 1967, and more recently he had become involved with Gram Parsons, the flamboyant, hugely charismatic country-rock singer who had worked with The Byrds and was currently fronting The Flying Burrito Brothers.

There is little denying that Terry developed a crush on 22-year-old Gram, who very quickly told him that he was not interested in that kind of a relationship whence they became close friends. The first time Gram visited Doris' house in Palm Springs – almost girlishly pretty, wearing shoulder-length hair and dressed in his trademark Nudie Cohen suit with its pills, marijuana and naked women embellishments – she considered him very strange indeed, though like Terry she soon succumbed to his charm. Gram Parsons, she declared, once she had heard him sing 'Hickory Wind' (her favourite Byrds' song which he had composed) would, with her son's backing, become a household name because his judgement had always been spot on.

Both Doris and Terry were traumatised when Gram almost died in a motorcycle accident. Terry also owned a powerful machine (which, on his mother's insistence, had not been taken out of the garage for some time) and Terry had been one of the first to ride pillion on Gram's new baby, a customised Harley Davidson with coffin-shaped fuel tank and starry-skies bodywork. This was a big bike for a big man and the two friends often roared around Gram's favourite Mojave Desert location without crash helmets. There, in the shade of the Joshua trees, they smoked pot and gazed up into the night sky, looking for UFOs. Like any proud 'parent', Gram had an aversion for mechanics, attending to minor repairs and servicing the machine himself. This included securing his loose front forks with a wire coathanger – a quick-fix which nearly cost him his life. One afternoon he was riding well within the speed limit through Bel Air when the coathanger snapped, causing him to swerve his front wheel and hit the kerb. The handlebars gave way, throwing him forwards and smashing his face into the tarmac. For a while it was touch and go. Doris and Terry regularly visited him at the nearby St Joseph's Hospital, where he underwent emergency surgery to relieve pressure on his brain. He remained in hospital for two weeks before he was allowed to return home to the bungalow that he was renting at the Château Marmont complex. Astonishingly, within days he was back on stage with The Flying Burrito Brothers.

In the autumn of 1969 it was Gram's turn to help out his friend when Terry found himself indirectly but dangerously connected to the horrific event that took place at 10050 Cielo Drive. This was the farmhouse built for French movie legend Michele Morgan and more recently purchased by Terry, who lived there with his actress girlfriend Candice Bergen. In August 1968 he and record scout Gregg Jakobson visited a 40-strong hippy commune founded by a certain Charles Manson, who had taken over the Spahn Ranch, a former Westerns' location near Topanga Canyon.

Born in 1934, Manson spent the better part of his life in corrective institutes, with his crimes ranging from shoplifting to armed robbery and from pimping to violent male rape. His commune was one of the first of such gatherings in America and Jakobson believed the set-up might have the makings of an interesting television documentary. For his part, Manson was more interested in securing a record deal with Terry, whose close friend The Beach Boys' Brian Wilson had befriended him the previous year. Returning from an engagement, Wilson picked up two female hitch-hikers and took them home with him. On learning that they were not only 'Manson Chicks' but also suffering from gonorrhea, as will be noted in the subsequent trial, he took them back to the commune anticipating fireworks from Manson, whose violence was legendary. Instead he expressed his gratitude by kissing Wilson's feet!

Wilson subsequently took the two girls under his wing and paid for their medical treatment, running up a bill of $100,000. He went on to enjoy jamming sessions with Manson and even paid for studio time to enable him to record a few of his neo-Pete Seeger compositions, convincing him of his 'talent' more through fear of not offending him than actually telling him the truth. This was where Terry and Gregg Jakobson entered the equation when they agreed to audition Manson and market the songs, should they deem them marketable. Terry, however, had other things on his mind: in December 1968 he split from Candice Bergen, blaming the break-up on pressures heaped on him as he had had to deal with the aftermath of Marty Melcher's death and declaring, oddly, that he wanted to suffer the pain of loneliness like his mother. He moved out of Cielo Drive and into Doris' beach house in Malibu, which had somehow been saved from the Receiver. The Cielo Drive property was rented out to Polish film director Roman Polanski and his actress wife Sharon Tate.

Though responsible for the ensuing carnage that would make his a household name, Charles Manson never actually killed anyone himself. On 8 August 1969 four members of his so-called 'Family' – Tex Watson, Susan Atkins, Patricia Krenwinkel and Linda Kasabian – turned up at the house, according to the FBI's initial report, looking for Terry. The concensus would later be that Manson sent them there, looking for no one in particular, and that he was eager to instigate his 'Helter Skelter' campaign in the wake of the April assassination of Martin Luther King, which would see him teaching white racists a lesson. Manson's yardstick was The Beatles' *White Album*, from which the name of his mission originated, which he claimed highlighted in code the world's projected social and racial turmoil. His proposed album, he declared, would similarly pave the way for the 'self-annihilation' of these racists.

Being a hard-headed businessman and impatient with time-wasters, Terry dismissed Manson's recordings as 'below average, nothing', though the real reason for not wanting to work with Manson owed more to the visit to the Spahn Ranch, where he witnessed him losing his temper and almost beating a drunken stuntman to death. According to the first FBI report, Manson therefore elected to exact his revenge. Unaware Terry was no longer living at Cielo Drive, his adherents instead murdered whoever else happened to be on the premises. Their first victim was 18-year-old Steven Parent, shot dead at the wheel of his car while approaching the building. Roman Polanski's friend, Wojciech Frykowski, was sleeping on the couch in the living room and battered almost beyond recognition, stabbed and shot twice. Frykowski's partner, coffee heiress Abigail Folger, was stabbed a total of 28 times on the front lawn as she tried to escape. Eight-months' pregnant Sharon Tate was stabbed 16 times and a rope tied around her neck while celebrity hairdresser Jay Sebring was stabbed and shot at close range. All the victims were mutilated after death and Tate's blood used to daub the word 'Pig' across the front door.

But the killing spree did not end there. It subsequently emerged that another Family member, Bobby Beausoleil, stabbed Family acquaintance Gary Hilman to death during a dispute over money. And the evening after the Cielo Drive murders, the same killers – accompanied by two more, and Manson himself, dissatisfied at the way they had dispatched Tate and her friend and eager to demonstrate 'how to do the job properly' – set off for an address in Los Angeles' Los Feliz district. This belonged to supermarket chief Leno LaBianca and his wife Rosemary. The house was next door to the one where the Family had attended a party the previous year and the LaBiancas are thought to have complained about the noise. Manson now ordered them to be tortured, stabbed and bayonetted. As before, their bodies were mutilated post-mortem, too.

For over a year anyone known to have been directly or indirectly involved with Charles Manson was pencilled in to be a witness at his trial and therefore deemed to be in grave danger. Even after

1 December, the date when the last of the killers was apprehended and put behind bars, on the outside people were still working for Manson. One of the prosecution witnesses, Barbara Hoyt, almost died when she ate a hamburger containing LSD. Another unnamed witness was found dead, presumed murdered. Ronald Hughes, one of the defence lawyers who fought against Manson having to take the stand and give evidence, disappeared and his decomposed body was later found on wasteground outside Los Angeles. Several 'Manson Chicks' very nearly succeeded in an attempt to hijack a plane and hold its passengers hostage – they planned on killing one every hour until Manson was released into their custody. When the police refused to help because he was not an 'A-class witness' Terry was forced to hire around-the-clock protection not just for himself, but also for Doris, who feared they might both be kidnapped.

The mere fact that Terry had once associated with Manson also earned him a place on the FBI's 'Suspicious Persons' list and he was interrogated at length; Doris, too, it is believed, just in case Terry had revealed any of Manson's plans to her. Several of the tabloids reported that he was actually a member of the Manson Family and involved in drug trafficking – untrue, of course. One reporter who collared him outside his house asked if the rumour was true that he had fathered several children in the commune, causing him to pull out from his wallet photos of Candice Bergen and other women he had dated and to offer the response, 'When I've got beauties like these to bed, why would I want to screw any of Manson's clap-ridden, unwashed dogs?'

At the Manson Family trial in January 1971 the case for the prosecution determined there had been no connection between the Tate and LaBianca killings and that the motive for both crimes appeared to have been to trigger off Manson's 'Helter Skelter' dream. Manson and his gang members were all found guilty and sentenced to death, though their sentences were later commuted to life. What is remarkable is that the verdicts were delivered without a single witness taking the stand so it turned out that Terry had been worrying over nothing. In May 2007 Manson appealed for the eleventh time against his sentence and again he was turned down. He is likely to remain in prison until he dies. Terry's former house was razed to the ground in 1994.

On 14 March 1971 CBS aired Doris' one-off television special, *The Doris Mary Anne Kappelhoff Show*, featuring special guest star Perry Como. This had been taped during the April of 1970 when she was at an all-time low though this does not show in the production. Following along the lines of the immensely popular Barbra Streisand specials (*Call Me Barbra*, etc.), it contained a series of song sketches and as much in-between patter as she could sensibly get away with. The major problem with the special is that at 51 minutes it is a good half-hour too short. It opens with an orange-clad dollybird Doris pedalling her bicycle through the town as she helps to deliver newspapers and milk while the overdub plays her recording of 'Secret Love'.

Ironically, considering what happened in the near future, in the next scene she reprimands a fleet of motorcyclists: 'Slow down, you move too fast!' Then the scenario cuts to the on-set garden, where she serenades several of her dogs with 'You Must Have Been A Beautiful Baby'. Enter Perry Como, who sings 'Didn't We?' before duetting beautifully with Doris on 'When You Were Sweet Sixteen', 'Everybody Loves A Lover' and several other standards. Wearing a fluffy yellow Elizabeth Taylor-like creation, Doris sings 'Quiet Nights' and then 'If I Had My Life To Live Over' – the tune is 'I'm Writing A Letter To Daddy', which a few years earlier was murdered by Bette Davis in *Whatever Happened To Baby Jane?*

There is a montage of her on-screen weeping scenes which leads to the 'surprise' not listed in the credits, of which Doris had of course been aware though the viewers were initially sucked in. She is wringing the tears out of her handkerchief and claiming to have cried more in her films than any other actress (which was probably true) when Rock Hudson marches up to her with a towel. Looking nothing like the heartthrob she had worked with in *Pillow Talk* (plumper and sporting a thick moustache), he was in the midst of shooting *Pretty Maids In A Row*, a decidedly unpleasant film which saw him playing very much against type as a psychopathic teacher who seduces under-age girls at his school and then murders them. In the 60-second sequence Doris introduces him as Roy Harold Fitzgerald (his real name), then as Tab Hunter. This was the real surprise for the in-joke slipped in by the scriptwriter – and which went over Doris' head – was that Tab Hunter had never made any secret of his homosexuality while Rock always fought to conceal his. In any case he returns for a kiss whence Doris sings 'Both Sides Now', a number which could not have been more appropriate for her at the time: she really had seen life from a good and bad perspective. She then closes with sensational versions of 'It's Magic' and 'Sentimental Journey' in a torchy setting, wearing white against a black background. Superb stuff!

Terry, who produced the television special, had wanted Doris to sing 'Que Sera, Sera' and the sequence was actually filmed. In the out-take she wears a beautiful pink flowing silk dress and dances with two male partners. For some reason, after viewing the rushes she decided the clip was inappropriate – in her depressive state she temporarily no longer believed in the maxim 'What will be, will be' – and there was a row with Terry when she demanded it be removed.

In fact Terry was feeling just as low as Doris and when she tried to offer him moral support once the special had been taped, he told her to mind her own business and promptly moved out of her beach house into a rented property in Benedict Canyon. She alone was responsible for the slump in his finances and morale, he declared, for marrying Marty Melcher in the first place. Although he retained the position of executive producer on her television series, for some months the title was nominal as he flung himself into his latest project – getting drunk and stoned out of his head every day aided by musician friends, most of whom have since died as a result of their excesses. Among them was acknowledged opiates expert Gram Parsons, who was drug addled much of the time though it would later emerge after his death that his accident had left him suffering from epilepsy. The 'strange turns' he kept having – one in front of Doris when Terry invited her for dinner – were on account of the medication he was taking.

Soon after this incident Terry moved to another rented property in Idyllwild, where he distanced himself from all but his very closest friends and lived off a diet of vodka and pills. Doris said at the time that she had been praying for something to happen which would bring him back into her life. Effectively, they were both brought to their senses – Gram Parsons persuaded Terry, very much against Doris' will to have his motorbike serviced and 'burn some serious rubber'. Terry was test-riding his bike, speeding on the road between Idyllwild and Palm Springs and supposedly en-route to make amends with his mother, when he crashed into an oncoming car while negotiating a precipitous mountain bend long designated an accident black spot. He catapulted over the handlebars and landed upright on his feet, shattering both legs on impact.

He was rushed to the nearby Hemet Valley Hospital, an establishment that in those days dealt with as many as 20 such accidents a week, all along the same stretch of road. Doris was contacted at once and when she arrived at the hospital she was told that her son had a total of 37 fractures and he might have to have both legs amputated below the knee. This did not happen but Terry suffered a relapse before surgeons could operate and he may well have been given the last rites when embolisms developed. Like Gram Parsons, whose turn it was now to visit him, he remained on the danger list for two weeks.

Doris, who had more or less abandoned her Christian Science beliefs in the year following Marty Melcher's death, readily agreed to Terry undergoing whatever surgery would be necessary to save him. Even so she left the last word to Mary Baker Eddy. The decision over whether her son would survive his ordeal was God's will, she said. If he died, this too would be God's will and she would have to deal with it accordingly. Gram Parsons' attitude was much more positive though his motives may have been slightly questionable: no less religious than Doris (in his youth he attended college to train as a pastor), he wanted his buddy fit and well so they could resume their good times together, top of the list being to complete the album they had discussed prior to the accident. When Doris felt that Mary Baker Eddy was not quite delivering the goods, she then turned towards other religious thinkers that she found more convincing. Her new inspirations, she said, were Joel Goldsmith and Kathryn Kuhlman. It was largely a case of searching for something to believe in since she had finally stopped believing in herself.

Goldsmith (1892–1964) started off with a Christian Science background and developed his own philosophies from the religion that were still regarded as foolhardy by critics and cynics. He claimed that his principles of study revealed the 'inner secrets' of the New Testament. 'God is Omnipresent, and therefore there is no escaping God, not even in sin,' he observed in *The Infinite Way*, published in 1948. 'In the moment that you have the actual feel of His Presence, which is Omnipresence, in that very moment these illusory appearances of sin, disease, death, lack, and limitation, evaporate.' Doris bought tape recordings of his lectures and played them on her bedside machine whenever she was unable to sleep.

Kuhlman (1907–76) travelled the world holding 'healing crusades'. In the 1960s and 1970s she had her own television show *I Believe In Miracles*. Her critics, however, denounced her as a crank and con-artist, something which annoyed Doris, who claimed to have been in the audience at Kuhlman's 'shrine' when a man who had not walked for 20 years suddenly got out of his wheelchair and marched onto the stage. To prove Kuhlman was genuine, in February 1975 she took her friend and several times co-star Billy De Wolfe to see her after he was diagnosed with terminal lung cancer. Once she had extended her arms towards him (she never touched her followers because, she claimed, the healing she effected came from God and not from herself), Kuhlman convinced him that he was cured. Four weeks later De Wolfe died. Doris is thought to have asked Kuhlman to visit Terry in hospital and to effect one of her 'miracles'. Once she learned the press would be there, Kulman declined, not wishing to be exposed as a fake, which she almost certainly was.

Terry's slow and painful recovery put he and Doris through the mill. Once the embolisms had been eradicated, the shattered bones in his legs needed to be manipulated back into place and the limbs reconstructed, an immensely traumatic procedure that had to be done without anaesthetic before surgeons could work on him. He remained in hospital off and on for six months while Doris tried her utmost to spend as much time with him as was possible between taping sessions at CBS. Otherwise Alma sat next to his bed while he cursed and raved. His abusive attitude towards his mother and grandmother was a combination of psychosis and cold turkey and anyone else might have given up on him. Doris, however, managed to persuade him to see a mental health specialist – a Dr Head, who offered a 'double-deal' and agreed to treat them both. She was still seeing Dr Head on a regular basis as late as 1975 when she published her autobiography.

In more lucid moments Terry welcomed visits from friends such as Gram Parsons and members of The Byrds – they were able to push him around the hospital grounds in his wheelchair and alleviated the tension by smoking pot when the nurses were not looking. To a certain extent reverting to his old habits calmed his temper tantrums and this was reflected in his attitude towards Doris and Alma, who, once he could get around with a walking frame, insisted on taking him back to Doris' house, where she had converted one of the guest-rooms into a mini-clinic. She made Terry agree never to get on a motorcycle again, a promise he made with his fingers crossed behind his back. She also gave her other 'children' – Philip Brown and Todd Starke, from her television show – a stern lecture about the dangers of two-wheel driving. While Brown listened, Starke did not, and Doris was devastated in May 1983 (shortly after declaring herself the happiest woman in the world following the birth of her only grandchild Ryan) to hear that Todd had been killed, aged just 21, in an accident remarkably similar to the one which almost claimed Terry.

Once he was out of hospital and almost recovered, Terry threw himself back into his work though he was still more interested in working with Gram Parsons than being involved in *The Doris Day Show*. It was he who persuaded Gram that he had been wasting his time over the last few years by being in a band – first, with The International Submarine band and then after his brief spell with The Byrds, fronting The Flying Burrito Brothers and squabbling much of the time because of the inferior talents of his fellow band members. For some time a co-produced album had been on the cards. Ten tracks were laid down during the winter of 1971–2 at Gram's expense – as co-heir to the Snively orange-groves millions, he was considerably wealthier than Terry would ever be and insisted on paying – but his friend's accident put paid to the project going any further. Terry had been home but after a few weeks A & M contacted him to say that they were withdrawing their funding. The album was abandoned and so too ended his friendship with Gram Parsons.

Gram left in a huff for England to work with the Rolling Stones while Terry returned to his mother's television series. On 20

September 1974 Terry received a telephone call from Parsons' entourage to inform him that his former friend had died, aged just 26, at the Joshua Tree Inn out in their favourite Mojave Desert location – not from a drugs overdose as was first suspected but due to a mix-up in the medication he had been taking for his epilepsy. What made his death all the more difficult for Terry to bear – and for Doris too for she had liked the young man – was that following an alleged pact with his road manager Phil Kaufman, made at the funeral of a friend wherein Gram is supposed to have declared his own horror of being buried, Kaufman and another friend stole his body from the mortuary and set fire to it in the desert. The songs that he and Terry worked on were posthumously released on an album that would remain timeless and unique: *Grievous Angel*.

Around this time Doris embarked on a mysterious one-year relationship with one of her former co-stars. She readily confesses this in her memoirs: how with tremendous difficulty she managed to keep it out of the press by neither admitting nor denying that she was having an affair with Don Genson, producer of her television series. Over the years there has been considerable speculation over her lover's identity. She gave away three clues: the man was married with three children; he had met her again on an adjacent studio lot while filming a television movie and had subsequently gone on to make his own series which was pulled after just one season. Finally, he had not been a leading man but a support with whom she had only acted in several scenes. This would more or less narrow things down to just four contenders: Steve Forrest, who had appeared in *It Happened To Jane*, had three children and had recently completed *The Hanged Man*; Cameron Mitchell, her love interest in *Love Me Or Leave Me*, similarly had three children and had appeared in any number of television movies that year. Neither of them, however, had had a series at the time of the affair. Clint Walker, on the other hand, had just finished filming *Killdozer* when he bumped into Doris at the CBS commissary –

along with four episodes of *Kodiak,* which saw him playing an Alaskan State Trooper tracking down killers. The series was dropped after just four episodes owing to poor ratings. On the negative side, so far as her 'evidence' was concerned, Walker had only one child. Then there was the outsider: Brian Keith, her co-star from *With Six You Get Eggroll.* Thrice-married Keith had just had the plug pulled on his own series *The Brian Keith Show.* He had fathered four children but adopted three more. It is possible of course that she juxtaposed certain aspects of the actors' careers to throw her readers off the scent. At the time of writing, for legal reasons it would not be deemed prudent to point a finger – which means that, like Doris herself, this author must be content in allowing the reader to keep on guessing!

There were rumours that she might return to the movies when, on 3 March 1974, Doris participated in the American Film Institute's tribute to James Cagney, who was presented with a Lifetime Achievement Award for his contribution to the film industry. The award was established the previous year when the recipient had been director John Ford. As such, from Doris' point of view the event that was watched by millions on TV turned out to be an evening of great hypocrisy. She was introduced onto the stage by Frank Sinatra as, 'The lady all of us love all of the time,' but graciously refrained from any response towards a man she despised. Of Cagney she enthused, 'Working with you was one of the happiest times of my life . . . and tonight you make the whole world feel good just because you are here!' Prior to the event the sponsors had asked her to sing 'Love Me Or Leave Me' but she made it very clear that she would not be singing in public again for the foreseeable future. Instead an out-take of her, aka Ruth Etting performing 'You Made Me Love You', was broadcast on a giant screen.

But that night only one thing was really on her mind: following a lengthy investigation, the next day Jerry Rosenthal was arraigned before the Superior Court of California on numerous charges of embezzlement. There was no jury and a staggering 2,550 exhibits submitted as evidence in a lengthy investigation that dragged on until the September. The case involved not just Doris but a whole host of celebrities swindled by the smooth-talking lawyer: Gordon MacRae, Ross Hunter, Van Johnson, Gogi Grant, Zsa Zsa Gabor, Kirk Douglas, Irene Dunne, Billy Eckstine, Dorothy Dandridge and George Hamilton represented but the tip of the iceberg. When the trial began, no one was sure if they would get their money back. Having placed his illegal earnings in a Swiss bank or so it was alleged, Rosenthal had no viable assets. However, the court listed six malpractice insurance companies so Doris was hoping she might be able to recover some of her missing millions from them.

It was a costly affair: the legal fees for the 12 prosecuting lawyers amounted to almost $300,000. For Doris, or so she claimed, the money Rosenthal had taken from her was less important than finding out, once and for all, whether her late husband was villain or dupe. By the end of the proceedings, no one would be any the wiser: Marty Melcher played his cards close to his chest and covered his tracks so well there was no way of knowing how involved he had been. One of the first revelations was that some years earlier he had paid $25,000 to an accounting company to 'investigate Rosenthal's investments' and their subsequent report condemned him as untrustworthy. Doris had known nothing of this. It also emerged that despite Melcher's protests that his partner had been on the level, Doris *had* suspected the lawyer of cooking the books and had apparently told him so to his face as a result of which on at least three occasions he attempted to sue her and have her declared a vexatious litigant.

Rosenthal also did his best to decimate Doris' good name by refusing to furnish her lawyer with the names of the witnesses that he would be bringing to court, something he was legally obliged to do. Doris, he declared, had given birth to an evil man, who, having been a member of the Manson Family, would arrange to have them bumped off before they set foot in the building! The judge, Lester E. Olson, threatened him with contempt of court should he fail to comply. One of the witnesses brought in by the other claimants petitioned for the judge to take into consideration that Dorothy Dandridge had killed herself after finding out that Rosenthal's dodgy investments had bankrupted her. Some time later it emerged that the *Carmen Jones'* star, almost certainly suffering from a bi-polar disorder, had most likely overdosed on a mixture of the Imipramine she had been taking for depression and the painkillers prescribed for an injury to her ankle.

Rosenthal's method of fleecing Doris had been to take 10 per cent of her earnings, then 10 per cent of the 25 per cent Marty Melcher had been paying himself. As had happened with Gordon MacRae, he also invested several million dollars of Doris' money in sham Land Bank bonds. Both MacRae and Doris were chided by the judge for not knowing they were being taken in when everyone around them apparently did. She sniffed back the tears as he pronounced, 'Miss Day, you have been too busy making movies to pay any attention to your real affairs!' Indeed, the mind boggles as to how she could not have known what had been going on almost the entire length of her marriage. Additionally, she had unwittingly paid astronomical fees for 'legal work' that had never been necessary in the first place and bought into non-existent oil wells, hotel developments, cattle franchises and fuel ventures. This had been going on for 20 years. It further emerged that Rosenthal had had a trust account into which he paid almost $3 million of her earnings and twice that amount from his other clients.

Jerry Rosenthal was found guilty as charged and Judge Olson announced, 'The Union Bank, Beverly Hills Regional Office, is ordered to pay over the trust funds presently on deposit the sum of $30,684,69.' Of this, Doris was to receive $22,835,646, detailed in the court records as follows:

Oil and gas ventures: $5,589,000, plus interest of
   $1,956,150.
Hotel ventures: $3,437,000, plus interest of $1,956,150.
Global Industries & Guided Space Transmissions:
   $137,500, plus interest of $48,125.
Land Bank Bonds & Tax Malpractice: $534,675, plus
   interest of $186,900.
House Purchase & Tax Malpractice: $15,763, plus interest
   of $5,517.
Damages re. fees paid to Rosenthal: $2,268,538, plus
   interest of $793,800.
Recovery of fees for the above: $252,600, plus interest of
   $88,410.
Recovery of loans made by Marty Melcher to Rosenthal:
   $219,375, plus interest of $76,781.
Damages re. wrongful retention of records by Rosenthal:
   $16,329.
Attorney's fees for Doris Day & Terry Melcher: $850,000.
Punitive damages to the above: $1,000,000.
Fraudulent trust fund damages: $2,965,358, plus interest of
   $1,037,875.

Naturally, she was ecstatic. 'It was over,' she later observed. 'God in his heaven had smiled upon Clara Bixby, and the forces of evil had been put to rout.' What she did not add was that Rosenthal's lawyers appealed against the judge's decision and this process endured until August 1985 when she ended up with but a fraction of the money originally swindled from her. The exact amount was not made public but is thought to have been no more than $3 million.

Chapter 11

'Gonna Take A Sentimental Journey'

'Much as I admired Doris Day for her work, I could only
condemn her for putting those goddam animals first and not
supporting Rock Hudson when he was dying.'

Marlene Dietrich

By the end of 1974, as her passion for animals took over,
Doris Day fans might have been forgiven for thinking
that she had started to wind down her career as an
entertainer. To her way of thinking, animals were far more
important than humans: they never answered back, they rarely
outlived you and they were always unyielding with their affection.
In a similar way to Brigitte Bardot they would take over her life and
offer an unselfish anodyne to the unsatisfactory marriages that had
blighted both actresses' lives. Writing for *American Weekly*,
Richard Gehman already summed this up as far back as the
summer of 1963 when he observed, 'It may well be that animals are
the beneficiaries of [Doris Day's] affections because she has
worked so hard all her life and simply hasn't had time enough to
cultivate more complicated relationships.' With the change of
direction would also come a change of tactics in so far as voicing
her opinion was concerned: for years she had suffered in silence,
on and off the set, when compelled to work on projects very much

against her will. Only on rare occasions had she ever complained or even opined about a co-star but now, in retirement, she would finally have her say on the issues that mattered to her and not care two hoots who she offended if she believed they were harming animals.

The Rosenthal trial proved to be her last public performance and with her debts finally settled (and still aged only 50) she made it clear outside the courthouse that there would be no more films. For the final day of the trial she even dressed down: wearing horn-rimmed spectacles and with her hair up under a tweed hat. She managed to age herself by a good ten years, not that many saw through the charade and behind the disguise she was still a beautiful woman. Additionally she was considered 'old hat' by her record company when her voice was actually still in its prime but it was she herself who decided there would be no more records. Of course she could have gone to another company – all the major studios would have snapped her up in an instance. The truth is, martinet or not, she simply could not function without the steering hand of a Svengali and the only one she had ever wanted had been Marty Melcher. From now on fans would have to make do with a handful of half-hearted chat show appearances, most of these around 1975 while promoting her autobiography. Time and again she was asked to sing; always she declined – and not always politely when the demands became too overzealous. On *The Tonight Show*, she almost snapped fellow guest Carole Wayne's head off when she told the audience that she disliked animals. 'Shut up,' she mouthed under her breath, before levelling, 'People don't take care of their own children so if they don't do that, they won't take care of their animals!'

Among the projects that she turned down over the coming years was *West Side Waltz*, based on the play by Ernest Thompson which in 1978 enjoyed a successful run on Broadway with Katharine Hepburn as the aging, arthritic pianist who cuts herself off from the rest of the world, the exception being crotchety neighbour, violinist Cara Varnum – the role *Teacher's Pet* director George Seaton originally wanted Doris to play. Fearing she might be pigeon-holed with the likes of latter-day schlock horror heroines Bette Davis and Joan Crawford, she turned the part down. The film was made in 1995 with Shirley MacLaine and Liza Minnelli. She was also short-listed for the role of Jessica Fletcher in the television series *Murder She Wrote*. 'Give it to Angela Lansbury,' she is said to have told the producers – who did just that. In 1993 she was approached for the part of an unnamed female detective in a proposed series to compete against Lansbury. Again, the answer was no. The only role she had ever been interested in playing, she declared, was mother to Terry and now her ever-increasing collection of dogs.

Back to 1974, and Doris travelled to Las Vegas to see her childhood heroine, Ella Fitzgerald, now said to be ailing but vocally perfect as ever. Ella was appearing with Frank Sinatra and the Count Basie Band at the Circus Maximus. Doris was offended by the comedian MC Pat Henry, who stared at her as he pulled an ice-cube out of his whisky glass and announced, 'Just like my wife – a lump of ice with a hole!' She then accused him of blasphemy for introducing Sinatra with, 'Fill this orchestra pit with water and Frank will walk on it. I wish they would make Frank the next Pope – then I'd only have to kiss his ring!'

Before the show she met Ella in her dressing room and Sinatra's aide invited her to sit at his table with 50 or so other 'personal guests' who had actually paid over the odds to get in. Sinatra ignored her completely; he had not enjoyed working with her in *Young At Heart*, and they had not seen each other since. What really peeved him, however, was that when Doris had entered the auditorium his fans had given her a standing ovation. After the show many of them eschewed waiting at the stage door to catch a glimpse of him dashing out to his car (ignoring those who had put him on the map and muttering obscenities under his breath) because Doris had the patience to stand in the foyer chatting to them and signing autographs.

In Las Vegas she stayed at the MGM Grand Hotel, where her entrances-exits to the building saw her mobbed by hundreds of fans. Several entrepreneurs contacted her, begging her to return to the city with her own one-woman show. The manager of the Tropicana Hotel offered her $50,000 for three concerts and promised to donate the same amount to what was then her main charity: Actors & Others For Animals. She told him she would do one show provided all the money went to the charity – she would permit this to be filmed, she added, but there would have to be no audience. But she had not sung live since leaving Les Brown and even in those days her nerves were shot to pieces before she even stepped onto the platform; she dreaded to think what they might be like now, 30 years on. The Riviera Club made a similar offer. Doris agreed that she would sing there but only 'for the lunchtime rush'. The establishment, of course, was closed during the day.

In February 1975 CBS aired her second and last television special, *Doris Day Today*, a mish-mash of comedy, song and animal politics where all of the guests did their utmost to steal the limelight. She opened the proceedings with a stomping 'Anything Goes' – into which first guest Sammy Davis Jr interjected with the line, 'And black's white today,' at her insistence. Also appreciated were her duets with John Denver and her reading of 'Day By Day' – not her former signature tune but the song from the musical *Godspell*. The quality of the show varied however. She was joined by Tom Conway and comedian and impersonator Rich Little – some of whose sequences are hard to watch. Doris went on to sing 'Everybody Loves A Lover', then 'Love Me Or Leave Me' and 'Secret Love' while Little pulls faces and clowns around, impersonating Doris Day co-stars Cagney, Sinatra, Grant and Gable. In Britain Morecambe and Wise were executing similar send-ups with personalities such as Shirley Bassey and Nana Mouskouri but the attempt at this type of humour was not so slickly pulled off, even when he sang the self-referential 'Que Sera, Sera'.

Around this time Doris was guest of honour when Terry married at a friend's house in Rancho Santa Fe. The press was in attendance but all they were really interested in was whether Doris was thinking of tying the knot again – obviously they were referring to her rumoured affair with producer Don Genson. Her response was that she had no intention of heading down the same road as Elizabeth Taylor and Zsa Zsa Gabor, who were jokes, she considered. Her three marriages, she added, had all been mistakes though some good had come out of one of them – Terry. A few months later she observed in her memoirs that if there ever was going to be another man in her life then he would have to be, 'Someone who will turn me on sexually, but also someone who is as turned on by listening to Joel Goldsmith tapes and reading his books as I am.' With such aspirations cynics at the time predicted she would probably die an old maid. Of course what they did not know was that she was still seeing her secret lover.

It therefore came as a big surprise when Doris announced that she was going to marry husband Number Four. Neither was the new spouse from her own side of the showbusiness fence. Forty-one-year-old prematurely greying Barry Comden, 11 years her junior, managed the Old World Eatery restaurant chain: Doris befriended him when, on her way out of his Palm Springs restaurant, he had given her a bag of meat scraps for her dogs. The ceremony took place at a friend's house in Carmel – the coastal town where Doris had filmed the locations for *Julie* – on 14 April 1976. 'At last, I'm romantically fulfilled,' she told journalists. 'Barry's a beautiful person and we have a marvellous relationship, the most marvellous I've ever had!'

Newfound joy more or less put paid to her ever working again though the popularity of her films and sales of her albums showed no signs of abating. Almost a decade after she last faced a camera, readers of *Film Weekly* voted her third most popular actress in America after Barbra Streisand and Julie Andrews. That same year she stepped up her work with animal charities. For some time she had been an active fund-raiser for Actors and Others for Animals, founded in 1971 by actor Richard Basehart and his wife. She was also involved with Cleveland Amory's high-profile Fund For Animals. In 1987, with $100,000 of her own money and regular injections of cash to keep the project going, she set up her own foundation, the Doris Day Animal League, primarily because the other organisations did not have funding for strays and most of her own dogs had been such. It was set up to provide veterinary care and food for these animals and to counteract animal abuse through a sub-organisation called Beyond Violence: The Human Connection. Doris firmly believed that animals, just the same as children, should have the best protection possible against abusive owners. In those days she was often seen walking the streets of Carmel, her home since 1981 – according to one ungallant report, 'looking like a bag-lady' while rounding up animals abandoned by their owners.

To help prevent unwanted puppies, Doris set up a National Spay Day to be held in February each year. Research on her behalf brought home the startling news that one in four American pets was being put to sleep for no other reason than they had been neglected by their owners. 'We're all here together, animals and people,' she told *OK! Magazine* in 1996, 'and animals have taught me such a lot. They're loyal and joyful, and they're *so* grateful. Even if you holler at them the dogs never get mad and people could learn from that.'

In the meantime what she had still not learned was how to hang onto a successful marriage: the relationship with Barry Comden, like those with Al Jorden and George Weidler, proved short-lived. By the end of 1979 they had drifted apart – there were no press reports of any feud or indeed any reason for this – and by 1981 they were divorced.

The next major event in her life involved her close friend Rock Hudson, whom she had not seen for a while – at least not in person, though she had been following his character's storyline on *Dynasty* with some trepidation. Rock began working on the TV series in October 1984 – the producer Esther Shapiro assigned him the part of ranch-owner Daniel Reece during a trip to Paris, where Rock had been secretly having experimental treatment not just for HIV but full-blown AIDS on the pretext that he was guest-of-honour at the Deauville Film Festival. Only his closest friends were aware of his illness or his sexuality for that matter – he even kept the diagnosis from his current lover Marc Christian, who Doris is thought to have once met.

Hudson's scenes in *Dynasty* playing Crystal Carrington's lover and the father of Sammy Jo (Heather Locklear) were unquestionably the most heartbreaking of his career. Occasionally he has to break a line to gasp for breath and in one scene, where Crystal (Linda Evans) gives him a gentle shove, he is hard pushed not to lose his balance. It is obvious that he is deteriorating rapidly between episodes. Yet everything he does remains utterly natural and charismatic in contrast to the frequently over-the-top amateurism of most of his colleagues who, when called to play opposite him in a scene, were automatically demoted to second-rate hams.

Doris had known for some time that Rock was gay and found part of the storyline hilarious: Daniel Reece's daughter is enamoured of Crystal's openly-gay stepson Steven and she tells her father, 'I never would have married Steven if I'd known he was gay, no matter how much money he had.' Like Rock, with whom she later compared notes, she was also amused by the more than probable 'fuck-buddies' relationship between Daniel and his best friend Dex Dexter played by Michael Nader. What she did not know was how much Rock agonised over the scene where he had to kiss Linda Evans for his doctors had warned him that the AIDS virus could be transmitted via saliva and he had open sores in his mouth. The scene was filmed but nothing more was said about it until July 1985 when thousands of Linda Evans' fans accused him of deliberately putting her life at risk.

Watching him fade before her eyes caused Doris considerable distress. Like everyone else not too closely connected to him, she assumed he was suffering from either anorexia or cancer – his press-office had suggested both. She became even more alarmed when, in January 1985, she saw pictures of Rock arriving at the Golden Globes, arms linked with Elizabeth Taylor and Liza Minnelli. By now his weight had dropped from 225 to 180 pounds. Aware he might not have long to live, she told herself that she would like to work with him one last time. Even so, it took her until June of that year to call her friend because it had taken her that long herself to pluck up the courage, at 61, to make another television series. This one was to be called *Doris Day's Best Friends* – there would be 26 episodes in all – for the Christian Broadcast Network and the first was to be taped on 16 July. Though she had no intention of singing in the series, Terry provided the theme song 'My Buddy' for her to record and sing over the credits. The 'best friends' of the title were not of the human genre but the pets she had collected along the way: dogs, cats and horses. Such was her enthusiasm for the project once she warmed to the idea – suggested to her by Terry, who would be part-scripting the series – that she allowed him to coax her back into the recording studio for the first time in almost 20 years, barring the backing vocals she added in 1974 to his *Terry Melcher* album.

Doris was convinced she was now vocally beyond her prime and there was seemingly no way of anyone persuading her otherwise. The *What A Day For Daydream* album which she would record over several afternoons in the September, contained 11 songs mostly with animal themes and she sounds as superb as ever! 'Stuval Was A Racehorse' had been popularised by Joan Baez, 'Crocodile Rock' was composed by Elton John and 'An Octopus' Garden' by The Beatles. The other tracks (see Appendix II) included such oddities as 'Disney Girls' and 'Ryan's On His Way To The Round-Up', the song about her only grandchild.

The show's producer set up a press conference in Carmel to which representatives of every major publication in the States were invited. *Life* magazine agreed to do a picture-spread: Doris and Rock would appear on the cover. One newspaper hailed the event as being 'the biggest show business reunion of the decade'. There was even talk of the two of them making another film together. 'Their bedroom banter was a hit in the racy-sounding but ultra-chaste movie *Pillow Talk*,' observed *People* magazine's Guy Garcia. 'Twenty-six years later, Doris Day and Rock Hudson are still chatting about petting – petting animals, that is.'

Rock's doctors and friends begged him not to do the show because he looked so dreadfully ill. He now weighed 170 pounds and could hardly stand on his feet on occasion. But he refused to listen. Well aware that this would be his swansong, on 15 July he flew out to Carmel. The actual taping of the show went well, though he turned up late, wearing old clothes and with unkempt hair and moustache. At one stage he stumbled and he trembled noticeably when Doris wrapped her arms round him and called him her 'best buddy'. She was so shocked by his appearance that she wanted to cancel the show until he was feeling a little stronger but he would not hear of it. Asked point-blank what was wrong with his client, his manager delivered the same spiel as he had to everyone else: Rock was suffering from the flu. For the moment the AIDS word would not be printed: to the layman, including Doris, his sunken eyes, hollow cheeks and ghastly yellow tinge indicated he must have cancer, possibly of the liver.

His contribution to *Doris Day's Best Friends* was a skit on *Pillow Talk* and opens with the familiar split screen. Two pals are chatting on the phone while she arranges roses in a vase and he is at home, getting ready to leave for the show. Doris expresses her delight that he has consented to appear. However, the budget cannot stretch to him flying so he must catch the bus – which he does, turning up in an old banger that she goes to meet in a country lane. They then drive off in a buttercup-yellow convertible. Finally, in Doris' garden and surrounded by her dogs, they talk over old times. Then Rock climbs back into his bus and as this drives away, she sings 'My Buddy'. Her original choice had been Elton John's 'Crocodile Rock', which she had been rehearsing in the studio with Terry and his long-time music partner Bruce Johnston with a view to putting it out as a single release. The tableau is intended to be hilariously funny but Rock looks so feeble, gaunt and prematurely aged that it is almost impossible to watch without shedding tears. Not only did Doris change her mind about releasing the single, she subsequently abandoned the album.

It has never been established whether Rock actually told her the truth about his illness or if she worked it out for herself. She has steadfastly refused to speak about this period in her friend's life and she was still biting back the tears when she brushed off the politely persuasive Gloria Hunniford at the end of 1994 in a British television interview to honour her seventieth birthday. 'It was shattering,' she responded, 'but enough of that. Let's think of him with laughter because he was *so* funny!'

By the end of July, two weeks after working with Doris, the truth came out when Rock was taken ill in Paris and the Hôpital Americain de Nevilly released a statement that he had AIDS. This came as double shock for his fans – most of them never had the slightest inkling that he was gay. The announcement coincided with the photographs of Rock and Doris taken in Carmel – in particular, an unposed head-and-shoulders taken from a larger picture of them together – being wired to press offices around the world. Over the next few days the public were fed the most lurid resumé of his personal life – very dubious 'exclusives' acquired from suspicious sources: insiders, talent scouts, so-called close friends and prominent doctors, who were of course unnamed and in almost every instance pure editorial fiction, the oldest trick in the book.

Rock was flown back to Los Angeles and he was transferred by helicopter, gravely ill, to the UCLA Medical Center where visitors were counselled before being ushered into the sickroom so that they would not let him see how shocked they were by his appearance. He received over 30,000 letters, get-well cards and gifts from fans and colleagues. Madonna, Ava Gardner and Marlene Dietrich were three who publicly expressed admiration for his courage. Elizabeth Taylor, always the champion of the oppressed gay man, put him in touch with the Shanti Foundation, a Los Angeles organisation which had set up a telephone hotline for AIDS sufferers who did not wish to be seen visiting their centre. Elizabeth visited him every day despite the fact that some days he could keep nothing down and the stench of the sickroom was overpowering. Nancy Reagan announced that she and Ronald would visit him once he got out of the hospital but this was prevented by the White House administration for fear of offending the moral majority. Likewise, Doris made no contact with him at all, leading to some speculation that, with her Christian Science background, she was prejudiced and among those who condemned AIDS as God's revenge on the gay community. Her lack of communication certainly put her in a bad light, considering the sheer size of her gay fan-base.

On 19 September Elizabeth Taylor and Shirley MacLaine, who had already raised a great deal of money for AIDS charities, organised a benefit dinner for Rock in Los Angeles. Their aim was to raise $250,000 – the same amount that Rock had donated to his own foundation. Among those who attended were Gregory Peck, Linda Evans and Burt Reynolds. Elizabeth's gay actor friends who gave generally insisted on anonymity and did not show up on the evening. Doris was invited but was unable to attend. 'She's more interested in her fucking animals than she is in saving human lives!' Rock's secretary Mark Miller told one journalist. However, on the broadcast of her show on 2 October 1985, which starred a very sick-looking Rock Hudson but was aired after his death, Doris gave a personal and touching eulogy. Later, Doris got into hot water with humanist groups. 'When they do find something they think might cure this thing,' she told Reuters in a statement that she would repeat over the years, 'I hope they test the drugs on convicted murderers and not on innocent animals. These people are getting clothed and fed at the expense of fools like you and me. It's about time it stopped.' Later, in another syndicated press release, she would add that maybe some of the nation's criminals might be willing to offer themselves up for testing. 'I think they would *want* to do it, to give back to society what they've taken from it,' she said. 'I think it would make them feel better. *I* would volunteer if I'd done something horrendous like those people on Death Row!'

Rock Hudson had some unexpected visitors before he left this world. During the last days of his illness when he was bedridden and attached to an intravenous drip, a woman – described by Tom Clark as 'a religious nut' – inveigled her way into his home, announcing that she had brought him a message from God. Despite being a lapsed Catholic, he received visits from ultra-clean-cut singer and born-again Christian Pat Boone, accompanied by his wife and three daughters. They turned up on the evening of 1 October for a laying-on-of-hands ceremony, claiming that if Rock – now down to a pitiful 98 pounds – dressed in the clothes they had chosen for him, the 'cancer' would leave his body. The next morning, at 8.45am, he died in his sleep.

While Elizabeth Taylor organised a crack security team to prevent the press from getting a shot of the corpse within three hours Rock was cremated. Doris finally broke her silence with a statement to the press:

> This is when our faith is tested. All of those years I worked with him, I saw him as big, handsome and indestructible. I'm saddened by this and all I can do is uplift myself: life is eternal – I hope we'll meet again.

The episode of *Doris Day's Best Friends* featuring Rock Hudson should have aired on 2 October 1985, the very day he died and the Christian Broadcast Network were all for putting it out until Doris contacted them, accusing them of 'crass insensitivity'. It was broadcast the following week, preceded by a filmed message – the first time any of Rock's friends had actually shown their faces on television to pay tribute to this much-loved, remarkable man, fearful that being associated with a gay man who had succumbed to AIDS might prove detrimental to their careers. 'All his friends, and there were many, could always count on Rock Hudson,' said Doris, tearfully concluding, 'I feel that without my deep faith I would be a lot sadder than I am today. I know that life is eternal and that something good is going to come from this experience.'

The series unfortunately proved little better than so-so. Millions tuned in to watch the episode with Rock Hudson, urged by curiosity and the tabloid furore brought about by his death. And when they discovered their idol was no longer interested in singing – despite her excitement at having Les Brown and His Band of Renown on the show, Doris *mimed* to an earlier recording of 'Sentimental Journey' – they turned off in their thousands. Only the faithful, and the animal lovers, stayed tuned in to hear her talking about vaccinations, veterinary care, dogs for the blind, cosmetics and drug-testing and other issues – that was when she was actually on the screen for as the series progressed, audiences saw less and less of her. In Britain despite heavy sales' tactics from the Christian Broadcast Network, none of the major channels were interested in buying the series.

From the end of 1985 Doris lived the life of a virtual recluse at her 11-acre estate in Carmel, emerging but rarely from her enforced solitude and mostly for functions concerned with her all-important animal charities. In 1988 she and Terry bought the Cypress Inn, a Spanish-style hotel in the centre of Carmel, simply because she had heard of clients complaining about its strict 'no animals' policy, and she wanted to change the rules.

In 1989 she appeared in a television documentary, *I Don't Even Like Apple Pie*, devised by Christopher Frayling of the BBC. Frayling and his team travelled to Carmel, where the 50-minute programme was filmed at the Cypress Inn – Doris would never allow cameras inside her home primarily because her dogs had the run of the place and she did not like to interrupt their routine. It is not exemplary. Much of the time she is shot in soft-focus, sitting next to a window, and she is more interested in speaking about her animal charities – her condition for appearing in the first place – than discussing her career. Frayling also appears to have left the best bits out. Like Elizabeth Taylor in her later years, Doris was fond of reaching for the Kleenex for best effect and there had certainly been almost as much drama in her life as there had in Elizabeth's. Her tears are only seen at the end of the piece when she thanks her fans – and sincerely so – for their loyal support over the years. Frayling also lets his cloying admiration get in the way of major issues such as discussing the men in her life. Only once does he become confrontational when he broaches the subject of Mamie Van Doren's nasty attitude towards her alleged 'temperamental' episode while they were making *Teacher's Pet*. Van Doren's memoirs had recently been published so she was currently in the media spotlight. 'She is not well,' Doris says of her.

'This lady is making it up . . . I feel sorry for her to say something like that. I don't *behave* like that!'

Another documentary, *Sentimental Journey*, was broadcast in the United States in November 1991. Two years later Doris appeared in two televised interviews filmed in Carmel at a *Doris Day's Best Friends'* fund-raiser. For the Christmas of that year, but only in Britain and Australasia, Vision Records released *The Love Album*, a collection of standards she had recorded early in 1968. At that time she handed the tapes over to Terry for safekeeping, and, as had later happened with his Gram Parsons' sessions, these were 'misplaced' – though to be fair, he had had his hands full in the wake of Marty Melcher's death.

Effectively her swansong (until her never-released sessions of 1985 resurface), this is a very intimate body of work, as if Doris is singing to the listener on a one-to-one basis. The work reflects her personal psychoses, joys, sorrows, hopes and ultimate peace of mind. Abject solitude is represented by Judy Garland's secondary theme 'All Alone', hope by way of 'If I Had To Live My Life Over' and tranquility is 'Sleepy Lagoon', long the theme of the British Radio 4 programme, *Desert Island Discs* which regularly features 'castaways' taking a Doris Day record to their imaginary island. In a class of their own are her dreamy interpretations of Ferde Gofe's 'My Wonderful One' and Elvis Presley's 'Are You Lonesome Tonight?'

In 1994 she was filmed for British television appearances on *Pebble Mill At One* and *The Des O'Connor Show*. The world's newspapers and magazines fared little better in their attempts to woo her out of retirement. In truth she was not interested in making a comeback though she pretended this might happen for the sake of keeping her name in lights – anything to raise money for her beloved animals. 'If I find the right role, I'll consider acting again just to take a break,' she would tell *OK! Magazine* in 1996. 'I've never worked so hard – I think making a movie might give me some free time!' Nor was she interested in discussing her personal life and career. If anyone wanted an audience, she declared, the subject would have to be animals – period. The tiny episode where her little dog was run over after dashing out into the road was ceaselessly repeated to eager media hounds who tolerated the same, now-dull anecdote in the hope that she might just release some snippet of information about the men in her life, or more importantly if there had been anyone else since Barry Comden but she always remained tight-lipped.

Doris Day was dead while Doris Kappellhoff was alive and well and living in Carmel. If one of her dogs died, she would talk for hours about its intellect and the way they had connected – her dogs loved watching her movies and the feedback, she said, was always positive, leading cynics to draw the conclusion that she might be spending too much time with her dogs. Whenever a co-star passed away, she would send no message of sympathy to the bereaved relatives. James Cagney, Howard Keel, Frank Sinatra, Jack Lemmon, David Niven, Gene Nelson and Gordon MacRae all went to their graves without comment, positive or otherwise, from Doris Day. As the re-committed (following her lapse, after Marty Melcher's death) Christian Scientist, in her world there were no such words as death and mourning.

Her last offer of a film role, so far as is known, occurred in 1995 when she was approached by actor-director Albert Brooks and asked to star in his *Mother*, which told of a failed, 40-something science-fiction writer. Having never got along with his mother, he elects to move back in with her to resolve their differences. Brooks' first choice had been long-retired actress Nancy Reagan, who expressed interest but eventually turned down the role for personal reasons – it later emerged that she was nursing husband Ronald through the latter stages of Alzheimer's. Doris refused the part for no other reason than she had always had a very close relationship with her own son and did not wish anyone to confuse the actress with the character. Brooks signed up Debbie Reynolds: the role won her numerous awards and she was also nominated for a Golden Globe.

On 23 June 2004, two months after her eightieth birthday, Doris (who had offended some of her peers by refusing an honorary Oscar) – 'If they couldn't offer me one before, why bother me now when I could be dying?' – was awarded the Presidential Medal of Freedom with the citation, 'In recognition of her distinguished service to her country'. 'Doris Day became an American icon as an actress and singer,' President George W. Bush told the gathering. 'She captured the hearts of Americans while enriching our culture and it was a good day for our fellow creatures when she gave her good heart to the cause of animal welfare.' But she was conspicuous by her absence: there was no way that she was getting on a plane at her age, she said, not even for an audience at the White House!

On 19 November 2004 the bottom dropped out of her world when, following a long battle against skin melanoma, Terry died, aged 62. One of his last public appearances had been in the BBC's *Hollywood Greats* series when he had shown the camera crew around his mother's former Los Angeles home. Bloated and pale, he had found walking difficult. Terry was survived by his second wife Terese and his son Ryan from his first marriage – the boy had appeared several times as a special guest on *Doris Day's Best Friends*. The press was merciless, gathering outside Doris' home around the clock in the hope of forcing her to emerge and to give an interview. But she did not, and so far as is known, she has never spoken about her greatest loss.

In October 2005, from behind the locked doors of her home, Doris donated $20,000 to mount 'Operation Paris' – to airlift 130 cats and dogs out of North Iberia, Louisiana, following one of the state's worst disasters. The animals were all taken to the Santa Cruz SPCA kennels. She told columnist Liz Smith, whom she had never liked, over the phone, 'These precious angels are the silent victims of Hurricane Katrina. I'm so grateful that we can contribute to this humanitarian effort.' In her syndicated column, Smith observed somewhat cynically, as was her wont, 'Doris is shaking the blues away – just don't expect to see her doing it in public any time soon.'

In September 2006 the Doris Day Animal Foundation joined forces with the Humane Society of the United States, the country's largest animal protection league that boasted over 10 million members. Her last public appearance of sorts (from within the safety of her Carmel home), took place in May 2007 when she established an annual vets scholarship in Terry's memory. 'The veterinarians and staff are miracle workers,' her press statement read, 'and I'm delighted that our gift will help train future veterinarians'. For once she even allowed a photographer into her home to snap the official portrait – the first glimpse most fans had had of her for some time. The photograph may have later been touched up by the studio: even so, she belied her 83 years, giving just the glimmer of hope that she might one day step back in front of a movie camera, even in a cameo role. She never did.

Epilogue

Unlike Lauren Bacall and Elizabeth Taylor, who since retiring from the movies have kept their names in lights – Bacall has been making personal appearances to reminisce over her glory years with Humphrey Bogart while Liz has been dominating the headlines with health scares and promoting her new range of jewellery – Doris Day seems to have been never more content to slip back into the shadows. Indeed, she has become so reclusive that many may be excused for wondering if she is still alive!

In September 2006, The Who's Pete Townshend caused a minor stir by writing a song, 'Mirror Door', which the group included in their first studio album since 1984. In this, Townshend laments some of his favourite dead icons: Elvis Presley, Buddy Holly, Bobby Darin, Eddie Cochran . . . and Doris Day! 'I was absolutely convinced she was dead,' he said at the time, 'but then I went to the internet and there she was, with a happening website!'

At least one of the organisers of the Grammy awards is thought to have believed this, too, when their board elected to give her a

Lifetime Achievement Award at the end of 2007. 'We had to check, just to make sure,' a spokesman said. Burt Bacharach, violinist Itzhak Perlman and the other recipients turned up at the bash in January 2008, but as had happened with all her previous awards, Doris was conspicuous by her absence.

Over the last few years there have been numerous reports of a figure – according to one Reuter story, 'looking like a little old bag-lady' – stealing through the streets of Carmel in the middle of the night, sometimes alone, most often with an assistant, rounding up stray dogs and emaciated cats and secreting them into her car. Could this be Doris Day, a latter day female St Francis, doing what she has always felt most comfortable with?

Maybe it is best to remember Hollywood's golden girl in her hey-day. Maybe we should just close our eyes and picture her smooching Rock Hudson – or maybe just drop that DVD into the machine and enjoy watching Calamity Jane riding the roof of the Deadwood Stage, giving those 'injuns' what for before setting our pulses racing with her stunning rendition of 'Secret Love'.

Appendix 1:
The Films Of Doris Day

ROMANCE ON THE HIGH SEAS   WARNER BROS, 1948
Director: Michael Curtiz. Screenplay: Julius J. & Philip G. Epstein.
With Jack Carson, Janis Paige, Don DeFore, Oscar Levant, S. Z. Sakall.
Doris was 4th billing. Released in the UK as *It's Magic*.

MY DREAM IS YOURS   WARNER BROS, 1949
Director: Michael Curtiz. Screenplay: Harry Kurnitz, Dane Lussier, based
on the story by Jerry Wald and Paul Moss. With Jack Carson, Lee Bowman,
Adolphe Menjou, Eve Arden, S. Z. Sakall. Doris was 2nd billing.

IT'S A GREAT FEELING!   WARNER BROS, 1949
Director: David Butler. Screenplay: Jack Rose, Mel Shavelson, based on the
story by I. A. L. Diamond. With Jack Carson, Dennis Morgan, Bill Goodwin,
Joan Crawford, Errol Flynn, Ronald Reagan. Doris was 2nd billing.

YOUNG MAN WITH A HORN   WARNER BROS, 1950
Director: Michael Curtiz. Screenplay: Carl Foreman, Edmund North,
based on the novel by Dorothy Baker. With Kirk Douglas, Lauren
Bacall, Hoagy Carmichael. Doris was 3rd billing.

TEA FOR TWO   WARNER BROS, 1950
Director: David Butler. Screenplay: Harry Clork, William Jacobs, based
on the play by Frank Mandel, Otto Harbach, Vincent Youmans, Emil

Nyitray. With Gordon MacRae, Gene Nelson, Patrice Wymore, Eve Arden, S. Z. Sakall. Doris was top billing.

THE WEST POINT STORY   WARNER BROS, 1950
Director: Roy Del Ruth. Screenplay: John Monks Jr, Charles Hoffman, Irving Wallace, based on the play by the latter. With James Cagney, Virginia Mayo, Gordon MacRae, Gene Nelson, Alan Hale. Doris was third billing.

STORM WARNING   WARNER BROS, 1951
Director: Stuart Heisler. Screenplay: Daniel Fuchs, Richard Brooks. With Ginger Rogers, Steve Cochran, Ronald Reagan. Doris was third billing.

LULLABY OF BROADWAY   WARNER BROS, 1951
Director: David Butler. Screenplay: Earl Baldwin. With Gene Nelson, Billy DeWolfe, Gladys George, S. Z. Sakall. Doris was top billing.

ON MOONLIGHT BAY   WARNER BROS, 1951
Director: Roy Del Ruth. Screenplay: Jack Rose, Melville Shavelson, based on the stories by Booth Tarkington. With Gordon MacRae, Jack Smith, Rosemary De Camp, Mary Wickes, Leon Ames. Doris was top billing.

STARLIFT   WARNER BROS, 1951
Director: Roy Del Ruth. Screenplay: Karl Kamb, John Klorer, based on a story by the latter. With Gordon MacRae, Virginia Mayo, James Cagney, Gene Nelson, Ruth Roman, Jane Wyman. Doris was top billing.

I'LL SEE YOU IN MY DREAMS   WARNER BROS, 1952
Director: Michael Curtiz. Screenplay: Jack Rose, Mel Shavelson, based on a story by Grace Kahn, Louis Edelman. With Danny Thomas, Frank Lovejoy, Patrice Wymore, James Gleason, Mary Wickes. Doris was top billing.

THE WINNING TEAM   WARNER BROS, 1952
Director: Louis Seiler. Screenplay: Ted Sherdeman, Seeleg Lester, Merwin Gerard. With Ronald Reagan, Frank Lovejoy, Russ Tamblyn, Eve Miller, James Millican. Doris was top billing.

APRIL IN PARIS WARNER BROS, 1953
Director: David Butler. Screenplay: Jack Rose, Mel Shavelson. With Ray Bolder, Claude Dauphin, Eve Miller. Doris was top billing.

BY THE LIGHT OF THE SILVERY MOON WARNER BROS, 1953
Director: David Butler. Screenplay: Robert O'Brien, Irving Elinson, based on the stories by Booth Tarkington. With Gordon MacRae, Leon Ames, Rosemary De Camp, Mary Wickes, Billy Gray. Doris was top billing.

CALAMITY JANE WARNER BROS, 1953
Director: David Butler. Screenplay: James O'Hanlon. With Howard Keel, Philip Carey, Allyn McLerie, Dick Wesson. Doris was top billing.

LUCKY ME WARNER BROS, 1954
Director: Jack Donohue. Screenplay: Robert O'Brien, Irving Elinson, James O'Brien, based on a story by the latter. With Robert Cummings, Phil Silvers, Martha Hyer, Nancy Walker, Eddie Foy Jr. Doris was top billing.

YOUNG AT HEART WARNER BROS, 1955
Director: Gordon Douglas. Screenplay: Liam O'Brien, Julius Epstein, Lenore Coffee, based on a story by Fannie Hurst. With Frank Sinatra, Ethel Barrymore, Gig Young, Robert Keith, Elizabeth Fraser, Dorothy Malone, Alan Hale. Doris was top billing.

LOVE ME OR LEAVE ME MGM, 1955
Director: Charles Vidor. Screenplay: Isobel Lennart, Daniel Fuchs, based on a story by the latter. With James Cagney, Cameron Mitchell, Robert Keith, Harry Bellaver, Tom Tully. Doris was top billing.

THE MAN WHO KNEW TOO MUCH PARAMOUNT, 1956
Director: Alfred Hitchcock. Screenplay: John Michael Hayes, based on a story by Charles Bennett and D. B. Wyndham-Lewis. With James Stewart, Bernard Miles, Christopher Olsen, Brenda De Banzie, Daniel Gelin. Doris was second billing.

JULIE   MGM, 1956
Director & Screenplay: Andrew Stone. With Louis Jourdan, Barry Sullivan, Frank Lovejoy, Jack Kelly. Doris was top billing.

THE PAJAMA GAME   WARNER BROS, 1957
Directors: George Abbott, Stanley Donen. Screenplay: Richard Bissell, based on his novel. With John Raitt, Carole Haney, Eddie Foy Jr, Reta Shaw, Jack Straw, Barbara Nichols, Thelma Pelish. Doris was top billing.

TEACHER'S PET   PARAMOUNT, 1958
Director: George Seaton. Screenplay: Fay & Michael Kanin. With Clark Gable, Gig Young, Mamie Van Doren, Nick Adams. Doris was second billing.

TUNNEL OF LOVE   MGM, 1958
Director: Gene Kelly. Screenplay: Jerome Chodorov, Joseph Fields, based on the play by the latter and the novel by Peter De Vries. With Richard Widmark, Gig Young, Elizabeth Fraser, Gia Scala, Elizabeth Wilson. Doris was top billing.

IT HAPPENED TO JANE   COLUMBIA, 1959
Director: Richard Quine. Screenplay: Norman Katkov, based on a story by Katkov and Max Wilk. With Jack Lemmon, Steve Forrest, Ernie Kovacs, Teddy Rooney, Gina Gillespie. Doris was top billing.

PILLOW TALK   UNIVERSAL, 1959
Director: Michael Gordon. Screenplay: Stanley Shapiro, Maurice Richlin, from the story by Russell Rouse and Clarence Green. With Rock Hudson, Tony Randall, Thelma Ritter, Nick Adams. Doris was second billing.

PLEASE DON'T EAT THE DAISIES   MGM, 1960
Director: Charles Walters. Screenplay: Isobel Lennart, based on the book by Jean Kerr. With David Niven, Janis Paige, Spring Byington, Patsy Kelly, Richard Haydn, Jack Weston. Doris was top billing.

MIDNIGHT LACE   UNIVERSAL, 1960

Director: David Miller. Screenplay: Ivan Goff, Ben Roberts, based on the play by Janet Green. With Rex Harrison, John Gavin, Myrna Loy, Herbert Marshall, Hermione Baddeley, Roddy McDowall. Doris was top billing.

LOVER COME BACK   UNIVERSAL, 1962

Director: Delbert Mann. Screenplay: Stanley Shapiro, Paul Henning. With Rock Hudson, Tony Randall, Jack Kruschen, Jack Oakie, Edie Adams. Doris was second billing.

THAT TOUCH OF MINK   UNIVERSAL, 1962

Director: Delbert Mann. Screenplay: Stanley Shapiro, Nate Monaster. With Cary Grant, Gig Young, Dick Sargent, Audrey Meadows, Allan Hewitt. Doris was second billing.

BILLY ROSE'S JUMBO   MGM, 1962

Director: Charles Walters. Screenplay: Sidney Sheldon, based on the play by Ben Hecht and Charles MacArthur. With Stephen Boyd, Jimmy Durante, Martha Raye, Dean Jagger. Doris was top billing.

THE THRILL OF IT ALL   UNIVERSAL, 1963

Director: Norman Jewison. Screenplay: Carl Reiner, based on Reiner and Larry Gelbart's story. With James Garner, Arlene Francis, ZaSu Pitts, Edward Andrews. Doris was top billing.

MOVE OVER, DARLING   20th CENTURY-FOX, 1963

Director: Michael Gordon. Screenplay: Hal Kanter, Jack Sher, based on the story-screenplay by Bella & Samuel Spewack. A remake of the 1940 film, *My Favourite Wife*. With James Garner, Polly Bergen, Thelma Ritter, Chuck Connors, Fred Clark. Doris was top billing.

SEND ME NO FLOWERS   UNIVERSAL, 1964

Director: Norman Jewison. Screenplay: Julius Epstein, based on the play by Norman Barasch, Carroll Moore. With Rock Hudson, Tony Randall, Edward Andrews, Clint Walker, Hal March, Paul Lynde. Doris was second billing.

DO NOT DISTURB   20th CENTURY-FOX, 1965
Director: Ralph Levy. Screenplay: Milt Rosen, Richard Breen, based on the play by William Fairchild. With Rod Taylor, Sergio Fantoni, Hermione Baddley. Doris was top billing.

THE GLASS BOTTOM BOAT   MGM, 1966
Director: Frank Tashlin. Screenplay: Everett Freeman. With Rod Taylor, Arthur Godfrey, John McGiver, Eric Fleming, Edward Andrews, Paul Lynde, Dick Martin. Doris was top billing.

CAPRICE   20th CENTURY FOX, 1967
Director: Frank Tashlin. Screenplay: Frank Tashlin, Jay Jason, based on a story by Martin Hale. With Richard Harris, Jack Kruschen, Ray Walston, Lilia Skala, Michael J. Pollard, Edward Mulhare. Doris was top billing.

THE BALLAD OF JOSIE   UNIVERSAL, 1967
Director: Andrew McLaglen. Screenplay: Harold Swanton. With Peter Graves, George Kennedy, Andy Devine, Elizabeth Fraser, Audrey Christie. Doris was top billing.

WHERE WERE YOU WHEN   MGM, 1968
THE LIGHTS WENT OUT?
Director: Hy Averback. Screenplay: Everett Freeman, Karl Runberg, based on the play by Claude Magnier. With Robert Morse, Patrick O'Neal, Terry-Thomas, Lola Albright, Jim Backus, Steve Allen. Doris was top billing.

WITH SIX YOU GET EGGROLL   WARNER BROS-PATHE, 1968
Director: Howard Morris. Screenplay: Gwen Bagni, Paul Dubov, Harvey Bullock, R. S. Allen. With Brian Keith, Pat Carroll, Barbara Hershey, George Carlin, John Findlater, Alice Ghostley. Doris was top billing.

Appendix 2:
Studio Albums & 78/45 Rpm Singles

There are literally scores of Doris Day compilation albums and retrospectives that persistently repeat the same items from her back catalogue and repackages of her film scores. The following represent her much sought-after vinyl studio albums.

10-inch Albums

YOU'RE MY THRILL   1949 Columbia CL6071
You're My Thrill; Bewitched, Bothered And Bewildered*; I'm Confessing That I Love You*; Sometimes I'm Happy*; You Go To My Head; I Didn't Know What Time It Was *; When Your Lover Has Gone; That Old Feeling. Reissued in 1955 with extra tracks as *Day Dreams*.
*With the Mellowmen.

YOUNG MAN WITH A HORN   1950 Columbia CL6106
The soundtrack from the film: Doris and Harry James. I May Be Wrong But I Think You're Wonderful (sung by Doris); The Man I Love; The Very Thought Of You (sung by Doris); Melancholy Rhapsody; Get Happy; Too Marvellous For Words (sung by Doris); Limehouse Blues; With A Song In My Heart (sung by Doris).

TEA FOR TWO   1950 Columbia CL6149

The soundtrack from the film. Crazy Rhythm *; Here In My Arms **; I
Know That You Know *; I Want To Be Happy ***; Do, Do, Do **; I Only
Have Eyes For You **; Oh Me! Oh My! Oh You! *; Tea For Two **

* Doris & Gene Nelson. ** Doris Day. *** The Page Cavanaugh Trio

LULLABY OF BROADWAY   1951 Columbia CL6168

Promoted as the film's soundtrack though all the songs are performed by
Doris with the Norman Luboff Choir and the Buddy Cole Quartet.
Lullaby of Broadway; Fine And Dandy (not in the film); A Shanty In Old
Shanty Town; Somebody Loves Me; Just One Of Those Things; You're
Getting To Be A Habit With Me; I Love The Way You Say Goodnight;
Please Don't Talk About Me When I'm Gone.

ON MOONLIGHT BAY   1951 Columbia CL6186

On Moonlight Bay; Till We Meet Again *; Love You *; The Christmas
Story; I'm Forever Blowing Bubbles *; Cuddle Up A Little Closer *;
Ever Little Movement; Tell Me Why Notes Are So Lonely.

* Sung with Jack Smith (Gordon MacRae duetted with Doris in the film)

I'LL SEE YOU IN MY DREAMS   1951 Columbia CL6198

Ain't We Got Fun *; The One I Love Belongs To Somebody Else; I
Wish I Had A Girl; It Had To Be You; Nobody's Sweetheart **; My
Buddy; Makin' Whoopee! *; I'll See You In My Dreams.

* Sung with Danny Thomas. ** Performed by the Norman Luboff Choir. Orchestra
conducted by Paul Weston, with the Lee Brothers

BY THE LIGHT OF THE SILVERY MOON 1953 Columbia CL6248

By The Light Of The Silvery Moon; Your Eyes Have Told Me So; Just
One Girl; Ain't We Got Fun; If You Were The Only Girl In The World;
Be My Little Baby; Bumble Bee; I'll Forget You; King Chanticleer.
Doris sings with The Norman Luboff Choir.

CALAMITY JANE   1953 Columbia CL6273
The Deadwood Stage *; I Can Do Without You **; The Black Hills Of
Dakota; Just Blew In From The Windy City; A Woman's Touch; Higher
Than A Hawk, Deeper Than A Well ***; 'Tis Harry I'm Plannin' To
Marry; Secret Love *

* Directly recorded from the film. The other tracks are studio-recorded. ** With Howard
Keel. *** Howard Keel Solo

YOUNG AT HEART   1954 Columbia CL6339
Till My Love Comes To Me *; Ready, Willing And Able *; Hold Me In
Your Arms *; Someone To Watch Over Me **; Just One Of Those
Things*; There's A Rising Moon *; One For My Baby **; You, My Love*

* Sung by Doris Day. ** Sung by Frank Sinatra.

12-inch Albums

LOVE ME OR LEAVE ME   1955 Columbia CL710
It All Depends On You; You Made Me Love You; Stay On The Right
Side, Sister; Mean To Me; Everybody Loves My Baby; Sam, The Old
Accordion Man; Shaking The Blues Away; Ten Cents A Dance; I'll
Never Stop Loving You; Never Look Back; Love Me Or Leave Me.

DAY DREAMS   1955 Columbia CL624
This is a re-issue of the 1949 *You're My Thrill* album with extra tracks:
Imagination; I've Only Myself To Blame; If I Could Be With You; Darn
That Dream.

DAY IN HOLLYWOOD   1955 Columbia CL749
Doris' first compilation of her movie hits: Tea For Two; Lullaby Of
Broadway; Cuddle Up A Little Closer; I May Be Wrong But I Think
You're Wonderful; Makin' Whoopee!; Be My Little Baby Bumble Bee;
Secret Love; Till We Meet Again; Ain't We Got Fun; Just One Of Those
Things; It Had To Be You, Love Me Or Leave Me.

DAY BY DAY   1956 Columbia CL942
The Song Is You; Hello, My Lover, Goodbye; But Not For Me; I
Remember You; I Hadn't Anyone Till You; But Beautiful; Autumn
Leaves; Don't Take Your Love From Me; There Will Never Be Another
You; Gone With The Wind; The Gypsy In My Soul; Day By Day.

THE PAJAMA GAME   1957 Columbia OL5210
The Pajama Game/Racing With The Clock (Eddie Foyle Jr &
Ensemble); I'm Not At All In Love (Doris & The Girls); I'll Never Be
Jealous Again (Eddie Foy Jr & Reta Shaw); Hey There (John Raitt);
Once-A-Year Day (Doris, John Raitt & Ensemble); Small Talk (Doris,
John Raitt); There Once Was A Man (Doris, John Raitt); Steam Heat
(Carol Haney, Kenneth Le Roy & Ensemble); Hernando's Hideway
(Carol Haney & Ensemble); Seven-And-A-Half Cents (Doris, Jack Shaw
& Ensemble); Finale; The Man Who Invented Love.

DAY BY NIGHT   1957 Columbia CS8089
I See Your Face Before Me; Close Your Eyes; The Night We Called It A
Day; Dream A Little Dream Of Me; Under A Blanket Of Blue; You Do
Something To Me; Stars Fell On Alabama; Moon Song; Wrap Your
Troubles In Dreams; Soft As The Starlight; Moonglow; The Lamp Is Low.

HOORAY FOR HOLLYWOOD Vol. 1   1958 Columbia CS8066
Cheek To Cheek; It's Easy To Remember; The Way You Look Tonight;
I'll Remember April; Blues In The Night; Over The Rainbow; Love Is
Here To Stay; In The Still Of The Night; Night & Day; Easy To Love;
I Had The Craziest Dream.

HOORAY FOR HOLLYWOOD Vol. 2   1959 Columbia CS8067
I've Got My Love To Keep Me Warm; Soon; That Old Black Magic;
You'll Never Know; A Foggy Day; It's Magic; It Might As Well Be Spring;
Nice Work If You Can Get it; Three Coins In The Fountain; Let's Face
The Music And Dance; Pennies From Heaven; Oh, But I Do.

CUTTIN' CAPERS   1959 Columbia CS8078

Cuttin' Capers; Steppin' Out With My Baby; Makin' Whoopee!; The Lady's In Love With You; Why Don't We Do This More Often?; Let's Take A Walk Around The Block; I'm Sitting On Top Of The World; Get Out And Get Under The Moon; Fit As A Fiddle And Ready For Love; Me Too; I Feel Like A Feather In The Breeze; Let's Fly Away.

WHAT EVERY GIRL SHOULD KNOW   1960 Columbia CS8234

What Every Girl Should Know; Mood Indigo; When You're Smiling; A Fellow Needs A Girl; My Kinda Love; What's The Use Of Wond'rin'; Something Wonderful; A Hundred Years From Today; You Can't Have Everything; Not Only Should You Love Him; What Does A Woman Do?; The Everlasting Arms.

SHOW TIME   1960 Columbia: CS261

Show Time; I Got The Sun In The Morning; Ohio; I Love Paris; When I'm Not Near The Boy I Love; People Will Say We're In Love; I've Grown Accustomed To His Face; The Surrey With The Fringe On Top; They Say It's Wonderful; A Wonderful Guy; On The Street Where You Live; The Sound Of Music; Show Time.

BRIGHT & SHINY   1961 Columbia: CS8414

Bright And Shiny; I Want To Be Happy; Keep Smilin', Keep Laughin', Be Happy; Singin' In The Rain; Gotta Feelin'; Happy Talk; Ridin' High; On The Sunny Side Of The Street; Clap Yo' Hands; Stay With The Happy People; Twinkle And Shine.

I HAVE DREAMED   1961 Columbia: CS8460

I Believe In Dreams; I'll Buy That Dream; My Ship; All I Do Is Dream Of You; When I Grow Too Old To Dream; We'll Love Again; I Have Dreamed; Periwinkle Blue; Someday I'll Find You; You Stepped Out Of A Dream; Oh What A Beautiful Dream; Time To Say Goodnight.

WONDERFUL DAY   1961 Columbia Limited Edition
Lover Come Back; Pillow Talk; Be Prepared; Whatever Will Be, Will
Be; It's Magic; Never Look Back; Should I Surrender; Teacher's Pet;
When You're Smiling; Possess Me; Julie; Till My Love Comes To Me.
This concept album was released in 2003 (Columbia 510867-2) as part of
a double-CD with *With A Smile And A Song*, with alternative/bonus
tracks: That Jane From Maine; A Perfect Understanding.

DUET WITH ANDRE PREVIN   1962 Columbia: CS8552
Close Your Eyes; Fools Rush In; Yes; Nobody's Heart; Remind Me;
Who Are We To Say; Daydreaming; Give Me Time; Control Yourself;
Wait Till You See Him; My One And Only Love; Falling In Love
Again. Accompanied at the piano by André Previn. Released in Great
Britain 12/61.

YOU'LL NEVER WALK ALONE   1962 Columbia: CS8704
If I Can Help Somebody; Nearer My God To Thee; The Prodigal Son;
Abide With Me; Bless This House; You'll Never Walk Alone; In The
Garden; Walk With Him; Scarlet Ribbons; Be Still And Know; I Need
Thee Every Hour; The Lord's Prayer.

BILLY ROSE'S JUMBO   1962 Columbia: OS2260
The Circus Is On Parade (Doris, Jimmy Durante, Martha Raye); Over
And Over Again (Doris); Why Can't I? (Doris, Martha Raye); This Can't
Be Love (Doris); The Most Beautiful Girl In The World (Stephen
Boyd); My Romance (Doris); The Most Beautiful Girl In The World
(Jimmy Durante); Little Girl Blue (Doris); Sawdust, Spangles And
Dreams (Entire Cast).

LOVE HIM   1963 Columbia: CS8931
More: Can't Help Falling In Love; Since I Fell For You; Losing You; A
Fool Such As I; As Long As He Needs Me; Funny; Softly As I Leave You;
Lollipops And Roses; Love Him; Moonlight Lover; A Whisper Away.

ANNIE GET YOUR GUN   1963 Columbia: OS2360
Doris and Robert Goulet perform songs from the film: Colonel Buffalo
Bill (Leonard Stokes) ; I'm A Bad, Bad Man *; Doin' What Comes
Naturally **; The Girl That I Marry *; You Can't Get A Man With A
Gun **; There's No Business Like Show Business (Ensemble); They
Say It's Wonderful ***; Moonshine Lullaby **; My Defenses Are
Down*; I'm An Indian Too **; I Got Lost In His Arms **; Who Do You
Love, I Hope? (Kelly Brown & Renee Winters); I Got The Sun In The
Morning **; Anything You Can Do ***
* Sung by Goulet ** Sung by Doris *** Sung by Doris & Goulet.

THE DORIS DAY CHRISTMAS ALBUM   1964 Columbia: CS9026
Silver Bells; I'll Be Home For Christmas; Snowfall; Toyland; Let It
Snow! Let It Snow! Let It Snow!; Be A Child At Christmas Time; Winter
Wonderland; The Christmas Song; Christmas Present; Have Yourself A
Merry Little Christmas; The Christmas Waltz; White Christmas; Deck
The Halls With Boughs Of Holly; I've Got My Love To Keep Me Warm;
Let No Walls Divide.

WITH A SMILE AND A SONG   1964 Columbia: CS9066
Give A Little Whistle; The Children's Marching Song (Nick Nack
Paddy Whack); Getting To Know You; Zip-A-Dee-Doo-Dah; The Lilac
Tree; High Hopes; Do Re Mi; Whatever Will Be, Will Be (1964
remake); The Inch-Worm; Swinging On A Star; Sleepy Baby; With A
Smile And A Song. With Jimmy Joyce & His Children's Choir.

DORIS DAY'S SENTIMENTAL JOURNEY   1965 Columbia: CS9160
The More I See You; At Last; Come To Baby Do; I Had The Craziest Dream/I Don't Want to Walk Without You; I'll Never Smile Again; I Remember You; Serenade In Blue; I'm Beginning To See The Light; It Could Happen To You; It's Been A Long, Long Time; Sentimental Journey.

LATIN FOR LOVERS   1965 Columbia: CS9110
Quiet Nights Of Quiet Stars; Fly Me To The Moon; Meditation; Dansero; Summer Has Gone; How Insensitive; Slightly Out Of Tune; Our Day Will Come; Be True To Me; Perhaps, Perhaps, Perhaps; Be Mine Tonight; Por Favor.

THE LOVE ALBUM (CD)   1994 Vision: VISCD2
Songs recorded in 1967, believed lost (see main text): For All We Know; Snuggled On Your Shoulder; Are You Lonesome Tonight?; Wonderful One; Street Of Dreams; Oh, How I Miss You Tonight; Life Is Just A Bowl Of Cherries; All Alone; Faded Summer Love; Sleepy Lagoon; If I Had My Life To Live Over; Let Me Call You Sweetheart.

Unreleased Studio Albums

Doris recorded 11 songs during the late summer/autumn of 1986 for an album provisionally titled *What A Day For A Daydream*, produced by her son Terry Melcher to complement her *Doris Day's Best Friends* television series. To date they have not resurfaced: You Are Beautiful To Me; Crocodile Rock; What A Day For A Daydream; Disney Girls; You Are So Beautiful To Me; In An Octopus' Garden; Heaven Tonight; This Is The Way I Dreamed It; Stewball Was A Racehorse; My Heart; Ryan's On His Way To The Round-Up.

78/45 rpm Singles

Love Somebody/Confess	1948 Columbia 38174
It's Magic/ Put ' Em In A Box	1948 Columbia 38188
My Darling, My Darling/That Certain Party	1948 Columbia 38353
Powder Your Face With Sunshine/I'll String Along With You	1949 Columbia 38394
Again/Everywhere You Go	1949 Columbia 38467
Now That I Need You/Blame My Absent-Minded Heart	1949 Columbia 38507
Let's Take An Old-Fashioned Walk (with Frank Sinatra)/Unknown	1949 Columbia 38513
Cuttin' Capers/It's Better To Conceal Than Reveal (with Dinah Shore)	1949 Columbia 38595
Bluebird On Your Windowsill/ The River Seine	1949 Columbia 38611
Quicksilver/Crocodile Tears	1949 Columbia 38638
Bewitched/Imagination	1950 Columbia 38698
Hoop-Dee-Do/Marriage Ties	1950 Columbia 38771
I Didn't Slip, I Wasn't Pushed, I Fell/ Before I Loved You	1950 Columbia 38818
A Bushel And A Peck/The Best Thing For You	1950 Columbia 39008
Lullaby Of Broadway/Would Love You?	1951 Columbia 39159
Shanghai/My Life's Desire	1951 Columbia 39423
A Guy Is A Guy/Who, Who, Who	1952 Columbia 39673
Sugarbush/How Lovely Cooks The Meat (both with Frankie Laine)	1952 Columbia 39693
When I Fall In Love/Take Me In Your Arms	1952 Columbia 39786
A Full-Time Job/Ma Says, Pa Says (both with Johnnie Ray)	1952 Columbia 39898
Mister Tap-Toe/Your Mother And Mine	1952 Columbia 39906

Let's Walk That-A-Way/Candy Lips
   (both with Johnnie Ray)   1953 Columbia 40001

Choo-Choo Train/This Too Shall Pass Away   1953 Columbia 40063

Secret Love/The Deadwood Stage   1953 Columbia 40108

I Speak To The Stars/The Bluebells
   of Broadway   1954 Columbia 40210

If I Give My Heart To You/Anyone
   Can Fall In Love   1954 Columbia 40300

I'll Never Stop Loving You/Never Look Back   1955 Columbia 40505

Que Sera, Sera/I've Gotta Sing Away
   These Blues   1956 Columbia 40704

Everybody Loves A Lover/Instant Love   1958 Columbia 41195

Move Over, Darling/Twinkle Lullaby   1963 Columbia 42912

The Bear Family CD Boxed Sets

Of tremendous importance to fans and collectors, this monumental project kicked off in 1993 when the German record label pledged to re-issue every single recording Doris Day made when assigned to Columbia from 1947–67. These boxed sets contain all of her commercially released work, along with unreleased songs, alternative takes and acetates. Each one has a high-quality hardback book with rare photos and extensive biographical notes.

It's Magic (1947–50)   1994 BCD15609FK
CD-1: It Takes Time; Pete; My Young And Foolish Heart; Tell Me, Dream Face; I'm Still Singing Under The Apple Tree; Just An Old Love Of Mine; A Chocolate Sundae On A Saturday Night; When Tonight Is Just A Memory; That's The Way He Does It; Why Should We Both Be So Lonely; Papa, Won't You Dance With Me; Say Something Nice About Me, Baby; It's Magic; Just Imagine; Pretty Baby; Confess*; Love Somebody*; Tacos, Enchilados And Beans; No Moon At All; Put 'Em In A Box, Tie 'Em With A Ribbon; Imagination; It's The Sentimental Thing To Do; I've Only Myself To Blame; Thoughtless; It's A Quiet Town.
* with Buddy Clark

CD-2: Someone Like You; My Dream Is Yours; I'm In Love*; It's You Or No One; My Darling, My Darling*; That Certain Party*; His Fraternity Pin*; If You Will Marry Me*; You Was*; I'll String Along With You*; Powder Your Face With Sunshine; Don't Gamble With Romance; I'm Beginning To Miss You; That Old Feeling; When Your Lover Has Gone; You Go To My Head; How It Lies, How It Lies, How It Lies; If I Could Be With You One Hour Tonight; Everywhere You Go; Again; Now That I Need You; Blame My Absent-Minded Heart; Let's Take An Old-Fashioned Walk.**

* with Buddy Clark ** with Frank Sinatra

CD-3: You're My Thrill; Bewitched; At The Cafe Rendezvous; It's A Great Feeling; It's Better To Conceal Than Reveal *; You Can Have Him*; Sometimes I'm Happy; Land Of Love; I Didn't Know What Time It Was; I'm Confessin';The Last Mile Home; Canadian Capers; Here Comes Santa Claus; Old Saint Nicholas; It's On The Tip Of My Tongue; The River Seine; Festival Of Roses; The Three Rivers; Bluebird On Your Windowsill; Crocodile Tears; The Game Of Broken Hearts; Quicksilver; I'll Never Slip Round Again; I Don't Wanna Be Kissed By Anyone But You.

* with Dinah Shore

CD-4: With You Anywhere You Are; Save A Little Sunbeam For A Rainy, Rainy Day; Mama, What'll I Do; I Said My Pajamas And Put On My Prayers; Enjoy Yourself; I May Be Wrong; The Very Thought Of You; Too Marvellous For Words; With A Song In My Heart; Spesh'lly You; Marriage Ties; Before I Loved You; I Went A Wooing; I Didn't Slip, I Wasn't Pushed, I Fell; Hoop Dee Doo; I Can't Get Over A Boy Like You; I've Forgotten You; I'll Be Around; Darn That Dream; Here In My Arms; Tea For Two; I Only Have Eyes For You; Do Do Do; Crazy Rhythm *

* with Gene Nelson

CD-5: I Know That You Know*; Oh Me! Oh My!*; I Want To Be Happy; He's Such A Gentleman; A Load Of Hay; I Love The Way You Say Goodnight; Orange Coloured Sky; The Comb And Paper Polka; Pumpernickel; You Are My Sunshine; The Everlasting Arms; David's Psalm; Christmas Story; I've Never Been In Love Before; A Bushel And A Peck; You Love Me; The Best Thing For You; If I Were A Bell; Silver Bells; It's A Lovely Day Today; From This Moment On; I Am Loved; Nobody's Chasing Me; Ten-Thousand Four Hundred Thirty-Two Sheep.

*with Gene Nelson

CD-6: You're Getting To Be A Habit With Me; Somebody Loves Me; Please Don't Talk About Me When I'm Gone; Just One Of Those Things; Lullaby Of Broadway; I Love The Way You Say Goodnight; In A Shanty In Old Shanty Town; Fine And Dandy; Lullaby Of Broadway; Would I Love You; Say Something Nice About Me, Baby; It's Magic; Pretty Baby; Thoughtless; It's You Or No One; My Darling, My Darling*; That Certain Party (1)*; That Certain Party (2)*; His Fraternity Pin*; Let's Take An Old-Fashioned Walk**; You're My Thrill; I Said My Pajamas And Put On My Prayers; Here In My Arms; I Only Have Eyes For You; Do, Do, Do; I Want To Be Happy

* with Buddy Clark ** with Frank Sinatra

Secret Love (1951–55)   BCD 15746EK

CD-1: It's So Laughable; Something Wonderful: We Kiss In A Shadow; Very Good Advice; Tell Me Why Nights Are Lonely; Till We Meet Again; Moonlight Bay; My Life's Desire; I'm Forever Blowing Bubbles*; Every Little Movement; Love Ya*; Cuddle Up A Little Closer; Shanghai; Lonesome And Sorry; Ask Me; Kiss Me Goodbye, Love; Got Him Off My Hands; Baby Doll; Oops; If That Doesn't Do It; Domino; Makin' Whoopee**; It Had To Be You; My Buddy; The One I Love Belongs To Somebody Else; *Moonlight Bay* interview.

* with Jack Smith ** with Danny Thomas

CD-2: I'll See You In My Dreams; I Wish I Had A Girl; Ain't We Got Fun*; Nobody's Sweetheart; How Lovely Cooks The Meat**; Sugar Bush**; A Guy Is A Guy; A Little Kiss Goodnight***; Gentle Johnny***; Who, Who, Who; Take Me In Your Arms; Make It Soon; My Love And Devotion; It's Magic; When I Fall In Love; The Cherries; April In Paris; No Two People****; You Can't Lose Me****; I Know A Place; That's What Makes Paris Paree; I'm Gonna Ring The Bell Tonight; The Second Star To The Right; Your Mother And Mine.

*with Danny Thomas **with Frankie Laine ***with Guy Mitchell ****with Donald O'Connor

CD-3: Mister Tap Toe; Ma Says, Pa Says*; A Full Time Job*; Beautiful Music To Love By; You Have My Sympathy; Let's Walk That-A-Way*; Candy Lips*; By My Little Baby Bumble Bee; King Chanticleer; I'll Forget You; If You Were The Only Girl In The World; Your Eyes Have Told Me So; Ain't We Got Fun; Just One Girl; Just One Girl; By The

Light Of The Silvery Moon; Ain't We Got Fun (remake); When The Red, Red Robin . . . ; A Purple Cow; Kiss Me Again, Stranger; The Black Hills Of Dakota (quartet); 'Tis Harry I'm Planning To Marry (quartet); Just Blew In From The Windy City; This Too Shall Pass Away; A Woman's Touch; Choo Choo Train; Secret Love; I Can Do Without You**; The Deadwood Stage; Secret Love (interv).

* with Johnnie Ray ** with Howard Keel

CD-4: Love You Dearly; Lost In Loveliness: I Speak To The Stars; What Every Girl Should Know; The Blue Bells Of Broadway; I Speak To The Stars; Kay Muleta; Anyone Can Fall In Love; Jimmy Unknown; Someone Else's Roses; If I Give My Heart To You; There's A Rising Moon; You My Love; Hold Me In Your Arms; Till My Love Comes To Me; Ready, Willing And Able; Two Hearts, Two Kisses; Foolishly Yours; I'll Never Stop Loving You; Love's Little Island (Take 9); Ooh Bang, Jiggily, Jang; Let It Ring; I've Gotta Sing Away These Blues; Live It Up; I'm A Big Girl Now; When I'm Happy; Love's Little Island (Take 11).

CD-5: It All Depends On You; You Made Me Love You; Stay On The Right Side, Sister; Mean To Me; Everybody Loves My Baby; Sam, The Old Accordion Man; Shaking The Blues Away; Ten Cents A Dance; I'll Never Stop Loving You; Never Look Back; At Sundown; Love Me Or Leave Me; Never Look Back (audition); Overture; It All Depends On You; You Made Me Love You; Stay On The Right Side, Sister; Everybody Loves My Baby; Mean To Me; Sam, The Old Accordion Man; Shaking The Blues Away; Ten Cents A Dance; I'll Never Stop Loving You; Never Look Back; At Sundown; Love Me Or Leave Me/Finale; Ten Cents A Dance (alternative version); Love Me Or Leave Me (alternative version).

Que Sera, Sera (1956–59)   BCD 15797
CD-1: Whatever Will Be, Will Be; Somebody, Somewhere; We'll Love Again; Julie; Love In A Home; Gone With The Wind; The Song Is You; Don't take Your Love From Me; The Gypsy In My Soul; Autumn Leaves; I Remember You; Hello My Lover Goodbye; Day By Day; But Beautiful; There Will Never Be Another You; But Not For Me; I Hadn't Anyone Till You; Today Will Be Yesterday Tomorrow; The Party's Over; Nothing In The World; Whad'ja Put In That Kiss; The Man Who Invented Love; Twelve O'Clock Tonight; Rickety Rackety Rendezvous; Through The Eyes Of Love.

CD-2: I'm Not An All In Love; Once A Year Day; Small Talk; There Once Was A Man; Seven And A Half Cents; Under A Blanket Of Blue; I See Your Face Before Me; Moon Song; Dream A Little Dream Of Me; You Do Something To Me; Wrap Your Troubles In Dreams; Close Your Eyes; Stars Fell On Alabama; The Night We Called It A Day; Soft As The Starlight; The Lamp Is Low; Moonglow; Cheek To Cheek; Nice Work If You Can Get It; I've Got My Love To Keep Me Warm; Let's Face The Music And Dance; Wrap Your Troubles In Dreams (alt).

CD-3: It's Easy To Remember; It Might As Well Be Spring; I'll Remember April; Three Coins In The Fountain; In The Still Of The Night; Soon; A Foggy Day; Love Is Here To Stay; Run Away, Skidaddle Skidoo; Teacher's Pet; Walk A Chalk Line; You'll Never Know; I Had The Craziest Dream; Over The Rainbow; Oh, But U Do; Easy To Love; That Old Black Magic; Pennies From Heaven; The Way You Look Tonight; Night And Day; Hooray For Hollywood; A Very Precious Love; Blues In The Night.

CD-4: Everybody Loves A Lover; The Tunnel Of Love (Tk 1); Instant Love; Possess Me; The Tunnel Of Love (Tk 14); Kissin' My Honey; That Jane From Maine (train-effect version); Steppin' Out With My Baby; The Lady's In Love With You; I Enjoy Being A Girl; Let's Fly Away; Why Don't We Do This More Often; Fit As A Fiddle; Let's Take A Walk Around The Block; Makin' Whoopee; You're Driving Me Crazy; Get Out And Under The Moon; I Feel Like A Feather In The Breeze; I'm Sitting On Top Of The World; Cuttin' Capers; Me Too; Love Me In The Daytime (double vocal); Any Way The Wind Blows (double vocal); Be Pepared; A Perfect Understanding; It Happened To Jane; He's So Married; Deck The Halls; Inspiration.

CD-5: Pillow Talk; Roly Poly; Heart Full Of Love; The Sound Of Music; Oh, What A Lover You'll Be; No; A Fellow Needs A Girl; What Every Girl Should Know; Mood Indigo; What's The Use Of Wond'rin'; My Kinda Love; When You're Smiling; You Can't Have Everything; A Hundred Years From Today; The Everlasting Arms; Something Wonderful; Not Only Should You Love him; What Does A Woman Do; Everybody Loves A Lover (alt take); Run Away, Skidaddle Skidoo; Teacher's Pet; Walk A Chalk Line; Possess Me; That Jane From Maine (without train effect); Makin' Whoopee; Love Me In The Daytime (single vocal); Any Way The Wind Blows (single vocal); Be Prepared (alt take); A Perfect Understanding (alt take).

Move Over, Darling (1960–68)   BCD 15800-HK
CD-1: What Does A Woman Do; Please Don't Eat The Daisies; Falling; The Blue Train; Daffa Down Dilly (fast version); Here We Go Again; *Show Time Part One:* On The Street Where You Live; When I'm Not Near The Boy I Love; I Love Paris; The Surrey With The Fringe On Top; Ohio; I've Grown Accustomed To His Face; They Say It's Wonderful; A Wonderful Guy; People Will Say We're In Love; I Got The Sun In The Morning. *Show Time Part Two:* Happy Talk; Ridin' High; Stay With The Happy People; Clap Yo' Hands; Singin' In The Rain; I Want To Be Happy; Make Someone Happy; On The Sunny Side Of The Street; Twinkle And Shine; Bright And Shiny; Gotta Feelin'.

CD-2: Keep Smilin', Keep Laughin', Be Happy; Oh What A Beautiful Dream; I'll Buy That Dream; Time To Say Goodnight; All I Do Is Dream Of You; My Ship; We'll Love Again; I Believe In Dreams; Periwinkle Blue; Let No Walls Divide; Look All Around; In The Secret Place; As A Child; Someday I'll Find You; You Stepped Out Of A Dream; I Have Dreamed; Let No Walls Divide (overdub version); When I Grow Too Old To Dream; Who Knows What Might Have Been; Should I Surrender; Lover Come Back; Close Your Eyes; Fools Rush In; Remind Me; Yes.

CD-3: Control Yourself; You're Good For Me; Nobody's Heart; Wait Till You See Him; Fools Rush In; Give Me Time; Who Are We To Say; Nobody's Heart; Day Dreaming; Close Your Eyes; My One And Only Love; In Love In Vain; Falling In Love Again; Nearer My God To Thee; I Need Thee Every Hour; Abide With Me; The Lord's Prayer; Walk With Him; In The Garden; The Prodigal Son; If I Can Help Somebody; Scarlet Ribbons; Bless This House; You'll Never Walk Alone; Be Still And Know.

CD-4: Let The Little Girl Limbo (single vocal); Move Over, Darling; Twinkle Lullaby; More; Lollipops And Roses; Can't Help Falling In Love; Softly As I Leave You; As Long As He Needs Me; Losing You; Since I Fell For You; Love Him; Night Life; A Fool Such As I; Funny; Moonlight Lover; Rainbow's End; Oo-Wee Baby; Have Yourself A Merry

Little Christmas; Toyland; The Christmas Song; Winter Wonderland; Silver Bells; White Christmas; Be A Child At Christmas Time; Snowfall; Let It Snow! Let It Snow! Let It Snow!; The Christmas Waltz.

CD-5: I'll Be Home For Christmas; Christmas Present; Getting To Know You; Sleepy Baby; With A Smile And A Song; Que Sera, Sera; Zip-A-Dee-Doo-Dah; Give A Little Whistle; The Inchworm; Swinging On A Star; The Lilac Tree; The Children's Marching Song; Do-Re-Mi; High Hopes; Send Me No Flowers; I Remember You; Sentimental Journey; It Could Happen To You; At Last; I'll Never Smile Again; Serenade In Blue; It's Been A Long, Long Time; The More I See You; I'm Beginning To See The Light; I Had The Craziest Dream/I Don't Want To Walk Without You; Come To Baby, Do; Slightly Out Of Tune; Quiet Night Of Quiet Stars.

CD-6: Meditation; Summer Has Gone; Fly Me To The Moon; Perhaps, Perhaps, Perhaps; Our Day Will Come; Be True To Me; Dansero; Por Favor; How Insensitive; Be Mine Tonight; Catch The Bouquet; Another Go Around; A Whisper Away; Do Not Disturb; Au Revoir Is Goodbye With A Smile; There They Are; Every Now And Then; The Glass Bottom Boat; Sorry; Caprice; Snuggled On Your Shoulder; Sweet Dreams; Life Is Just A Bowl Of Cherries; If I Had My Life To Live Over/Let Me Call You Sweetheart; Are You Lonesome Tonight?; All Alone; Sleepy Lagoon; Faded Summer.

CD-7: Oh, How I Miss You Tonight; For All We Know; Wonderful One; Blue Train (without chorus version); Daffa Down Dilly; Let The Little Girl Limbo (single vocal); Let The Little Girl Limbo (double vocal); Catch The Bouquet (alt take); Another Go Around (alt take); Do Not Disturb (alt take); Glass Bottom Boat (alt take); The Circus Is On Parade; Over And Over Again; Why Can't I; This Can't Be Love; The Most Beautiful Girl In The World (1 Stephen Boyd); My Romance; The Most Beautiful Girl In The World (2); Little Girl Blue; Sawdust, Spangles And Dreams.

CD-8: Annie Get Your Gun (overture); Colonel Buffalo Bill (Leonard Stokes); I'm A Bad, Bad Man (Robert Goulet); Doin' What Comes Naturally; The Girl That I Marry (Robert Goulet); You Can't Get A

Man With A Gun; They Say It's Wonderful; My Defences Are Down (Robert Goulet); Moonshine Lullaby; I'm An Indian Too; I Got Lost In His Arms; Who Do You Love, I Hope (Kelly Brown); I Got The Sun In The Morning (Doris plus full cast); Anything You Can Do; There's No Business Like Show Business (full cast).

Appendix 3:
Selected Television Work

The Doris Day Show
CBS, United States. Season One: 24/9/68 to 6/5/69. Season Two: 22/9/69 to 6/4/70. Season Three: 14/9/70 to 15/3/71. Season Four: 13/9/71 to 6/3/72. Season Five: 11/9/72 to 12/3/73. Cast includes: Doris Day, Denver Pyle, Philip Brown, Todd Starke, Lord Nelson (dog), Fran Ryan, James Hampton, Bernie Kopell, Naomi Stevens, Kaye Ballard, Patrick O'Neal, Billy De Wolfe, Peter Nelson.

The Doris Mary Anne Kappelhoff Special
CBS, United States. March 1971. Guests: Perry Como, Rock Hudson (see main text).

John Denver & Friends
ABC, United States. December 1974. Doris guested and duetted with Denver on 'By The Light Of The Silvery Moon', 'I'll See You In My Dreams', 'On Moonlight Bay'.

Doris Day Today
CBS, United States. February 1975. Guests: Tim Conway, John Denver, Rich Little (see main text).

Doris Day's Best Friends

Christian Broadcast Network, United States. 26 episodes aired 16/7/85 to 9/1/86. One guest per show in the following order: Rock Hudson, Les Brown, Bobby Benson, Denver Pyle, Earl Holiman, Biggest, Joan Fontaine, Cleveland Amory & Ryan Melcher (grandson), Gretchen Wyler, Mickey Gilley, Danny Cooksey, California Rescue Dogs Association, Alan Shepard, Howard Keel, Kaye Ballard, Monterey County SPCA, Angie Dickinson, Robert Wagner, Tony Randall & Ryan Melcher; Loni Anderson, Jull St John, Gary Collins, Gwen Wynn, Tony Bennett, Connie Edney & Biggest, Leslie Nielsen (see main text).

Bibliography

Amory, Cleveland: "Doris Day: I Even Cry Funny", *Parade*, 8/96

Anger, Kenneth: *Hollywood Babylon I & II*: Arrow, 1986

Bret, David: *Clark Gable: Tormented Star*, JR Books, 2007

Bret, David: *Piaf: A Passionate Life*, JR Books, 2007

Bret, David: *Rock Hudson*, Robson Books, 2004

Bret, David: Interviews with Marlene Dietrich and Kris Kirk, c.1990

Braun, Eric: *Doris Day*, Orion, 1991

Cahn, Sammy: *I Should Care*, Arbor House, 1974

Callan, Paul: "All In A Day's Work", *Radio Times*, 10/80

Desser, Fuller and Lloyd: *The Illustrated Who's Who Of The Cinema*, Orion, 1983

Eames, John Douglas: *The MGM Story*, Octopus, 1979

Frayling, Christopher: "A Life In The Day"; *Time Out*, 3/89

Gale, Patrick: "Armistead Maupin: How I Outed Rock Hudson", *Guardian*, 6/99

Gelb, Alan: *The Doris Day Scrapbook*, Gresnet & Dunlap, 1977

Gow, Gordon: "Rock Hudson: Actors Always Try!", *Films & Filming*, 6/76

Greif, Martin: *The Gay Book of Days*, W. H. Allen, 1985

Hotchner, A. E.: *Doris Day: Her Own Story*, W. H. Allen, 1975

Hudson, Rock & Davidson, Sara: *Rock Hudson: His Story*, Weidendeld & Nicholson, 1986

Norman, Barry: *The Hollywood Greats*, Hodder & Stoughton, 1979

Parker, John: *Five For Hollywood*, Lyle Stuart, 1991
Quinlan, David: *Quinlan's Film Stars; Quinlan's Illustrated Directory of Film Character Actors* (Batsford, 1981,1986)
Russo, Vito: *The Celluloid Closet*, Harper and Row, 1981
Van Doren, Mamie & Aveilke: *Playing The Field*, Headline, 1987

Index